United Nations Facing Global Economic Disorder: Assessing 20 Policy Proposals

Raúl de Arriba
Editor

United Nations Facing Global Economic Disorder: Assessing 20 Policy Proposals

palgrave
macmillan

Editor
Raúl de Arriba
Department of Applied Economics
University of Valencia
Valencia, Spain

ISBN 978-3-032-21951-0 ISBN 978-3-032-21952-7 (eBook)
https://doi.org/10.1007/978-3-032-21952-7

Cover credit: Shana Novak | Getty Images

This Palgrave Macmillan imprint is published by the registered company Springer Nature Switzerland AG
The registered company address is: Gewerbestrasse 11, 6330 Cham, Switzerland

Contents

Notes on Contributors

Juan Francisco Albert is an Assistant Professor at the University of Valencia, Spain. He holds a PhD in Economics. His research focuses on monetary policy and applied macroeconomics. His doctoral thesis was awarded by the *Real Academia de Doctores de España* as the best dissertation in sustainable finance. He has published in several peer-reviewed journals of international impact and has been a visiting scholar at the London School of Economics (LSE) and De Nederlandsche Bank (the Central Bank of The Netherlands).

Olga Blasco-Blasco is an Associate Professor at the University of Valencia, Spain. She holds a PhD in Economics. Her research focuses on the quantitative methods applied to culture, education, and communication, with a particular interest in developing indicators for public policy assessment.

Manuel Couret Branco is a Full Professor at the University of Évora, Portugal. He holds a PhD in Economics delivered by the École des Hautes Études en Sciences Sociales, Paris. His research interests concern Development Studies, Social Policy, and Human Rights. He has authored or co-authored four books and numerous articles in several indexed journals.

Marta R. Casanova is an Associate Professor at the University of Valencia, Spain. She holds a PhD in Economics. Her research focuses on regional and environmental economics, and she has published in several academic journals, like *Papers in Regional Science* or *Journal of Geographical Systems*. She has undertaken research stays at universities and research centers, such as the University of Toronto (Canada) and the Kiel Institute for the World Economy (Germany).

María Ángeles Tortosa Chuliá is an Associate Professor at the University of Valencia, Spain. She holds a PhD in Applied Economics. She directed the 'La Nau Gran als Pobles' program for older people and the Master's Degree in Economic Policy and Public Economics at the UV. She has published in several indexed journals on topics related to public economics and gerontology.

Carlos Ochando Claramunt serves as an Associate Professor at the University of Valencia, Spain, where he teaches Economic Policy within the Department of Applied Economics. His main publications are related to the welfare state, incomes policy, social security reforms, and income distribution. He was director of the master's degree in Economic Policy and Public Economy at the University of Valencia from 2020 to 2025.

Artur Colom-Jaén is an Associate Professor at the University of Barcelona, Spain. He holds a PhD in Economics. His research focuses on the Political Economy of Development, with a particular emphasis on Africa and East Asia. He has extensively published on this topic and has been a visiting scholar at SOAS (University of London), Peking University, and IFAN (Senegal), among others.

Raúl de Arriba is currently an Associate Professor at the University of Valencia (Spain) and director of the POLAR Research Group (Policies, Actors and Globalization). He holds a PhD in Applied Economics. His research interests concern International Political Economy and Economic Policy. He has authored more than one hundred books, chapters, and articles in several indexed journals.

Gherardo Girardi is an Associate Professor at St Mary's University, UK. He holds a PhD in Economics. His research interests include International Political Economy, Industrial Economics, Business Ethics, and Climate Change. He has authored book chapters and articles in several indexed journals.

Marta Pedrajas Herrero is the Deputy Assistant Director for Multilateral Development Policies at the Directorate-General for Sustainable Development Policies within the Spanish Ministry of Foreign Affairs, European

Union and Cooperation. Marta holds a PhD in Philosophy and is a trained economist. Her research and work focus on human and sustainable development and in Spain's engagement with the United Nations. She has worked at UNDP and the Vatican, and previously conducted research with Amartya Sen at Harvard University.

Spartak Keremidchiev is a Professor at the Economic Research Institute at the Bulgarian Academy of Sciences, Bulgaria. He holds a PhD in Economics. His research interests focus on economics and management of infrastructure sectors and economic reforms. He has published over 130 works, including books, book chapters, and journal articles.

Julián Martinez-Moya is an Assistant Professor at the University of Valencia, Spain. He holds a PhD in International Economics. His research specializes in the design and evaluation of transportation economic policies. He has contributed to advancing evidence-based policymaking through both academic publications and applied research projects.

María Sabrina Nola is a PhD candidate in the Doctoral Programme in Social Sciences at the University of Valencia, Spain. She is member of the POLAR Research Group (Policies, Actors, Globalization). She holds a degree in Political Science and International Relations from the University Federico II of Naples (Italy) and a Master's degree in Economic Policy and Public Economics from the University of Valencia

Paula Granell is a Pre-doctoral Researcher at the University of Valencia, Spain. He is a PhD candidate at the Department of Tax Law. Her research interest concerns International Taxation, with a particular focus on Transfer Pricing. She has authored book chapters and articles in several journals.

Carlos H. Ramirez is an Associate Professor in the Faculty of International Studies at Kindai University, Osaka, Japan. He is an Associate Professor of International Relations and Political Economy. His current research focuses on IR theory, globalization, and development issues and has published widely on these topics in indexed and other industry journals.

Joan Sanchis is an Assistant Professor at the University of Valencia, Spain. He holds a Master's Degree in Economic Policy and Public Economics and a PhD in Social Sciences. His research interests are political economy, post-work studies, and public policy. He has authored a book and several chapters in academic publications.

Jordi Sanjuán is an Assistant Professor of Applied Economics at the University of Valencia, Spain. Holding a PhD in the field, he specializes in teaching and research related to economic policy. His research interests include cultural economics and economic policy. He has authored or co-authored nearly twenty academic publications, including books, chapters, technical reports, and articles in indexed journals.

Paula Simó-Tomás is an Assistant Professor at the University of Valencia, Spain. She holds a PhD in International Economics and Tourism from the University of Valencia. Her research explores the intersection of cultural and creative industries with tourism, focusing particularly on music as a driver of territorial development and urban branding. She has authored articles and book chapters on music cities, cultural tourism, and regional economic dynamics, and actively collaborates with international networks such as the Music Cities Network. Her work contributes to understanding how culture and tourism shape local economies and foster innovative development strategies.

Victòria Soldevila-Lafon is an Associate Professor at Universitat Rovira i Virgili, Spain. She holds a PhD in Economics from University of Barcelona. Her research interests concern Agricultural Economics, Rural Development and Economic Policy. She has published several articles and book chapters about food security, food policies, and agri-food chains.

Néstor Vercher is an Assistant Professor at the University of Valencia, Spain. He holds a PhD in Local Development and International Cooperation. His main research interests are territorial development policy and innovation, with a strong intersdiciplinary background. He has participated in several international projects, actively collaborating with social economy organizations and policy-makers.

CHAPTER 1

Challenges to the International Economic Order and the Role of the United Nations

Raúl de Arriba

1 The Failure of Globalisation

Over recent decades, globalisation has fundamentally restructured the global economy. This system, anchored in open markets, was predicated on the promise of enhanced efficiency, well-being, and a stable world order. It was widely anticipated that economic interdependence would mitigate social and international conflict, while fostering the global expansion of liberal democracy. However, far from generating the efficient and harmonious balances predicted by the orthodox liberal paradigm, globalisation has produced structural tensions that affect the economic, social, environmental, and geopolitical stability of the international system.

The first set of tensions centres on the relationship between globalisation and efficiency. While globalisation has undeniably catalysed economic growth and diversified consumer goods, these results cannot be attributed exclusively to market liberalisation or the self-regulating

R. de Arriba (✉)
University of Valencia, Valencia, Spain
e-mail: dearriba@uv.es

R. de Arriba (ed.), *United Nations Facing Global Economic Disorder: Assessing 20 Policy Proposals*,
https://doi.org/10.1007/978-3-032-21952-7_1

paradigm. Indeed, the most successful examples of economic dynamism—most notably China—have strategically blended global integration with robust, interventionist industrial policies.

Furthermore, the premise that globalisation inherently fosters competition has proven hollow. Contrary to orthodox theoretical expectations, corporate concentration has accelerated across strategic sectors, leading to the emergence of global oligopolies. These entities now wield sufficient structural power to distort market dynamics and exert disproportionate influence over sovereign political decisions.

Globalisation has fundamentally accelerated the financialisation of the global economy. The unprecedented volume and velocity of capital flows have introduced chronic systemic volatility, decoupling financial markets from the real economy. This fragility is exacerbated by a staggering surge in global debt, which soared to $251 trillion in 2024 (235% of global GDP). The crisis is particularly acute in the Global South, where nations are struggling with record-high external debt, debilitating debt-servicing costs, and severe fiscal erosion (IMF, 2025).

The second block of tensions centres on the relationship between globalisation and well-being. Although global poverty has decreased, deep inequalities persist. Differences in per capita income, life expectancy, or access to education between developed and low-income countries, especially in Sub-Saharan Africa, remain enormous (UNDP, 2025).

Globalisation has produced winners and losers. The middle class in wealthy countries has seen stagnant or declining relative incomes, while the emerging Asian middle class and the world's richest 1% have benefited significantly (Milanovic, 2016). Corporate offshoring and competition with developing economies have negatively affected wages and industrial employment in the West, while favouring the rise of China, India, and other emerging economies.

Extreme poverty, defined by the low-income threshold of USD 3.0 per person/day, currently affects 808 million people. However, when applying more realistic poverty lines—such as the USD 8.30 benchmark for upper-middle-income countries—the global impoverished population surges to over 3.7 billion, revealing a far more precarious reality for nearly half of humanity (World Bank, n.d.). The prevalence of undernourishment affected 8.2% of the global population in 2024; however, the scale of the crisis is even broader, with 28% of people worldwide facing moderate or severe food insecurity (FAO et al., 2025). Both problems are particularly severe in regions afflicted by conflict, institutional fragility, or climate crises.

In this context, tax evasion has become a central problem. Large corporations and wealthy individuals use tax havens to avoid taxation, generating annual losses of around USD 500 billion (Tax Justice Network, 2024). This erosion of public revenues limits governments' ability to finance the welfare state and exacerbates inequality.

The third group of tensions concerns the relationship between globalisation and nature. Economic growth and the expansion of trade exert unsustainable pressures on ecosystems. According to the Stockholm Resilience Centre, six of the nine planetary boundaries have already been exceeded, including climate change, biosphere integrity, nitrogen and phosphorus cycles, land use, and freshwater consumption (SRC, n.d.).

Climate change stands out as the principal challenge. The year 2024 marked a global temperature record, with an average of more than 1.5 °C above pre-industrial levels. Despite the Paris Agreement, emissions from fossil fuels continue to rise. Low-income countries exhibit the highest levels of climate vulnerability. Although they are not primary emitters, they are asymmetrically affected by the rising intensity and frequency of climate-driven catastrophes.

Moreover, pressure on essential resources such as water and land is directly linked to global production and trade systems. Meanwhile, the proliferation of synthetic chemicals exceeds ecosystems' capacity for regeneration. This environmental panorama reflects a structural contradiction between the expansionary logic of globalisation and the planet's limits.

The fourth set of tensions concerns security. Far from consolidating a stable order, globalisation has heightened geopolitical rivalries. China's rise is key to understanding these dynamics. The country has become an industrial, technological, and commercial superpower, competing with the United States for global hegemony. It leads sectors such as solar panels, batteries, drones, electric vehicles, etc.; and projects its global influence through the Belt and Road Initiative, especially in developing countries. Simultaneously, the expansion and consolidation of BRICS+ represents a significant institutional challenge to Western hegemony. By fostering financial cooperation outside the dollar's orbit and creating alternatives to the International Monetary Fund (IMF) and the World Bank, the bloc is actively seeking to redefine the global financial architecture in favour of a multipolar framework.

International trade has been increasingly weaponised as an instrument of foreign policy. The global landscape is now defined by a surge in protectionist interventions, where tariffs and subsidies are strategically deployed not just for economic advantage, but as tools of geopolitical coercion and national security. The trade and technology war between the United States and China, initiated in 2018, symbolises this protectionist shift, intensified by Trump's return to the White House in 2025.

Technological competition has deepened in critical sectors such as AI and semiconductors. Access to critical raw materials—such as cobalt, lithium, or rare earths—is a major geopolitical battleground. Dependence on a handful of suppliers, such as China, fuels strategic tensions during the energy and digital transitions and amid renewed military build-ups.

Finally, global economic interdependence has not prevented the proliferation of armed conflicts, undermining the idea that trade guarantees peace.

2 The Dispute for Global Hegemony

Traditionally, economic and corporate priorities dictated the globalisation agenda and much of foreign policy. In recent years, however, the weight of economic decisions has shifted towards political and security strategists. As Rodrik (2022) states: "The problem with hyper-globalization was that we allowed big banks and multinational corporations to write the rules of the global economy… Today they are handing the keys of the global economy to their national security establishments, jeopardising global peace and prosperity."

The growing rivalry among major powers explains this shift. China's economic, technological, and military rise has moved US policy priorities towards national security and strategic autonomy. The aim of the United States is now to safeguard its hegemony by excluding its rivals from the technological revolution. In this context, almost anything can be weaponised in foreign policy: supply chains, migration flows, trade, humanitarian aid, etc.

The United States has enjoyed a hegemonic position since the collapse of the Soviet bloc in the late 1980s. Today, the main challenges to US dominance come from China—economically and technologically—and from Russia—militarily, especially in certain regions such as Europe and

Africa. This implies a transition from a unipolar world dominated by the American hegemon to an international order where several major powers both compete and cooperate. Beyond the US, China and Russia, other actors such as the European Union, India, and Saudi Arabia seek to assert their geo-strategic and economic interests. This places geopolitics at the centre of strategic decision-making over who controls certain regions, resources, and routes (Biscop, 2024).

The demographic and economic weight of the West has declined significantly, and its technological supremacy is increasingly questioned. Meanwhile, new centres of power have emerged in the Global South. The BRICS+ group constitutes an economic institutional alternative that challenges the Bretton Woods framework. The Shanghai Cooperation Organization is shaping a pragmatic axis between China, Russia, Iran, and other Global South countries, with India playing a distinct and independent role. These dynamics do not create a monolithic bloc, but rather tactical alliances aimed at contesting leadership in strategic sectors (Borrell & Morillas, 2025).

Nevertheless, the United States retains its global primacy, underpinned by four strategic pillars. Financially, it dominates capital markets. Monetarily, the dollar remains hegemonic over the euro and the renminbi. Technologically, it maintains leadership despite China's rapid ascent. Lastly, its military power is unquestionable (Sapir et al., 2025).

The real challenge to US hegemony comes from China. Unlike twentieth-century rivals (Germany, Japan, or the USSR), which never surpassed two-thirds of US productive capacity, China's rise has been extraordinary: its GDP moved from 18% of the US level in 1995 to 89% in 2024, with projections of reaching 135% by 2035 (Fàbregues & Farrés, 2025). This expansion is not merely quantitative; it encompasses technological leadership in critical sectors and a deepening commercial dominance across global markets. Beijing's influence is now global. It has become the main creditor of developing countries and expanded its presence in Europe.

By contrast, Russia's economy is fragile and poorly diversified, and does not offer an attractive development model. Moscow plays other cards. It uses arms sales, disinformation, and nuclear energy to assert influence in the Global South, especially in Africa and Central Asia (Sumner & Klingebiel, 2025). For its part, the European Union sees its geopolitical influence diluted, often reduced to its traditional soft normative power. Despite Brussels' ambition to strengthen strategic autonomy, progress remains modest, constrained by structural vulnerabilities: chronic dependence on US security guarantees, technological lag in the digital race, and high commercial exposure to Beijing. This fragile external balance is aggravated by growing internal division, where the rise of national-populism hinders the cohesion needed to articulate a unified foreign policy.

3 The Crisis of Multilateralism

The UN Charter of 1945, the Universal Declaration of Human Rights of 1948 and the Bretton Woods system laid the foundations for a multilateral order which, with periodic adaptations, has shaped international economic relations to the present day. Its legitimacy rested on a normative framework and a distribution of power which, although unequal, provided predictability in countries behaviour. This Western-designed architecture consolidated a rules-based order: a system of laws and institutions intended to promote cooperation and guarantee global stability by resolving disputes peacefully.

However, this system should not be idealised. It has always been an imperfect multilateralism, tolerating certain discretionary behaviours, especially those undertaken or endorsed by the United States. This exceptionalism is institutionalised through the US veto power in key bodies such as the UN Security Council and the Bretton Woods organisations.

Multilateralism is now in crisis. It no longer governs the world in several critical domains. Moreover, the main institutions of global governance are malfunctioning: the UN suffers a major legitimacy crisis (particularly its Security Council), the World Trade Organization (WTO) is paralysed (due to the blockage of its Appellate Body and ongoing trade wars), and the IMF and World Bank have proved unable to address challenges in financial stability and development (Mani, 2025).

This crisis has accelerated following Trump's return to the White House in 2025. The United States has inflicted severe damage on rule-based global governance. Its rejection of the existing international order is reflected both in its withdrawal from multiple international organisations and agreements, and in its disregard for international law through increasing interference in other countries.

Trump initially withdrew from the OECD global tax deal, the UN Framework Convention on International Tax Cooperation, the Paris Agreement, the World Health Organization, the UN Human

Rights Council, UNESCO, and categorically rejected the 2030 Agenda and the Sustainable Development Goals. Later, in January 2026, he announced the US withdrawal from 66 additional multilateral organisations, including: UN Framework Convention on Climate Change, Intergovernmental Panel on Climate Change, UN Oceans, Department of Economic and Social Affairs, UN Conference on Trade and Development, United Nations Collaborative Programme on Reducing Emissions from Deforestation and Forest Degradation, UN Energy, UN Population Fund, or UN Water (The White House, 2026).

Although formally still a WTO member, Washington effectively left the organisation on 2 April 2025 (the so-called "Liberation Day"), after imposing a chaotic, unilateral, and indiscriminate wave of disproportionate tariffs on virtually every country. Moreover, the US has turned tariffs into a coercive political instrument, used unpredictably to secure objectives unrelated to trade.

Parallel to its withdrawal from multilateral agreements, the US has multiplied interventions in other countries, using various forms and for multiple motives. The list is long: a short invasion of Venezuela to capture its president; threats of intervention in Cuba, Mexico or Colombia; bombings in Nigeria, Iran, Yemen, Somalia, Syria, or the Caribbean; insults and threats towards traditional allies such as the EU or Canada; support for Israel's invasion of Gaza; interference in elections in Argentina or Honduras; or threats to annex the Panama Canal, Canada, and—most recently and dangerously—Greenland.

The international order is now viewed as an obstacle to US primacy and national interest. American foreign policy is characterised by discretionality, unilateralism, and aggressiveness, generating instability, uncertainty, and mistrust. The erosion of US credibility as a reliable partner is pushing the rest of the world to move forward without its leadership. At the multilateral level, this is evident in the holding of key summits (G20, COP30, etc.) without Washington's centrality, and in the creation of alternative cooperation mechanisms.

Examples of such minilateral or club-based diplomacy include: BRICS + (steadily expanding its membership and deepening cooperation channels), AUKUS (a 2021 trilateral security pact between Australia, the UK, and the US), Quad (a security, infrastructure and critical supply chain alliance between the US, Japan, India, and Australia), I2U2 (India, Israel, the US and the UAE cooperating in water, energy, transport, and more), the Chip4 Alliance (US, Japan, South Korea, and Taiwan for semiconductor coordination), the Minerals Security Partnership (US, EU, Canada, Australia, Japan, the UK, and others, acting as a buyers' club for critical minerals), or the Multi-Party Interim Appeal Arbitration Agreement (an alternative dispute-settlement system to the WTO). More recent initiatives include the Board of Peace (a coalition created by Trump to rival the UN in conflict resolution) and Pax Silica (an alliance about chips/AI value chain between US, Japan, South Korea, Singapore, the Netherlands, the UK, Israel, UAE and Australia, with Taiwan, the EU, and Canada as invited participants).

Meanwhile, other major blocs are also advancing their agendas. China is redirecting its trade flows towards the European Union. Furthermore, it defends multilateralism and the United Nations, a vision crystallised in its 2025 Global Governance Initiative unveiled at the Shanghai Cooperation Organization Summit. For its part, the EU has accelerated its trade agenda, reaching agreements with New Zealand, Chile, and Kenya, and more recently with Indonesia, Mexico, Mercosur, and India.

Against this backdrop, the twin objectives of reshoring and reindustrialising strategic sectors have gained significant momentum globally. States promote self-sufficiency to reduce external dependency, primarily through industrial and trade policies. Corporations have also shifted strategies, adopting risk-management approaches (de-risking and friendshoring): diversifying suppliers and seeking geographically closer production hubs is becoming standard practice (Blázquez, 2024). Vertical integration has experienced a strategic revival. This is very evident in the automotive sector, where almost every company has invested directly in its electric vehicle supply chains rather than purchasing batteries and electronic components from third parties (Levinson, 2021).

In essence, the world is moving beyond the era of US-supported multilateralism into a volatile multipolarity defined by American unilateralism. This transition carries distinct imperial overtones, where the traditional rules-based order is increasingly supplanted by the unilateral threat of force.

4 The Role of the United Nations

The United Nations system is a complex structure comprising six original principal organs, numerous funds and programmes (funded primarily through voluntary contributions), and specialised agencies and related bodies. Specialised agencies are autonomous and have cooperation agreements with the UN (such as World Health Organization, International Labour Organization, Food and Agriculture Organization, etc.). The relationship of WTO, IMF, and World Bank with the UN system is particular and often described as an institutional partnership.

Despite being the cornerstone of the post-Second World War institutional architecture, the UN system presents several structural problems:

- Institutional design based on outdated power relations. The Security Council includes five permanent members with veto power. This allows recurrent blockages in conflicts where their interests are at stake and reveals a democratic deficit, eroding legitimacy. Moreover, the advantage of universal representation is undermined by the limited real influence of most countries, pushing emerging powers towards alternative platforms such as BRICS + or the G20 (Weiss & Abdenur, 2014).
- Financial dependence. A small minority of states funds most of the UN budget, essentially the US. The system is vulnerable to political pressure from major contributors. The system is also sustained by supplementary voluntary funding, which is inherently tied to the individual preferences and geopolitical priorities of its contributors.
- Liquidity crisis. Many states do not pay their contributions in full or on time. The US has accumulated arrears of USD 1.5 billion in the regular budget and USD 1.2 billion in peacekeeping operations (Landay & Pamuk, 2025). The impact is enormous, as the US accounts for roughly 22% of the regular UN budget and nearly a third of total system financing (Ferragamo & Roy, 2025).
- Fragmentation. The UN comprises more than 30 organisations, funds, and programmes, leading to overlaps and coordination problems. As Boutros-Ghali noted in 1995: "Such coordination has to date proved difficult to achieve. Each of the agencies concerned has its own intergovernmental legislative body and its own mandate." He added that "multifunctional peacekeeping operations and peacebuilding transcend the competence and expertise of any one department, programme, fund, office or agency" (United Nations Secretary-General, 1995).
- Excessive bureaucracy. Decision-making is slow and complex, often preventing timely responses to new global challenges such as digital

governance, disruptive technologies, environmental crises, cybersecurity, etc.

- Erosion of leadership. The UN now operates within a congested landscape of competing actors that challenge its traditional primacy. These include public institutions (G7 or G20 for example), regional blocs (EU or others), informal groups (such as BRICS +), major corporations (especially tech firms), and semi-private organisations (GAVI for example).
- Weak executive capacity. The UN does not constitute a global government and is fundamentally dependent on states and global financial bodies for the implementation of its decisions. It lacks the autonomous enforcement mechanisms required to ensure compliance with treaties or mandates and possesses no coercive instruments to effect structural change (Ocampo, 2016).
- Limited transformative power. The UN remains relevant in technical assistance and humanitarian aid but has not succeeded in transforming the fundamental structures of global trade, finance, and debt (Babb & Chorev, 2016).

However, these shortcomings do not justify its marginalisation within global governance. A key aspect of the UN's work is its role as a laboratory of analysis and policy proposals. The UN functions as an ideas factory that has shaped the most influential development paradigms (basic needs, human development, gender, sustainable development, etc.) and defined development and global public goods agendas (Ghai, 2008). Although its formal power is modest, its strength lies in generating and disseminating ideas. Some of its reports—such as the UNDP Human Development Report or the Sustainable Development Goals—receive more media attention than those of the World Bank, extending their influence on public opinion and political agendas (Joshi & O'Dell, 2017).

Some of its proposals have materialised into agreements. The most significant in recent decades include: the Millennium Development Goals (2000), the Stockholm Convention on Persistent Organic Pollutants (2001), the UN Convention on the Contract for the International Carriage of Goods Wholly or Partly by Sea (2008), the Paris Agreement (2015), the 2030 Agenda and the SDGs (2015), and the High Seas Treaty (2023), among others.

The chapters that follow compile the proposals of the United Nations for addressing 20 contemporary challenges: global governance, new international economic order, human rights, trade, international financial system, international monetary system, taxation, intellectual property and patents, artificial intelligence, climate change, water and sanitation, transport, development cooperation, external debt, food security, poverty, inequality, decent work, migration, and tourism. Each chapter provides a description and diagnosis of the corresponding challenge, details the policies proposed by the United Nations, and offers an assessment of the measures suggested.

References

Babb, S., & Chorev, N. (2016). International Organizations: Loose and Tight Coupling in the Development Regime. *Studies in Comparative International Development, 51*, 81–102.

Biscop, S. (2024). *This Is Not a New World Order: Europe Rediscovers Geopolitics, from Ukraine to Taiwan*. Owl Press

Blazquez, I. (2024). Tecnología y geopolítica: Sobre una teoría del cambio en las relaciones internacionales. *Información Comercial Española, 935*, 135–150.

Borrell, J., & Morillas, P. (2025). El mundo en 2025: del fin de la posguerra a la brutalización del orden internacional. *Anuario Internacional CIDOB 2026*. https://www.cidob.org/publicaciones/mundo-2025-del-fin-posguerra-brutalizacion-del-orden-internacional

Fàbregues, F., & Farrés, O. (2025). Introduction. *Anuario Internacional CIDOB 2026*. https://www.cidob.org/publicaciones/anuario-internacional-cidob-2026-introduccion

FAO, IFAD, UNICEF, WFP and WHO. (2025). *The State of Food Security and Nutrition in the World 2025*. Food and Agriculture Organization, International Fund for Agricultural Development, United Nations Children's Fund, World Food Programme and World Health Organization.

Ferragamo, M., & Roy, D. (2025, 25 de septiembre). *How Much Does the U.S. Fund the United Nations?*. Council on Foreign Relations. www.cfr.org/articles/funding-united-nations-what-impact-do-us-contributions-have-un-agencies-and-programs

Ghai, D. (2008). UN Contributions to Development Thinking and Practice. *Development in Practice, 18*(6), 767–773.

IMF. (2025, September). *Global Debt Monitor*. International Monetary Fund. https://www.imf.org/external/datamapper/GDD/2025%20Global%20Debt%20Monitor.pdf

Joshi, D., & O'Dell, R. (2017). The Critical Role of Mass Media in International Norm Diffusion: The Case of UNDP Human Development Reports. *International Studies Perspectives, 18*(3), 343–364.

Landay, J. & Pamuk, H. (2025, April 15). Trump Administration Proposes Scrapping UN Peacekeeping Funding. *Reuters*. https://www.reuters.com/world/trump-administration-proposes-scrapping-un-peacekeeping-funding-2025-04-15/

Levinson, M. (2021, December 20). *Deglobalization: The New Normal?* ISPI. https://www.ispionline.it/en/publication/deglobalization-new-normal-32758

Mani, L. (2025). The Self-Inflicted Crisis of Global Governance. In ISPI, ORF, & PCNS (Eds.), *Annual Trends Report: Beyond Global Polarization: New Cooperation wanted. Policy Center for the New South*. https://www.policycenter.ma/publications/beyond-global-polarization-new-cooperation-wanted

Milanovic, B. (2016). *Global Inequality: A New Approach for the Age of Globalization*. Belknap Press of Harvard University Press.

Ocampo, J. A. (2016). *Global Governance and Development*. Oxford University Press.

Rodrik, D. (2022, November 7). *Don't Let Geopolitics Kill the World Economy*. Project Syndicate. https://www.project-syndicate.org/commentary/us-china-high-tech-trade-restrictions-by-dani-rodrik-2022-11

Sapir, A., Kirkegaard, J. F., & Zettelmeyer, J. (2025). *Geopolitical Shifts and Their Economic Impacts on Europe: Short-Term Risks, Medium-Term Scenarios and Policy Choices*. Bruegel Report 1/2025). https://www.bruegel.org/report/geopolitical-shifts-and-their-economic-impacts-europe-short-term-risks-medium-term-scenario

SRC. (n.d.). *Planetary Boundaries*. Stockholm Resilience Centre. https://www.stockholmresilience.org/research/planetary-boundaries.html

Sumner, A. & Klingebiel, S. (2025, December 17). The Big Flag Issues for Global Development Policy in 2026: Trump 2.0, China's status, Russia the Spoiler, Multi-Alignment and 80% Autocracy. *Global Policy Journal*. https://www.globalpolicyjournal.com/blog/17/12/2025/big-flag-issues-global-development-policy-2026-trump-20-chinas-status-russia

Tax Justice Network. (2024). *The State of Tax Justice 2024*. Tax Justice Network

The White House. (2026, January 7). *Withdrawing the United States from International Organizations, Conventions, and Treaties that are Contrary to the Interests of the United States* (Presidential Memorandum). https://www.whitehouse.gov/presidential-actions/2026/01/withdrawing-the-united-states-from-international-organizations-conventions-and-treaties-that-are-contrary-to-the-interests-of-the-united-states

UNDP. (2025). *Human Development Report 2025*. United Nations Development Programme.

United Nations Secretary-General. (1995). *Report of the Secretary-General on the Work of the Organization. Supplement to an Agenda for Peace*. Position Paper of the Secretary-General on the Occasion of the Fiftieth Anniversary of the United Nations (A/50/60* S/1995/1*). United Nations.

Weiss, T. G., & Abdenur, A. E. (2014). Introduction: Emerging Powers and the UN—What Kind of Development Partnership? *Third World Quarterly, 35*(10), 1749–1758.

World Bank. (n.d.). *Poverty and Inequality Platform*. World Bank. https://pip.worldbank.org/home

CHAPTER 2

Global Governance

Raúl de Arriba

1 The Challenge

Global governance has relied on rules-based multilateralism and institutions until now (Belhaj, 2024). This way of articulating international relations has advantages: it fosters cooperation between States, promotes collective problem-solving, and facilitates the resolution of conflicts via diplomatic channels (Nye & Welch, 2011). This system is founded on the role that the United States has played as the guarantor of the international order.

Now, the liberal multilateralism of globalization is being seriously questioned from several fronts. This is the result of a trend marked by diverse structural factors (Vinjamuri, 2025). On the one hand, United States hegemony is compromised both by China's economic rise and its global projection of power, and by the renewed Russian imperialism in the geopolitical and military sphere. Additionally, the Global South's frustration with the international *status quo* has led to the creation of alternative

R. de Arriba (✉)
University of Valencia, Valencia, Spain
e-mail: dearriba@uv.es

R. de Arriba (ed.), *United Nations Facing Global Economic Disorder: Assessing 20 Policy Proposals*,
https://doi.org/10.1007/978-3-032-21952-7_2

institutions. On the other hand, growing inequality and deindustrialization in developed countries fuels population discontent with a global order perceived as the cause of the deterioration of their quality of life. Finally, the expansion of national-populism across the world challenges traditional schemes of international integration and cooperation.

With Trump's return to the White House in January 2025, the United States has ended up dismantling the global order through its disdain for international law and multilateralism. Washington has threatened the sovereignty of Venezuela, Iran, Canada, Greenland, and the Panama Canal; it has undermined the transatlantic alliance through disparagement and ultimatums toward its allies; it has retreated from international leadership by exiting the Paris Agreement and various global bodies (such as the World Health Organization, the Human Rights Council, the UN Framework Convention on International Tax Cooperation, the UN Framework Convention on Climate Change, the Department of Economic and Social Affairs, the UN Conference on Trade and Development, or the UN Population Fund, among others); it has rejected the 2030 Agenda and the Sustainable Development Goals; and it has destabilized global trade by imposing disproportionate and unilateral tariffs on a global scale.

These decisions directly undermine the role of the United Nations (UN).

According to Secretary-General António Guterres, the organization is facing its most critical juncture since its founding, with its very credibility called into question. This crisis stems from a confluence of factors.

The Security Council remains paralyzed and deeply divided over key conflicts such as Palestine, Iran and Ukraine, while the General Assembly's repeated resolutions have limited efficacy. Furthermore, the UN system proves incapable of responding adequately to climate, poverty, migration, or humanitarian crises.

Chronic financial instability continues to hamper the organization's operational capacity. Delays in assessed contributions from major member states—notably the United States and China—alongside a decline in voluntary funding, are of particular concern given the U.S. position as the primary budget contributor. Finally, the systemic assault on multilateralism, driven by a global wave of ultra-nationalist populism led by Trump, calls into question the legitimacy and future of global cooperation, particularly regarding the UN.

Trump's policies have engendered profound uncertainty in international economic relations and eroded global trust in American leadership.

According to Gordon Brown, we are in a scenario that is now "neither global nor liberal nor orderly" (Brown, 2023). The institutional architecture of globalization is no longer capable of ensuring economic cooperation, social prosperity, or global peace. Consequently, a fundamental overhaul of the global governance system is imperative, beginning with its central pillar: the United Nations.

2 UN Proposals

The United Nations has approved two main documents aimed at improving governance tools:

- The Secretary-General's report, *Our Common Agenda*, published by the United Nations in 2021, is designed to accelerate the implementation of existing agreements, including the Sustainable Development Goals.
- The *Pact for the Future*, adopted by the UN General Assembly in 2024, represents a roadmap to modernizing global governance and revitalizing international cooperation.

Our Common Agenda (United Nations Secretary-General, 2021) defends a form of multilateralism that is "more networked, more inclusive and more effective in addressing the challenges of the twenty-first century", with the aim of improving the governance of global public goods and managing risks. By more networked multilateralism, the United Nations understands the need to combine existing institutional capacities, overcoming fragmentation, and improving coordination between regional and global actions. To be more inclusive, the system must allow, on the one hand, developing countries to have more influence on global decisions and, on the other, include other actors such as intergovernmental organizations, parliaments, local and regional governments, civil society, faith-based organizations, universities, researchers, trade unions, private sector, and local and grassroots movements.

More specifically, the document includes some proposals for improving the United Nations system itself, such as:

- Revitalizing the United Nations Trusteeship Council, suspended in 1994, to convert it into a multi-stakeholder body for addressing new emerging challenges and, specifically, serves as a debate forum to impart advice.

- Reforming the Security Council to accurately reflect twenty-first-century realities, with a specific focus on rectifying the under-representation of Africa and incorporating a broader range of stakeholders. To enhance inclusivity, the proposal advocates for deeper consultation with regional organizations and the expanded use of informal mechanisms, such as *Arria-formula* meetings. Additionally, it calls for the establishment of an emergency platform to streamline responses to complex global shocks.
- Revitalizing the General Assembly, simplifying its resolutions, and leveraging the Assembly High-Level Week to secure concrete commitments by heads of State and government.
- Enhancing the role of the Economic and Social Council (ECOSOC) by strengthening its synergy with the G20. A key proposal involves convening a Biennial Summit between the G20, ECOSOC, the Secretary-General, and the heads of international financial institutions to ensure seamless coordination in global economic governance.

Subsequently, the UN Secretary-General tasked the *High-Level Advisory Board on Effective Multilateralism* with drafting concrete, viable recommendations for a transformative shift in global governance. Building upon the "Our Common Agenda" report, these proposals served as the foundation for the 2024 Summit of the Future. The Board's report outlines ten guiding principles for effective multilateralism: it must be people-centred, representative, transparent, equitable, networked, resourced, mission-focused, flexible, accountable, and future-oriented (High-Level Advisory Board on Effective Multilateralism, 2023). These principles are integrated into six transformative shifts:

1. Rebuild trust in multilateralism through inclusion and accountability.
2. Deliver for people and planet by regaining balance with nature and providing clean energy for all.
3. Ensure sustainable finance that delivers for all.
4. Support a just digital transition that unlocks the value of data and protects against digital harms.

5. Empower equitable, effective collective security arrangements.
6. Strengthen governance for current and emerging transnational risks.

Shift 1 focuses on reinforcing multilateralism: "Rebuild trust in multilateralism. Improve Legitimacy and Effectiveness through Inclusion and Accountability". The Advisory Board contends that for global governance to be effective, it must be more inclusive, networked, and accountable. To this end, it outlines a series of strategic proposals:

- Ensure that "we the peoples" are better represented in the multilateral system through placing gender equality at the heart of the multilateral architecture, creating more meaningful space for the participation of civil society, and supporting a UN Youth Office with stronger accountability structures for youth inclusion.
- Design institutions, policies, and practices that represent and account for future generations.
- Provide formal status to cities, subnational governments, and private sector actors in key multilateral processes.
- Shift toward qualified decision-making on crucial issues of global concern and agree to a code of conduct on inclusive multilateral processes.

The *Pact for the Future*, adopted at the Summit of the Future held in September 2024 in New York, contains the key UN proposals to overcome the crisis of global governance (United Nations General Assembly, 2024). This plan recognizes the need to reinforce and renew the multilateral system and its institutions. While the document is notably ambitious in its principles -even proclaiming "the beginning of a new era for multilateralism", its specific proposals for global governance remain broad and largely aspirational.

The document outlines 56 actions distributed across five main axes: (I) sustainable development and financing for development; (II) international peace and security; (III) science, technology, innovation, and digital cooperation; (IV) youth and future generations; and (V) transforming global governance. Chapter V sets forth several key commitments, most notably the following:

- *Action 38.* A commitment to ensuring the multilateral system, with the UN at its core, becomes more effective, prepared, and equitable. It advocates for a more inclusive and networked architecture that possesses greater financial stability. Crucially, Action 38 emphasizes representativeness, asserting that all Member States - particularly developing nations- must participate meaningfully in the decision-making processes of multilateral institutions.
- *Action 39.* Reforming the Security Council by addressing the urgent need for a more representative, inclusive, and transparent body. The goal is to ensure the Council becomes more efficient, effective, and democratic, while establishing more robust mechanisms for accountability.
- *Action 42.* Revitalize the work of the General Assembly.
- *Action 43.* Strengthen the Economic and Social Council to accelerate sustainable development.
- *Action 45.* Action 45. Strengthen the United Nations system so that it remains effective, efficient, and fit for purpose.

In line with *Our Common Agenda* and the *Pact for the Future*, the UN Secretary-General launched the *UN80 Initiative* in March 2025. This landmark initiative is designed to address a fundamental question: "How can the UN adapt to be more agile, integrated, and equipped to respond to today's complex global challenges in a context of increasingly limited resources?" (United Nations, 2025a). The objective of the Initiative is to "strengthen the UN's capacity to respond to current global challenges, ranging from conflicts, displacement, and inequality to climate shocks and rapid technological change, while responding to external pressures such as shrinking budgets and growing political divisions in the multilateral space" (United Nations, 2025b). This mandate encompasses all United Nations agencies, funds, and programs, serving as a strategic response to the dual pressure of mounting global challenges and diminishing financial resources.

The strategy is structured around three core reform axes:

- Improvement of internal efficiency and effectiveness, reduction of bureaucracy, and optimization of the UN's global presence by relocating some functions to lower-cost duty stations.

- Review of mandate implementation, which implies the examination of nearly 4,000 documents, with the aim of streamlining the workload, eliminating duplications, and expediting execution.
- Structural changes and program realignment throughout the United Nations system to ensure coherence, effectiveness, and the optimal use of resources.

The implementation of these changes is being driven by the UN80 Working Group, which has been structured into seven distinct thematic streams to ensure a comprehensive and specialized approach to the reform: peace and security, humanitarian action, development, human rights, training and research, and specialized agencies. Its mission is to deliver concrete proposals aimed at reducing institutional fragmentation. Moving beyond the rhetoric of efficiency, the measures discussed to date include the consolidation of agencies with overlapping mandates, significant budgetary contractions, and a reduction in the workforce over the coming years (Ferragamo & Roy, 2025). The 2026 budget approved by the General Assembly, totaling $3.45 billion, already incorporates the Secretary-General's mandate for a 15% reduction in financial resources and an unprecedented 19% cut in staffing levels (United Nations, 2025c).

Finally, it is worth mentioning the *4th International Conference on Financing for Development* held in Sevilla in the summer of 2025. This summit was dedicated to the critical issue of development finance, addressing key pillars such as global tax cooperation and sovereign debt sustainability. However, the final declaration (*Sevilla Commitment*) also mentions some issues regarding the reform of global governance. Basically, the text emphasizes that the governance of the global economy must be more inclusive, representative, equitable, and effective. This entails: (1) amplifying the voice and participation of developing countries in international decision-making, and (2) recalibrating quotas, mandates, and governance structures within international financial institutions to better reflect today's global economic reality (United Nations, 2025d).

3 Assessment

The overall assessment of the United Nations' reform proposals remains largely critical. While the current challenges are both significant and urgent, the UN continues to prioritize broad normative principles over concrete, transformative actions. This creates a perceptible gap between its rhetorical ambition and its substantive policy output. In addition to fiscal consolidation, the UN's strategy focuses on three critical fronts: administrative simplification, the expansion of Global South representation in international governance, and the creation of operational synergies between ECOSOC and the G20.

Although *Our Common Agenda* and the *Pact for the Future* have laid the foundations for important reforms, the main challenge remains implementation. Ambitious proposals, such as the reform of the Security Council, face a structural deadlock. Implementation is exceptionally difficult as it requires the consensus of the permanent members—the very actors whose unilateral influence and veto power would be diminished by such reforms. The current geopolitical landscape presents an unprecedented barrier to institutional evolution. The systemic rivalry between the USA, Russia, and China has created a strategic deadlock within the Security Council. As long as these powers prioritize mutual obstruction over collective governance, the window for implementing key reforms remains critically narrow.

However, the urgency of reform transcends political debate and enters the realm of fiscal necessity. The UN is currently grappling with a severe liquidity crisis, fueled by the systematic failure of Member States to meet their assessed contributions in full and on schedule. This financial asphyxiation compromises the organization's very ability to maintain its basic operations (ISHR, 2025). The financial fragility of the United Nations is worrying, and the roadmap marked by the *UN80 Initiative* has awakened deep disquiet. There is a well-founded fear that the *Initiative* is, ultimately, a disguised austerity exercise rather than a true political revitalization (United Nations, 2025b). Tensions with primary donors further destabilize the UN's position. The growing unpredictability of the U.S. financial commitment creates a climate of instability that undermines the reforms the organization seeks to implement, making long-term operational planning very complicated. Inevitably, these cuts will force the de-prioritization of essential programs. The most vulnerable areas to these fiscal constraints are, paradoxically, those that constitute the normative core of the organization: human rights, gender equality, and sustainable development (Ferragamo & Roy, 2025).

In short, the United Nations appears committed to maintaining the existing institutional architecture of global governance without significant alterations. To date, its strategy fails to radically address the underlying drivers of international (dis)order, opting instead for institutional survival over systemic transformation.

References

Belhaj, F. (2024). *The Shift from Multilateralism to Plurilateralism: A Challenge for the Bretton Woods Institutions and the UN as They Turn 80?* Policy Center for the New South, Policy Brief, 26/24. https://www.policycenter.ma/sites/default/files/202405/PB_26_24%20%28Ferid%20Belhaj%29.pdf

Brown, G. (2023, September 11). A New Multilateralism. How the United States can Rejuvenate the Global Institutions it Created. *Foreign Policy*. https://foreignpolicy.com/2023/09/11/us-china-russia-multilateralism-diplomacy-alliances-trade/

Ferragamo, M., & Roy, D. (2025, September 15). *The UN80 Initiative: What to Know About the United Nations' Reform Plan*. Council on Foreign Relations. https://www.cfr.org/articles/un80-initiative-what-know-about-united-nations-reform-plan

High-Level Advisory Board on Effective Multilateralism. (2023). *A Breakthrough for People and Planet: Effective and Inclusive Global Governance for Today and the Future*. United Nations University.

ISHR. (2025, September 18). *UN80 Initiative: Proposed Budget Cuts Disproportionately Hit the Human Rights Pillar*. International Service for Human Rights. https://ishr.ch/latest-updates/un80-initiative-proposed-budget-cuts-disproportionately-hit-the-human-rights-pillar

United Nations. (2025a). *What is the UN80 Initiative?* United Nations. https://www.un.org/un80-initiative/en/news/what-un80-initiative

United Nations. (2025b). *UN80 Initiative: What It Is and Why It Matters to the World*. United Nations News. https://news.un.org/en/story/2025/06/1164836

United Nations. (2025c, December 30). *Fifth Committee Approves $3.45 Billion Proposed Budget for 2026, Reflecting Deep Cuts in Financial Resources*. United Nations [Press release]. https://press.un.org/en/2025/gaab4507.doc.htm

United Nations. (2025d). *Sevilla Commitment. Final Outcome Document of the Fourth International Conference on Financing for Development*. A/CONF.227/2025/L.1. https://docs.un.org/en/A/CONF.227/2025/L.1

United Nations General Assembly. (2024). *Pact for the Future*. Resolution A/RES/79/1. United Nations. https://docs.un.org/en/A/RES/79/1 (27/12/2025)

United Nations Secretary-General. (2021): *Our Common Agenda*. United Nations. https://www.un.org/en/content/common-agenda-report/ (27/12/2025)

Nye, J. S, & Welch, D. A. (2011). *Understanding Global Conflict and Cooperation: An Introduction to Theory and History*. Longman

Vinjamuri, L. (ed.) (2025). *Competing Visions of International Order. Responses to US Power in a Fracturing World*. Research Paper, Royal Institute of International Affairs. https://doi.org/10.55317/9781784136383

CHAPTER 3

New International Economic Order

Manuel Couret Branco

1 The Challenge

In 1986, the United Nations General Assembly, recalling the provisions of the International Covenant on Economic, Social and Cultural Rights and the International Covenant on Civil and Political Rights, which bound the state parties to comply with what had been adopted in the Universal Declaration on Human Rights, and other relevant agreements, recommendations, and instruments of the United Nations and its specialized agencies concerning the integral development of the human being, adopted the Right to Development, which, among other provisions, stated the following (United Nations General Assembly, 1986):

- Article 1. The right to development is an inalienable human right by virtue of which every human person and all peoples are entitled to participate in, contribute to, and enjoy economic, social, cultural and political development, in which all human rights and fundamental freedoms can be fully realized.

M. C. Branco (✉)
University of Évora, Évora, Portugal
e-mail: mbranco@uevora.pt

R. de Arriba (ed.), *United Nations Facing Global Economic Disorder: Assessing 20 Policy Proposals*,
https://doi.org/10.1007/978-3-032-21952-7_3

- Article 3. States have the duty to cooperate with each other in ensuring development and eliminating obstacles to development. States should realize their rights and fulfil their duties in such a manner as to promote a new international economic order based on sovereign equality, interdependence, mutual interest and co-operation among all States, as well as to encourage the observance and realization of human rights.

From these two articles it follows that for the international community at the time, development is not just a laudable objective of economic policy but also a full human right, and that its realization must result in a new international economic order. Clearly, for the UN, the prevailing International Economic Order at the time was a major responsible for the deep inequalities existing within and between countries and the deprivation affecting a large part of the world's population.

Almost forty years later the United Nations defined its most ambitious package for development, the Sustainable Development Goals, which in its own words, constitute a universal call to action to end poverty, protect the planet, and improve the lives and prospects of people around the world (DESA, 2015). Is the challenge of a new international economic order still in the United Nations' agenda for development and how? December 2024, the General Assembly of the UN adopted a resolution on the New International Economic Order recalling many resolutions and concerns about the negative impacts of international trade, financial governance, and environmental disregard, and the fact that progress toward ending extreme poverty has been reversed by three to four years at the global level (United Nations General Assembly, 2024a). The general secretary of the UN's report "Our Common Agenda" stresses that "now is the time to re-embrace global solidarity and find new ways to work together for the common good" (United Nations Secretary-General, 2021). How, then, does the United Nations 2030 Agenda on Sustainable Development incorporate the claim for a new international economic order?

2 UN Proposals

After the concept of new international economic order was first proposed in a political declaration adopted at the Fourth Conference of Heads of State or Government of the Non-Aligned Countries, held in Algiers from September 5 to 9, 1973, the United Nations General Assembly adopted the Declaration on the Establishment of a New International Economic Order in May 1974 (United Nations General Assembly, 1974). This declaration defined the new order, among other features, as follows:

1. Just and equitable relationship between the prices of raw materials, primary commodities, manufactured and semi-manufactured goods exported by developing countries and the prices of raw materials, primary commodities, manufactures, capital goods and equipment imported by them with the aim of bringing about sustained improvement in their unsatisfactory terms of trade and the expansion of the world economy.
2. Extension of active assistance to developing countries by the whole international community, free of any political or military conditions. Specifically, it seeks to increase official aid from industrialized countries to 0.7% of their GDP and eliminate any conditionality for such aid, and, finally, to alleviate the burden of foreign debt, including forgiving debt for less developed countries.

To check the presence of the new international economic order as defined above, within 17 Sustainable Development Goals, those most likely to contain references to a new international economic order were selected. These are Goal 1 No Poverty; Goal 2 Zero Hunger; Goal 8 Decent Work and Economic Growth; Goal 10 Reduced Inequalities; and finally, Goal 17 Partnerships for the Goals.

When one wishes to look for traces of a new international economic order within Sustainable Development Goals and particularly within goal 1 No Poverty, the first step is to look for the identified causes of poverty and the actions proposed to eradicate it. Poverty has many dimensions, with causes including unemployment, social exclusion, and the high vulnerability of certain populations to disasters, diseases, and other phenomena that hinder their productivity.

Priority actions on poverty eradication include (DESA, 2015):

- improving access to sustainable livelihoods, entrepreneurial opportunities and productive resources;
- providing universal access to basic social services;

- progressively developing social protection systems to support those who cannot support themselves;
- empowering people living in poverty and their organizations;
- addressing the disproportionate impact of poverty on women;
- working with interested donors and recipients to allocate increased shares of ODA (Official Development Aid) to poverty eradication;
- intensifying international cooperation for poverty eradication.

The only significant mention to the new international economic order as defined by the United Nations itself in 1974 among the actions proposed to achieve Goal 1 is a reference to increase shares of aid, the target of 0.7% of donor's GDP later in SDG 17. One must recall that this specific goal concerning the percentage of GDP to be donated to developing countries has been adopted at every international summit on development since the late 1960s and has never been achieved by donor countries except for half a dozen of them (DESA, 2015). This objective is reaffirmed in UN's Pact for the Future (United Nations General Assembly, 2024b) and in the Sevilla Commitment (United Nations, 2025). In its resolution on a New International Economic Order, the UN:

> calls upon Member States and international financial institutions to provide more liquidity and long-term finance for development, especially in all developing countries, in order to enable them to achieve sustainable development, emphasizes the need to strengthen development cooperation and to increase the volume of and access to concessional finance and grants, and calls upon developed countries that have not done so to fulfil their respective official development assistance commitments, particularly to least developed countries. (United Nations General Assembly, 2024a: 6)

One of the crucial elements of a new international economic order, as defined by the United Nations (i.e. improving unsatisfactory terms of trade) is not mentioned, even though it could reasonably be considered one of the major causes of poverty. The International Trade Union Confederation, an organization that works closely with the International Labour Organization, shows, for instance, that only 0.8%, or 0.18 euros of a shirt sold 29 euros in a European retail shop goes to a worker in the developing world (ITUC, 2016).

The Sevilla Commitment does call for "a universal, rules-based, fair, open, transparent, predictable, inclusive, non-discriminatory and equitable multilateral trading system", but nothing is specified regarding what "fair", "inclusive", and "equitable" should mean in this context (United Nations, 2025: 24). The same commitment adds that value addition and beneficiation of critical minerals and commodities in developing countries should be promoted (United Nations, 2025: 25). However, we are far from the 1974 statement on a new international economic order, which clearly pointed to mitigating unequal trade.

Therefore, it may seem odd that a different distribution of the value generated within the international value chain is not included on the list of actions proposed to fight poverty. One of the reasons for this may be found in the very definition of poverty itself, as even those workers who receive only 0.8% of the value they create are usually situated above the official poverty line, regardless of what it really means to be situated just above the poverty line in terms of real human well-being.

Concerning the new international economic order in goal 2 Zero Hunger, along with a slight reference to increase cooperation, mention is made to limit price volatility and correct and eliminate trade restrictions and distortions in world agricultural markets, inter alia, through the parallel elimination of all forms of agricultural export subsidies and all export measures with equivalent effect, in accordance with the mandate of the Doha Development Round of the World Trade Organization (DESA, 2015). However, if developing countries hold some 70% of the votes at the WTO, their influence in informal decision-making forums, such as the "Green Room" consultations, is disproportionately smaller which constitutes one of the reasons for the unequal status quo in the distribution of trade benefits (Branco, 2009: 124).

Moving on to goal 8, Decent Work and Sustainable Growth, references to a new international economic order are made when mentioning that achieving Goal 8 will requires a profound reform of the financial system to address rising debt, economic uncertainty, and trade tensions, while promoting equitable remuneration (United Nations, 2015). However, this formulation is rather vague. What kind of reform of the financial system? What are the trade tensions that need to be addressed? Some more information can be obtained from other UN publications referred to below in the discussion of Goal 10.

Regarding goal 10 Reduced Inequalities, the objective is to reduce inequalities between and within countries. The goals of this objective also remain somewhat vague, but key elements of a new international economic order are more explicit (United Nations, 2015). Concrete objectives concern:

- Improving the regulation and oversight of global financial institutions and markets and strengthen the enforcement of these regulations.
- Ensuring greater representation and involvement of developing countries in decisions made by international economic and financial institutions to increase the effectiveness, reliability, accountability, and legitimacy of these institutions (at the IMF, for example, only seven countries still hold most of the votes).
- Implementing the principle of special and differential treatment for developing countries, particularly least developed countries, in accordance with World Trade Organization agreements.
- Promoting official development assistance and financial flows, including foreign direct investment, to countries with the greatest needs.

More recently the UN Pact for the Future and the Sevilla Commitment stress the need to reform the international financial architecture, particularly to strengthen the voice and representation of developing countries, with the clearly stated objective of mobilizing additional financing for the Sustainable Development Goals (United Nations General Assembly, 2024b; United Nations, 2025: 26).

The Secretary-General of the UN, for instance, calls for action for a new allocation of special drawing rights by the International Monetary Fund, which should be handled according to developing countries' needs (United Nations General Assembly, 2024a: 6). The Sevilla Commitment calls for ensuring that all companies, including multinationals, pay taxes (United Nations, 2025: 8) and recognizes the need "to assist developing countries in attaining long-term debt sustainability through coordinated policies aimed at fostering debt financing, debt relief, debt restructuring and sound debt management" (United Nations, 2025: 30). Despite the many references to the vulnerable position of developing countries within the world's financial architecture, few references are made to their unequal position in this same architecture, aside from explicit calls for rating agencies to review developing countries' debt ratings.

Finally Goal 17 Partnerships for the Goals. The characteristics of this goal probably make it the most favorable context for the emergence of actions aimed at promoting a new international economic order. One of the most important issues of the new international economic order, if not its very essence, concerns the establishment of new political and economic relations between developed and developing countries. This is precisely the nature of goal 17.

Specific targets within this goal clearly point to a new international economic order. Target 17.2 states that developed countries should fully implement their official development assistance commitments, including the commitment by many developed countries to achieve the target of 0.7 percent of ODA/GNI for developing countries and 0.15 to 0.20 percent of ODA/GNI for least developed countries. ODA providers are encouraged to consider setting a target to provide at least 0.20 percent of ODA/GNI for least developed countries (DESA, 2015).

Target 17.4, in turn, demands that developed countries assist developing countries in attaining long-term debt sustainability through coordinated policies aimed at fostering debt financing, debt relief and debt restructuring, as appropriate, and address the external debt of highly indebted poor countries to reduce debt distress (United Nations, 2015), a request reiterated in the Sevilla Commitment, as seen above.

Finally target 17.10 intends to promote a universal, rules-based, open, non-discriminatory, and equitable multilateral trading system under the World Trade Organization, including through the conclusion of negotiations under its Doha Development Agenda (United Nations, 2015). This goal recaptures the idea of equitable trade that was referred to in the 1974 definition of a new international economic order but, as in SDG goal 1, does not define equitable and once again does not mention the need to improve the unsatisfactory terms of trade that affect developing countries clearly stated in the 1974 declaration. In the WTO terminology equity primarily refers to lifting barriers to trade, while improving unsatisfactory terms of trade involves a different distribution of international trade benefits. Two very different approaches.

3 Assessment

Many aspects of what was defined as a new international economic order in the 1974 declaration are represented in the SDGs, highlighting their importance in the United Nations agenda for socially and environmentally sustainable development, in line with its human rights-based development approach, inaugurated with the adoption of the right to development. However, optimism regarding the proposals for a new international economic order contained in the SDGs should be tempered. Firstly, the actions, that are in theory aiming at establishing a new international economic order are largely vague and imprecise, and secondly, they repeat objectives already present in previous United Nations' declarations, as in the case of development aid. This repetition could, ultimately, be taken as an evidence of United Nations' failure to promote this new international economic order over at least the past forty years. Should we expect, then, the advent of a new international economic order by 2030? Only time will tell.

References

Branco, M. (2009). *Economics Versus Human Rights*. Routledge.

ITUC (2016) *Frontlines Report 2016-Scandal*. International Trade Union Confederation. Retrieved from https://www.ituc-csi.org/frontlines-report-2016-scandal (03/06/2025).

UN DESA. (2015). *Sustainable Development*. Department of Economic and Social Affairs. United Nations. Retrieved from https://sdgs.un.org/goals (17/05/2025).

United Nations. (2025). *Sevilla Commitment*. Fourth International Conference on Financing for Development-Draft Resolution Submitted by the President of the Conference. A/CONF.227/2025/L.1. United Nations. Retrieved from https://docs.un.org/en/A/CONF.227/2025/L.1 (27/12/2025).

United Nations. (2015). *Transforming Our World: The 2030 Agenda for Sustainable Development*. UN General Assembly Resolution a/RES/70/1. United Nations. Retrieved from https://www.un.org/sustainabledevelopment (17/05/2025).

United Nations General Assembly. (1974). Programme of Action on the Establishment of a New International Economic Order. Resolution A/RES/3202(S-VI). United Nations. Retrieved from https://digitallibrary.un.org/record/218451?ln=es&v=pdf

United Nations General Assembly. (1986). *Declaration on the Right to Development*. Resolution a/RES/41/128. United Nations. Retrieved from https://www.ohchr.org/en/instruments-mechanisms/instruments/declaration-right-development (15/05/2025).

United Nations General Assembly. (2024a). *Towards a New International Economic Order*. Resolution a/RES/79/215. United Nations. Retrieved from https://docs.un.org/en/A/RES/79/215] (27/12/2025).

United Nations General Assembly. (2024b). *Pact for the Future*. Resolution a/RES/79/1. United Nations. Retrieved from https://docs.un.org/en/A/RES/79/1 (27/12/2025).

United Nations Secretary-General. (2021). *Our Common Agenda*. United Nations. Retrieved from https://www.un.org/en/content/common-agenda-report/ (27/12/2025).

CHAPTER 4

Human Rights

Maria Sabrina Nola and Raúl de Arriba

1 The Challenge

The concentrated power held by transnational corporations (TNCs) is a decisive factor in shaping the contemporary global economy. Their capacity for investment, innovation, and the organization of value chains enables them to stimulate economic development in numerous countries, generating employment, attracting capital, and driving strategic sectors. However, this same power carries deep and persistent risks for the protection of human rights and the achievement of sustainable and inclusive development.

The relocation of production to countries with weaker labor and environmental regulations has turned millions of workers into expendable components of a system designed to maximize profits. In many such contexts, economic savings take precedence over human dignity,

M. S. Nola (✉) · R. de Arriba
University of Valencia, Valencia, Spain
e-mail: mano7@alumni.uv.es

R. de Arriba
e-mail: dearriba@uv.es

R. de Arriba (ed.), *United Nations Facing Global Economic Disorder: Assessing 20 Policy Proposals*,
https://doi.org/10.1007/978-3-032-21952-7_4

with visible outcomes including excessive working hours, inadequate wages, and labor conditions that fall below the minimum standards recommended by the international community. Global production chains, particularly in labor-intensive sectors such as textiles, agriculture, or light manufacturing, reproduce exploitative practices reminiscent of the harshest forms of economic neocolonialism (Columbia Center on Sustainable Investment, 2021).

The International Labour Organization (ILO) has documented in detail how TNCs, despite their transformative impact on global trade and production, simultaneously generate structural precariousness, characterized by unstable employment, downward pressure on wages, and restrictions on the exercise of basic collective rights such as freedom of association. Although these corporations have undeniably created new jobs, the quality of such employment often falls far short of the goals set out in the 2030 Agenda concerning decent work and sustainable economic growth (ILO, 2017). This reality underscores the urgent need for stricter regulation, capable of guaranteeing dignified working conditions and reducing the imbalances stemming from regulatory competition between countries.

Environmental impact constitutes another critical dimension of TNC activities. These corporations are among the largest emitters of CO_2 and are directly linked to large-scale deforestation, water pollution, and the degradation of local ecosystems (UNCTAD, 2022). The priority accorded to short-term profit irreversibly undermines the sustainability of the territories where they operate, damaging not only the environment but also the communities that depend on it for their livelihoods.

Beyond these, it is possible to list other internationally protected rights that are often harmed by the conduct of transnational corporations. These include: the right to democratic participation along with the right to freedom of expression and information, which are frequently threatened by practices such as Strategic Lawsuits Against Public Participation; the right to an adequate standard of living and the right of indigenous peoples to access land and natural resources; the right to access to justice and effective remedy, which in many cases is affected by transnational corporations'recourse to international tribunals (such as ICSID) that tend to favor corporate interests (Columbia Center on Sustainable Investment, 2021).

Finally, an increasingly salient dimension of TNC power concerns the digital sphere. Technology-based TNCs exercise growing influence through mass surveillance, data extraction, and algorithmic governance. The Pegasus scandal exposed how spyware developed by a private company (NSO Group) was used to monitor journalists, activists, and political opponents, resulting in serious violations of fundamental rights such as privacy and freedom of expression (Amnesty International, 2024). At the same time, a paradigmatic example of this type of conflict is the Snowden case in 2013. This instance illustrates how several transnational corporations, including Google, Microsoft, Apple, Yahoo, Facebook, and Skype, collaborated with the U.S. National Security Agency (NSA) by providing access to users' data under the PRISM surveillance program (Amnesty International, 2015). Such practices proved highly detrimental to human rights, particularly by violating the right to privacy on a massive scale. Moreover, the extraterritorial nature of these violations exposed significant gaps in the global governance of human rights. Corporate complicity is also evident, as these TNCs prioritized the national security interests of their home states over the protection of human rights worldwide, raising critical questions regarding their accountability and responsibility in this domain.

To these adverse effects must be added the absence of a binding international regulatory framework that establishes clear and enforceable responsibilities for TNCs with respect to human rights. In practice, international trade agreements tend to safeguard the economic interests of corporations while rarely regulating their social and environmental obligations in an effective manner.

Although self-regulation and voluntary adherence instruments have helped disseminate the notion of corporate social responsibility, they present structural limitations that are difficult to overcome: their optional nature leads to uneven application, the absence of sanctions weakens accountability, and the lack of effective monitoring systems hinders the evaluation of the actual implementation of proclaimed principles (Ramasastry, 2015). In this context, the need to move toward stronger and more coherent forms of international governance is increasingly evident.

2 UN Proposals

With distinctive features in the international sphere, the two International Covenants adopted in 1966 occupy a central position. The International Covenant on Civil and Political Rights (ICCPR) recognizes, among others: the right to life; the prohibition of torture and of cruel, inhuman, or degrading treatment or punishment; the right to liberty and security of person; the right to privacy; freedom of thought, conscience, and religion; as well as freedom of expression (United Nations General Assembly, 1966). The International Covenant on Economic, Social and Cultural Rights (ICESCR), for its part, encompasses rights such as: the right to work; the right to just and favorable conditions of work; freedom of association and trade union rights; the right to an adequate standard of living, including adequate food, clothing, and housing; the right to the highest attainable standard of physical and mental health; and the right to enjoy the benefits of scientific progress (OHCHR, 1966).

In particular, Article 2 of the ICCPR establishes that: "Each State Party undertakes to respect and to ensure to all individuals within its territory and subject to its jurisdiction the rights recognized in the present Covenant" (United Nations General Assembly, 1966, Art. 2.1). However, the Human Rights Committee, in its General Comment No. 31, has clarified and expanded the territorial scope of States' obligations, stating that: "Each State Party must respect and ensure the rights laid down in the Covenant to anyone within the power or effective control of that State Party, even if not situated within the territory of the State Party" (United Nations Human Rights Committee, 2004, para. 10).

The United Nations' approach to transnational corporations is articulated through a complex and multidimensional framework of international bodies and instruments, each playing a particular role in promoting corporate responsibility and safeguarding human rights. This system did not emerge spontaneously but rather as a response to the growing influence of corporations on the global stage and the recognition that national regulatory frameworks are insufficient when faced with economic actors capable of exerting influence simultaneously across multiple jurisdictions. Aware of these limitations, the UN has sought to create a flexible yet ambitious normative framework, combining the promotion of universal ethical standards with the articulation of practical implementation mechanisms.

A fundamental milestone in this process is the *Guiding Principles on Business and Human Rights*, adopted in 2011 after an extensive process of consultations, negotiations, and debates among governments, corporations, and civil society (OHCHR, 2011). Also known as the Ruggie Principles, in reference to their main architect, they mark a turning point as they clearly define standards of corporate social responsibility in terms of human rights. Beyond their non-binding character, the Guiding Principles advance a framework that places the individual at the center of economic activity, reaffirming that economic progress cannot be achieved at the expense of dignity and fundamental rights.

The three pillars on which they are built are particularly significant. The first, *Duty to Protect*, reminds states of their obligation to safeguard human rights and prevent violations committed by corporations, whether within their territory or through transnational activities with extraterritorial impact. The second, *Responsibility to Respect*, establishes that companies must not only refrain from infringing human rights but also adopt proactive measures to ensure that their operations and supply chains remain consistent with these principles. Finally, the third pillar, *Access to Remedy*, stresses that states must guarantee rapid, effective, and accessible avenues for redress, both judicial and non-judicial, to ensure that victims of abuses are not left without protection.

The 2030 Agenda and the Sustainable Development Goals (SDGs) further reinforced this orientation. En su párrafo 10, establece que "la Agenda se basa en la Declaración Universal de Derechos Humanos, los tratados internacionales de derechos humanos y otros instrumentos." In particular, Goal 8, aimed at promoting sustained, inclusive, and sustainable economic growth, and Goal 10, focused on reducing inequalities, represent concrete attempts to realign the economy within ethical and social parameters[1]. These goals underscore that business profitability and social well-being are not mutually exclusive but rather must be articulated within a logic of complementarity. Linking corporate strategies to the SDGs also makes their commitment more tangible, as the goals are accompanied by measurable indicators that facilitate the evaluation of the real impact of corporate activities (United Nations, 2015).

Within this framework, the *Global Compact* has emerged as a key platform for cooperation among corporations, institutions, and civil society. Its significance lies not only in its reach—more than 12,000 signatories across 170 countries, including over 8600 companies—but also in its ability to bring together actors that traditionally operate under different logics: governments, corporations, and civil society organizations (United Nations Global Compact, 2022). The *Global Compact* goes

[1] Of course, these are not the only ones. There are other goals that align with human rights (for instance: education, health, water, housing, gender equality, justice, etc.).

beyond the formulation of abstract principles by proposing an actionable framework inspired by universally recognized values drawn from foundational documents such as the Universal Declaration of Human Rights (United Nations General Assembly, 1948), the ILO Declaration (ILO, 1998), the Rio Declaration (United Nations, 2018), and the United Nations Convention against Corruption (United Nations General Assembly, 2003).

Launched in 1999 by then-UN Secretary-General Kofi Annan at the World Economic Forum in Davos, the *Global Compact* marked a turning point by inviting corporations to become active participants in the protection of fundamental rights (United Nations Global Compact, 2016). In his speech, Annan urged business leaders to "embrace, support and enact a set of core values in the areas of human rights, labour standards, and environmental practices." This appeal addressed not only the ethical responsibility of corporations but also their capacity to transform realities within their value chains.

The *Global Compact* is structured around ten principles that cover key areas. The first two relate to the respect and promotion of human rights, calling on companies to avoid complicity in human rights violations. The next four principles (3–6) focus on labor rights, including freedom of association, the elimination of forced and child labor, and the fight against workplace discrimination. Principles 7–9 address environmental issues, encouraging the adoption of sustainable technologies and environmentally responsible practices. The tenth principle, added in 2004, commits companies to combat corruption in all its forms, including extortion and bribery.

The *Global Compact* also proposes a dynamic model of six steps to integrate its principles: public commitment by business leaders, continuous risk and impact assessment, definition of objectives and action plans, implementation through policies and training, measurement of progress with clear indicators, and transparent communication with stakeholders. This methodology is designed to ensure not only formal adherence but also the substantive incorporation of the principles into daily business practices. Companies that advance in this process can achieve "Advanced" status, reserved for those meeting stricter criteria in governance, alignment with the SDGs, operational implementation, transparency, and stakeholder engagement.

Nevertheless, the limitations of the *Global Compact* are clear: its voluntary nature, the absence of sanctions, and the lack of rigorous verification mechanisms have prevented it from becoming a fully effective tool (Ruiz-Morales, 2016). Aware of these shortcomings, the UN launched in 2003 the *Norms on the Responsibilities of Transnational Corporations and Other Business Enterprises with Regard to Human Rights* (Sub-Commission on the Promotion and Protection of Human Rights, 2003). This document represents a more ambitious step, as it introduces the concept of direct legal obligations for corporations, subjecting them to periodic, transparent, and independent monitoring with the participation of NGOs and other social actors. While reaffirming the primacy of states in the promotion and protection of human rights, these norms impose specific duties on TNCs, including the obligation to remedy harm caused to individuals or communities.

The obligations contained in the 2003 Norms are broad: equal treatment and non-discrimination, the right to workplace safety, respect for national sovereignty, protection of workers' rights, consumer protection, and environmental stewardship. However, despite their innovative scope, the norms failed to acquire binding status in international law due to strong resistance from several states and business associations, notably the United States, Russia, China, and multiple European Union member states. In a subsequent effort, a binding international treaty on business and human rights was proposed under the coordination of the Open-Ended Intergovernmental Working Group. Yet, this project also stalled, failing to achieve significant progress, and by 2022 had produced no concrete results.

In this context, other non-binding instruments have gained prominence. The ILO's *Tripartite Declaration of Principles concerning Multinational Enterprises and Social Policy* (ILO, 2001) serves as a fundamental guide for the adoption of inclusive, responsible, and sustainable labor practices. It specifies corporate duties related to freedom of association, the abolition of forced labor, the elimination of child labor and discrimination, as well as the provision of safe working conditions, fair wages, and social protection. It also emphasizes the importance of cooperation among governments, businesses, and workers as a means of improving social and economic welfare.

Taken together, these instruments reflect the international community's determination to move toward a model in which transnational corporations assume clearer responsibilities regarding human rights and sustainable development. Yet, the tension between voluntariness and binding regulation remains the central challenge. While *soft law* initiatives have helped build consensus and raise expectations regarding corporate behavior, their lack of enforcement mechanisms continues to limit effectiveness. For this reason, it is increasingly urgent to reflect on forms of global governance capable of balancing the economic power of TNCs with the effective protection of human rights and the environment.

3 Assessment

The regulation of transnational corporations requires a more incisive multilateral approach, capable of overcoming the limitations inherent to *soft law* instruments. Although the current proposals of the United Nations represent a significant step forward, they still demand stricter monitoring mechanisms and the consolidation of a binding legal framework.

The main difficulty lies in the fact that international human rights conventions are, by definition, directed at states and not at private actors, including corporations. One way of reconciling state sovereignty with the protection of human rights would be to impose conventional obligations on states, requiring them to introduce domestic rules directly applicable to companies, establishing regimes of civil and criminal liability for conduct that infringes upon human rights.

In this regard, the French Law on the Duty of Vigilance (Loi 339/2017, 2017) offers an illustrative example of how national legal systems can contribute to filling global regulatory gaps, fostering corporate responsibility in the fields of human rights and environmental protection. This legislation obliges large French companies to design and implement vigilance plans aimed at identifying, preventing, and mitigating risks related to human rights, health, safety, and the environment throughout their entire supply chain, including foreign operations. In cases of non-compliance, the law provides civil liability mechanisms that enable victims to seek effective judicial remedies.

Complementarily, Principle 9 of the United Nations Guiding Principles on Business and Human Rights reminds states of their obligation to "maintain an adequate national regulatory framework to ensure respect for their own human rights duties when they conclude agreements on activities" (OHCHR, 2011).

In a context of growing global interdependence, denying or opposing the influence of transnational corporations would amount to rejecting a structural process of contemporary economic development, with the risk of producing unintended and counterproductive consequences. Therefore, rather than questioning their predominant role, it is more realistic and effective to learn how to manage their influence in ways that promote balanced economic and social development. Accordingly, the issue is not to advocate for a drastic reduction in the activity of transnational corporations, but to rethink the governance mechanisms that regulate their conduct. These entities should not be regarded as adversaries, but as actors whose influence, if properly managed, can be incorporated into a more just global framework. In this sense, the initiatives promoted by the United Nations provide a valuable foundation for cultivating favorable expectations regarding the future of more effective international regulatory frameworks.

References

Amnesty International. (2015, June 4). Two Years After Snowden: Protecting Human Rights in an Age of Mass Surveillance (Briefing). *Amnesty International*. https://www.amnesty.nl/content/uploads/2015/06/two_years_after_snowden_final_report_en_a4.pdf?x32866

Amnesty International (2024). Case study: The Pegasus Project. *Amnesty International*. https://securitylab.amnesty.org/case-study-the-pegasus-project/

Columbia Center on Sustainable Investment. (2021, December). *Cartilla: Tratados Internacionales de Inversión y Solución de Controversias Inversor Estado*. https://ccsi.columbia.edu/sites/ccsi.columbia.edu/files/content/Cartilla%20%20Tratados%20Internacionales%20de%20Inversio%CC%81n%20y%20Solucio%CC%81n%20de%20Controversias%20Inversor-Estado.pdf.

ILO. (1998). Declaration on fundamental principles and rights at work and its follow-up. In Adopted by the international labour conference at its 86th session, Geneva, 18 June 1998. Organization.

ILO. (2001). Tripartite declaration of principles concerning multinational enterprises and social policy (3rd ed.). International Labour Office.

ILO. (2017). Tripartite declaration of principles concerning multinational enterprises and social policy (updated edition). International Labour Office.

Loi 339/2017. (2017). Loi 399/2017 du 27 mars 2017 relative au devoir de vigilance des sociétés mères et des entreprises donneuses d'ordre. *Journal officiel de la République française.*. https://www.legifrance.gouv.fr/jorf/id/JORFTEXT000034290626/

OHCHR. (1966, 16 December). International Covenant on Economic, Social and Cultural Rights. *Office of the United Nations High Commissioner for Human Rights*. https://www.ohchr.org/en/instruments-mechanisms/instruments/international covenant-economic-social-and-cultural-rights.

OHCHR. (2011). Guiding principles on business and human rights: Implementing the United Nations "protect, respect and remedy" framework. *Office of the United Nations High Commissioner for Human Rights*. https://www.ohchr.org/sites/default/files/documents/publications/guidingprinciplesbusinesshr_en.pdf

Ramasastry, A. (2015). Corporate social responsibility versus business and human rights: Bridging the gap between responsibility and accountability. *Journal of Human Rights, 14*(2), 237–259. https://doi.org/10.1080/14754835.2015.1037953

Ruiz-Morales, C.-A. (2016). Influencia de la internacionalización de la empresa en la implementación de los 10 principios del Pacto Mundial de Naciones Unidas. *Revista de Comunicación de la SEECI, 41*, 155–178.

Sub-Commission on the Promotion and Protection of Human Rights. (2003, August 13). *Draft Norms on the Responsibilities of Transnational Corporations and Other Business Enterprises with Regard to Human Rights* (UN Doc. E/CN.4/Sub.2/2003/12/Rev.2). United Nations Economic and Social Council.

UNCTAD. (2022). *World Investment Report 2022: Development prospects in a fractured world*. United Nations Conference on Trade and Development.

United Nations. (2015). Transforming our world: The 2030 agenda for sustainable development. UN general assembly resolution a/RES/70/1. *United Nations*. https://www.un.org/sustainabledevelopment

United Nations. (2018). *Global Compact for Safe, Orderly and Regular Migration: Intergovernmentally negotiated and agreed outcome*. A/CONF.231/3. United Nations.

United Nations General Assembly. (1948). Universal declaration of human rights. Resolution 217 a (III). *United Nations*.

United Nations General Assembly. (1966). International covenant on civil and political rights. Resolution 2200A (XXI). *United Nations*.

United Nations General Assembly. (2003). United Nations convention against corruption. Resolution A/RES/58/4. *United Nations*.

United Nations Global Compact. (2016). The ten principles of the United Nations global compact. *United Nations Global Compact.*. https://unglobalcompact.org/what-is-gc/mission/principles

United Nations Global Compact. (2022). Annual Report 2022. United Nations Global Compact.

United Nations Human Rights Committee. (2004). General comment no. 31: The nature of the general legal obligation imposed on states parties to the covenant (CCPR/C/21/Rev.1/Add.13). United Nations Human Rights Committee.

CHAPTER 5

Trade

Artur Colom-Jaén

1 The Challenge

In May 1974, the United Nations General Assembly adopted the Declaration on a New International Economic Order (NIEO), calling for comprehensive reforms in trade, finance, technology transfer, and global governance. Its aim was to redress historical inequalities and affirm the right to development of what then was commonly called the Third World (United Nations General Assembly, 1974). Prominently supported by the Group of 77 [1], the NIEO embodied a coordinated push for reform through multilateral institutions. However, it remained largely aspirational, lacking binding mechanisms, facing resistance from developed countries, and ultimately sidelined by shifting global dynamics. The structural vulnerabilities it sought to address (narrow export bases,

[1] The Group of 77 (G77) is a coalition of developing countries established in 1964 at the United Nations to promote their collective economic interests and enhance the collective bargaining capacity of developing countries, then commonly referred to as the Third World.

A. Colom-Jaén (✉)
University of Barcelona, Barcelona, Spain
e-mail: artur.colom@ub.edu

R. de Arriba (ed.), *United Nations Facing Global Economic Disorder: Assessing 20 Policy Proposals*,
https://doi.org/10.1007/978-3-032-21952-7_5

commodity price volatility, dependence on external credit, and chronic balance-of-payments constraints) have persisted in many countries.

Concerns about the developmental implications of the post-war trade system had already emerged in the 1950s. Raúl Prebisch (1950) and Hans Singer (1949) argued that the terms of trade systematically moved against primary commodity exporters, undermining industrialization prospects and exposing them to external shocks. With a different approach, Arghiri Emmanuel (1972) highlighted how wage differentials and labour market asymmetries facilitated value transfer from poorer to richer countries through international trade. These critiques shared a common diagnosis: the structure of international trade was inherently unfavourable to the Global South.

At the same time, the international trade system was expanding rapidly, generating efficiency gains and productivity growth in the world economy. Yet the distribution of these gains was highly uneven, with advanced economies consolidating their technological lead while many developing countries remained locked into primary exports. Thus, the debate was never about trade per se, but about the conditions under which it could become a key driver of development.

Half a century later, the international trade system continues to fall short of promoting inclusive, long-term development. Despite recurring promises of shared prosperity, many developing countries remain reliant on raw material and commodity exports. 66% of developing economies were commodity-dependent in 2021–2023, with around 85% in Africa. In several cases, a single product made up more than 80% of export earnings (UNCTAD, 2025a). These patterns reflect enduring structural asymmetries rooted in colonial trade regimes and post-independence specialization.

These vulnerabilities were exacerbated by the global shocks of the 1970s, including oil price volatility and rising interest rates. The resulting debt crisis of the 1980s (particularly acute in Latin America and sub-Saharan Africa) exposed the fragility of many developing economies. With limited available finance and high debt burdens, many countries were compelled to adopt structural adjustment programmes supervised by the IMF and World Bank. These programmes mandated trade liberalization, fiscal austerity, and privatization to restore macroeconomic stability. However, they often led to deindustrialization, unemployment, poverty, and renewed external vulnerability, entrenching a model of dependence and stagnation (Arrighi, 1994; Mkandawire & Soludo, 1998).

The collapse of the Soviet Union in the early 1990s cemented neoliberal dominance and intensified global integration, setting in motion what Rodrik (2011) later termed '*hyperglobalization*'. In this regard, the establishment of the WTO in 1995 marked a turning point in global trade governance. As the first international body with a binding dispute settlement mechanism and comprehensive rules on goods, services, and intellectual property, the WTO institutionalized a market-oriented regime reflecting the post–Cold War *Zeitgeist*. Unlike the GATT, it expanded into domestic regulation through agreements such as TRIPS and TRIMs[2], embedding rules aligned with the interests of advanced economies and transnational capital.

Despite its ambitions, the WTO has struggled to advance new multilateral agreements. Since the Uruguay Round (1986–1994), no global trade round has been concluded. The Doha Development Round, launched in 2001, remains stalled amid persistent Global North–South disagreements over subsidies, market access, intellectual property, and regulatory asymmetries. The WTO's inability to deliver its development agenda has prompted critique from the Global South, which argues the system imposes obligations without offering equivalent developmental gains or flexibility, reflecting an entrenched *rapport de force* favouring advanced economies.

The dominant paradigm of development through trade openness has yielded mixed outcomes. Deep integration has often required tariff reductions, liberalized investment regimes, and curtailed industrial policy, limiting autonomy in development strategy design. As Rodrik (2011) formulates in his famous trilemma, economic globalization, national sovereignty, and democratic politics cannot be simultaneously pursued; one must be sacrificed. In practice, many developing countries have surrendered policy space to align with global rules privileging market access over structural transformation.

[2] TRIPS (Trade-Related Aspects of Intellectual Property Rights) is a WTO agreement that sets binding minimum standards for the protection and enforcement of intellectual property rights, often criticized for favouring the interests of multinational corporations and restricting access to essential goods such as medicines. TRIMs (Trade-Related Investment Measures) prohibits certain investment-related policies, such as local content requirements or trade-balancing measures, that were historically used by developing countries to support domestic industries, thereby limiting their policy space for industrial development.

Even those developing countries that have integrated into global value chains (GVCs) and achieved some degree of industrialization are often confined to low-value-added activities like assembly or resource extraction, with limited opportunities for technological upgrading or diversification. The current trade regime has facilitated GVC expansion under institutional conditions that reinforce global and domestic inequality. Trade liberalization, investor protections, and intellectual property regimes have enabled transnational corporations (primarily based in developed countries) to capture a disproportionate share of value. The limited transfer of knowledge, combined with widespread use of tax havens and regulatory arbitrage, has further constrained the developmental benefits of GVC participation for the Global South. Many remain trapped in commodity exports or low-value GVC segments, with restricted autonomy in policy design and limited prospects for upgrading (UNCTAD, 2018; Whitfield et al., 2020).

These tensions have intensified with recent shifts in global trade geopolitics. Since 2018, the resurgence of national-populist protectionism, led by the United States, has reintroduced tariffs and export controls. This trend has been accompanied by the paralysis of the WTO's Appellate Body since 2019 (a result of sustained US obstruction) and by a renewed proliferation of bilateral and regional trade agreements, further fragmenting the multilateral system. While developing countries still face structural constraints, they must now navigate a more unpredictable and incoherent trade landscape. The reassertion of protectionist measures in advanced economies, often on flawed security or industrial grounds, narrows the scope for export-led growth in the Global South and exposes contradictions in the openness narrative.

The 2025 Trump tariff shock crystallized these dynamics by exposing the deeper logic underpinning the current trade regime. The emerging global economic order is increasingly disengaged from a structured and predictable rule-based liberalization and instead organized around contested policy sovereignty, in which powerful states selectively suspend multilateral commitments while maintaining openness requirements for others. In this context, unilateral tariff hikes operate less as instruments of productive transformation than as geopolitical signals, amplifying uncertainty and asymmetry (Ing & Rodrik, 2026).

2 UN Proposals

Since the 1960s, the United Nations (especially through UNCTAD) has advanced proposals to reorient global trade towards development and structural transformation. These efforts responded to persistent asymmetries in global trade, as diagnosed by economists such as Prebisch and Furtado through ECLAC[3] among others. Rather than treating trade as an end, the UN has often framed it as a means for long-term economic transformation.

These proposals have taken shape through specific instruments like non-reciprocal trade preferences, notably the Generalized System of Preferences (GSP), endorsed at UNCTAD II in 1968. Alongside the GSP, the principle of Special and Differential Treatment (SDT) has become a cornerstone of UNCTAD's trade vision. Both aimed to address structural disadvantages by offering market access and flexibility in trade obligations. While GSP challenged the reciprocity principle in GATT, SDT was integrated into WTO agreements. However, both tools were diluted over time, weakened by limited eligibility, non-binding terms, and political resistance. As such, they offered only marginal correction to global trade asymmetries.

The shrinking of policy space has emerged as a central concern in UNCTAD's analysis of the contemporary trade regime. UNCTAD's *Trade and Development Reports* have repeatedly warned that WTO rules, as well as North–South regional and bilateral trade and investment agreements, constrain tools such as subsidies, local content requirements, capital controls, and public procurement preferences. Agreements such as NAFTA (now USMCA)[4] and the Economic Partnership Agreements

[3] The United Nations Economic Commission for Latin America and the Caribbean (ECLAC), commonly known as CEPAL in Spanish, was established in 1948 to promote economic development in Latin America. Its first Executive Secretary was Raúl Prebisch, a key figure in structuralist development theory.

[4] The North American Free Trade Agreement (NAFTA), in force from 1994 to 2020, was a trilateral trade agreement between the United States, Canada, and Mexico. It was replaced in 2020 by the United States–Mexico–Canada Agreement (USMCA).

between the European Union and ACP countries[5] typify these kinds of arrangements.

Restrictions also extend to technology transfer, industrial licensing, and intellectual property flexibility, instruments once central to now-developed countries' strategies. These constraints, often embedded in frameworks claiming to promote development, limit the capacity of developing countries to pursue strategic interventions for economic transformation and technological upgrading (Chang, 2002).

In response, the UN has called for greater coherence between trade, finance, and development. Through its flagship reports[6], UNCTAD has proposed rethinking preference schemes to support industrial upgrading, governing GVCs for fairer value distribution, easing technology transfer through more flexible intellectual property regimes, and restoring the use of local content rules and targeted subsidies. These proposals reflect a fundamental critique: the global trade and financial architecture must enable autonomous strategies, not merely facilitate deeper integration into global markets. Beyond addressing structural disadvantages, these proposals were also conceived as systemic reforms. By widening access, easing asymmetries, and promoting technology diffusion, UNCTAD argued they would strengthen the multilateral trade regime itself, reducing tensions and fostering a more predictable environment for all participants in the global economy. Yet the institutional environment has come to treat liberalization as a panacea, sidelining its role as a strategic instrument for structural transformation.

The adoption by the UN of the Sustainable Development Goals (SDGs) in 2015 marked a turning point in global development discourse. Framed as a universal blueprint for sustainable development, the SDGs widened the scope of cooperation across social, environmental, and economic dimensions (United Nations General Assembly, 2015). Compared to earlier UN frameworks like the NIEO, the SDGs reflect a shift from questioning global power imbalances towards technocratic

[5] The African, Caribbean and Pacific (ACP) Group of States is a coalition of countries that have historically maintained a special partnership with the European Union, particularly through development cooperation and trade agreements such as the Cotonou Agreement.

[6] Besides the *Trade and Development Report*, UNCTAD publishes several other flagship reports, including the *World Investment Report*, the *Least Developed Countries Report*, and the *Economic Development in Africa Report*.

consensus. Although trade is not a central pillar of the SDGs, it features in Goal 17: Partnerships for the Goals, which includes several trade-related targets. Specifically, Target 17.10 calls for the promotion of a *universal, rules-based, open, non-discriminatory and equitable multilateral trading system under the WTO, including through the conclusion of negotiations under its Doha Development Agenda*. Target 17.11 seeks to increase exports from developing countries, especially from least developed countries (LDCs), and Target 17.12 calls for timely duty-free, quota-free access for LDCs.

These targets signal institutional alignment between the SDG framework and the multilateral trade regime. Whereas earlier UN trade proposals challenged somehow global capitalism's structure, SDG trade targets are framed within WTO norms. This reveals a tension: the SDGs endorse a system that, in practice, has constrained Global South policy autonomy, reinforced commodity dependence, and limited industrialization prospects. The underlying assumption that market integration, operating within existing rules, automatically fosters development stands in contrast to decades of structuralist analysis. Moreover, SDG trade targets lack binding commitments or enforcement mechanisms. Calls to increase LDC exports or to establish a 'rules-based' system are often made without addressing agricultural subsidies in the Global North, restrictive intellectual property regimes, or investor–state dispute settlement mechanisms. As a result, the SDG trade agenda lacks the political traction needed for meaningful change.

UNCTAD, while formally supportive of the SDGs, has offered a more critical reading. For instance, in its *Trade and Development Report 2020*, it argued that achieving the 2030 Agenda requires not only financing but deep reform of global trade, finance, and technology governance (UNCTAD, 2020). The report stressed that openness alone cannot deliver development. Yet these insights remain marginal within mainstream SDG discourse, which favours public–private partnerships, investment facilitation, and regulatory harmonization. The SDG framework risks reproducing, rather than transforming, the conditions that constrain Global South development.

A comparison with the earlier UN Millennium Development Goals (MDGs), set in 2001, underscores the shift in logic (United Nations Secretary-General, 2001). The MDGs, although also technocratic and limited in scope, treated trade as a supporting mechanism for development, focusing on market access, 'aid for trade', and tariff preferences.

In contrast, the SDGs frame trade as a system-wide process, participation in the WTO and global economic integration. This represents a shift from trade as a means of development assistance to trade as a presumed pathway to development in itself, regardless of the structural constraints that may persist.

These institutional continuities have been further tested by the resurgence of trade protectionism in recent years, revealing the fragility of the existing trade architecture. Since 2018, the international trade landscape has been destabilized by a surge in protectionist measures largely triggered by the United States under the Trump administration. The escalation of these tariff tensions risks mutating into a systemic trade war with global consequences. A careful analysis stresses that the shockwaves of these conflicts are not confined to the principal actors, but extend to developing countries, which are often deeply embedded in global value chains and vulnerable to shifts in demand, investment, and rules of origin. Moreover, these tensions are exacerbating structural fragilities in the Global South, particularly for commodity-dependent economies that lack diversification and bargaining power (UNCTAD, 2025b).

Recent global assessments further confirm that the sharp rise in U.S. tariffs in 2025 has increased trade policy uncertainty and disrupted supply chains, weakening export prospects and amplifying financial volatility in developing economies (UN DESA, 2026). This episode has further constrained the developmental policy space of developing countries, reinforcing a fragmented multilateral landscape in which weaker economies remain exposed to shocks they neither initiate nor control.

Taken together, these recent developments reaffirm the developmental asymmetries that have long underpinned UN proposals since the emergence of the post-war development agenda in the 1950s. Confronted with the current rise of national-populist protectionism in the Global North and the increasingly contested nature of the multilateral order, UNCTAD's response highlights the urgency of reclaiming developmental space. Without a recalibration of trade and investment rules to reflect the asymmetries of global capitalism, the trade wars risk reinforcing the very inequalities the UN system has long sought to overcome.

3 Assessment

The proposals advanced by the United Nations (particularly through UNCTAD) reflect a longstanding commitment to reorienting the international trade system towards global developmental equity and structural transformation in developing countries. From the 1974 New International Economic Order (NIEO) declaration to more recent calls for increased policy space, technology transfer, and fairer governance of global value chains, these initiatives have consistently challenged the dominant liberal orthodoxy. Yet, despite their analytical consistency and historical relevance, they have struggled to reshape the core architecture of global trade governance.

This contradiction is especially visible when contrasting UNCTAD's analyses with the content of the 2030 Agenda for Sustainable Development. While the Sustainable Development Goals (SDGs) include several trade-related targets as seen above that implicitly endorse the existing neoliberal rules-based framework under the World Trade Organization, without confronting how those same rules restrict the developmental autonomy of the Global South. The SDG framework celebrates participation in global trade but does not question the asymmetries embedded in trade liberalization, intellectual property rights, or investor protections. As a result, it risks reinforcing rather than disrupting the patterns of dependency it purports to address.

UNCTAD, by contrast, has repeatedly called attention to the structural constraints imposed by global trade and financial architecture. Its successive Trade and Development Reports stress the importance of industrial policy, strategic opening, and capital controls, not as exceptions, but as essential tools of development strategy. However, these insights have remained largely marginal in mainstream development discourse, sidelined by a technocratic consensus that prioritizes liberalization, efficiency, and market integration. This institutional incoherence reflects a deeper clash between two visions of global economic governance: one centred on sovereignty, autonomy in policy design, redistribution, and developmental justice; the other on predictability, market access, and investor security.

This tension came into sharp relief with the adoption of a new resolution on the New International Economic Order by the G77+China in December 2024, marking the fiftieth anniversary of the original NIEO (United Nations General Assembly, 2024). The resolution was endorsed by the UN General Assembly on 19 December 2024 with a strong majority: 134 votes in favour, 3 against, and 48 abstentions, highlighting widespread support among developing countries. More than a commemorative gesture, the 2024 declaration signalled a powerful reassertion of Global South discontents with the prevailing order. It denounced the continued marginalization of developing countries within trade and financial institutions and reaffirmed the urgent need for policy space, technology sharing, and a fairer distribution of value in GVCs and global markets. As the declaration states: *'The promise of a fair and inclusive global economic order remains unfulfilled. A renewed multilateralism must place development at its core, not at its periphery'*. This intervention underscores the widespread dissatisfaction with a system that has, for decades, delivered less transformation than it promised.

Against this backdrop, the dominant framing of current trade tensions as a binary contest between free trade and protectionism is not analytically sufficient. The real challenge lies in reconstructing multilateralism as a collective developmental project, not simply a forum for liberalization or dispute settlement. Trade governance should not be reduced to a battleground of great power rivalry, nor a vehicle for enforcing the prerogatives of transnational capital. It must instead become a site of meaningful redistribution of voice, opportunity, and technological capacity, enabling countries to pursue autonomous development strategies.

While the shortcomings of existing multilateral institutions are well documented, the alternative must not be isolationism or the unchecked proliferation of power asymmetries. Abandoning multilateralism altogether risks accelerating a shift towards a world increasingly governed by *lex mercatoria*, a fragmented system in which commercial law, investor contracts, and the power of transnational corporations outweigh cooperation, sovereign policy, and democratic oversight. If development is to remain a global public good, it must be institutionally embedded within the rules and norms of the international trade regime.

UNCTAD's voice remains indispensable in articulating this alternative vision. Yet its influence has been gradually eclipsed by institutions whose mandates are more aligned with liberalization than development. If the United Nations is to reclaim its historic role in shaping a fairer global trade order, it must not only continue producing rigorous analysis, but also find new mechanisms of enforcement, coalitions of like-minded states, and alliances with civil society and labour movements to shift the balance of power within the global trade system.

References

Arrighi, G. (1994). *The long twentieth century: Money, power, and the origins of our times*. Verso.

Chang, H.-J. (2002). *Kicking away the ladder: Development strategy in historical perspective*. Anthem Press.

Emmanuel, A. (1972). *Unequal exchange: A study of the imperialism of trade*. Monthly Review Press.

Ing, L. Y., & Rodrik, D. (2026). *The new global economic order*. Routledge.

Mkandawire, T., & Soludo, C. C. (1998). *Our continent, our future: African perspectives on structural adjustment*. CODESRIA.

Prebisch, R. (1950). *The economic development of Latin America and its principal problems*. United Nations Economic Commission for Latin America.

Rodrik, D. (2011). *The globalization paradox: Democracy and the future of the world economy*. W. W. Norton & Company.

Singer, H. W. (1949). *Post-war price relations between under-developed and industrialized countries* (UN Department of Economic Affairs, Bulletin no. 6). United Nations.

UN DESA. (2026). *World economic situation and prospects 2026*. United Nations Department of Economic and Social Affairs.

UNCTAD. (2018). *Trade and development report 2018: Power, platforms and the free trade delusion*. United Nations Conference on Trade and Development.

UNCTAD. (2020). *Trade and development report 2020: From global pandemic to prosperity for all: Avoiding another lost decade*. United Nations Conference on Trade and Development.

UNCTAD. (2025a). *State of commodity dependence 2025*. United Nations Conference on Trade and Development.

UNCTAD. (2025b). *Sparing the vulnerable: The cost of new tariff burdens*. United Nations Conference on Trade and Development.

United Nations General Assembly. (1974). *Declaration on the establishment of a new international economic order*. UN General Assembly Resolution A/RES/3201(S-VI). United Nations.

United Nations General Assembly. (2015). *Transforming our world: The 2030 agenda for sustainable development*. UN General Assembly Resolution A/RES/70/1. United Nations.

United Nations General Assembly. (2024). *Towards a new international economic order*. UN General Assembly Resolution A/RES/79/215. United Nations.

United Nations Secretary-General. (2001). *Road map towards the implementation of the United Nations Millennium Declaration: Report of the Secretary-General*. UN Doc. A/56/326. United Nations.

Whitfield, L., Staritz, C., & Morris, M. (2020). Global value chains, industrial policy and economic upgrading in Ethiopia's apparel sector. *Development and Change, 51*(4), 1018–1043.

CHAPTER 6

International Financial System

Gherardo Girardi

1 The Challenge

The post-World War II financial system, centered on the IMF, World Bank, WTO, and regional development banks, has historically provided a foundation for global economic growth and stability. Significant achievements include the introduction of the Generalized System of Preferences (GSP), a scheme which enables developing countries to export goods to developed markets at reduced or zero tariffs with the aim of promoting developing countries' economic growth (UNCTAD, 2025), and the Heavily Indebted Poor Countries (HIPC) Initiative and the Multilateral Debt Relief Initiative (MDRI), launched in 1996 by the IMF and World Bank, which have delivered over $100 billion in debt relief to more than 30 of the world's poorest countries, allowing them to increase investment in essential social services (World Bank, 2025).

However, the system faces several acute challenges. The most critical challenge is probably the rise of nationalist-populism in the Trump era. The Trump administration's "America First" and "Make America

G. Girardi (✉)
St Mary's University, London, UK
e-mail: gherardo.girardi@stmarys.ac.uk

R. de Arriba (ed.), *United Nations Facing Global Economic Disorder: Assessing 20 Policy Proposals*,
https://doi.org/10.1007/978-3-032-21952-7_6

Great Again" policies mark a stark challenge to the international financial order. The U.S. has withdrawn from key multilateral agreements and organizations, including the World Health Organization, questioned the legitimacy of institutions such as the WTO, and has imposed tariffs that have disrupted global trade (Bown & Irwin, 2019). This approach undermined decades of multilateral cooperation and weakened the institutional frameworks the UN relies on to coordinate global economic governance. The Trump era exemplifies how nationalist-populist politics can erode international financial cooperation, emboldening other countries to pursue unilateral policies that risk escalating economic fragmentation, and highlights the sensitivity of multilateral institutions to domestic political changes in major powers.

A second major challenge to the international US-led financial system today is China's rapid economic growth and strategic international initiatives. Through the Belt and Road Initiative[1], China has invested vast amounts in infrastructure projects across Asia, Africa, and Europe, enhancing its geopolitical and economic influence in a manner that circumvents Western-led development institutions. The Asian Infrastructure Investment Bank, inaugurated in 2016, presents a competing multilateral financial institution that challenges the World Bank's dominance in infrastructure financing. The rise of China as the second largest economy by GDP is very significant when one considers the words of Christine Lagarde, President of the European Central Bank (ECB): "We are witnessing a fragmentation of the global economy into competing blocs, with each bloc trying to pull as much of the rest of the world closer to its respective strategic interests and shared values. And this fragmentation may well coalesce around two blocs led respectively by the two largest economies in the world" (Lagarde, 2023). For some commentators, this fragmentation could spell the end of the global financial order as we know it: "A global economy fragmented into two or more competing blocs, likely led by the US and China, poses an existential threat to the currently truly global financial system" (Buckley & Trzecinski, 2022)[2].

[1] This is also known as the One Belt One Road, the Silk Road Economic Belt and the twenty-first-century Maritime Silk Road, or just the New Silk Road.

[2] While all of these developments pose, at least in theory, both opportunities and risks to individual countries, the overall picture appears negative. The World Trade Organization provides an estimate that the fragmentation of the global economy into two trading blocs

Furthermore, China's promotion of the renminbi as an international currency directly challenges the dollar's hegemony, which has underpinned global trade and finance since World War 2. In 2022, the People's Bank of China (PBOC) announced a plan to create a yuan reserve pool with the Bank for International Settlements together with Indonesia, Malaysia, Hong Kong, Singapore, and Chile to provide liquidity to member economies in times of market volatility (South China Morning Post, 2022). Not only China, but other countries too are promoting the de-dollarization of trade and financial flows. In 2022, for example, China and India paid for Russian commodities in renminbi, rupees, and UAE dirhams, and India has launched a rupee settlement mechanism for its international transaction (Pozsár, 2023). The international financial system is further challenged by what appears to be the forthcoming introduction of central bank digital currencies; according to Müller and Kerényi, these are the digital dollar, the digital euro, and the digital yuan (Müller & Kerényi, 2024). Furthermore, according to the same authors, the launch of a central bank digital currency called the Universal Monetary Unit by the Digital Currency Monetary Authority (DCMA) diminishes the IMF's role as the protector of the stability of the international monetary system.

Russia's 2022 invasion of Ukraine represents a third challenge to international peace and economic cooperation. The conflict precipitated a series of unprecedented Western sanctions targeting Russia's financial institutions, energy exports, and oligarchs, severely isolating the country from the global financial system. The EU and the US have imposed a number of sanctions on Russia, such as the freezing of a considerable amount of the Russian central bank's foreign exchange reserves and the exclusion of various Russian banks from SWIFT, the dominant financial network used to facilitate international payments (see Müller & Kerényi, 2024). The UN has been constrained in its ability to mediate this crisis due to Security Council vetoes and diverging member state interests. The fragmentation of financial markets and sanction regimes has complicated global trade flows and financial stability, with spillover effects felt in energy markets and commodity prices worldwide.

As with the war in Ukraine, the ongoing conflicts and political instability across the Middle East represent a major source of uncertainty

could reduce global GDP by around 5% in the long term, with emerging and developing economies bearing the brunt of the impact (Buckley & Trzecinski, 2022).

for the international financial system. The region's strategic importance due to its energy resources means that disruptions can quickly reverberate through global markets, affecting commodity prices, investment flows, and financial stability. States such as Syria, Yemen, and Libya remain mired in protracted conflicts, while the Israel-Palestine dispute continues to undermine regional cooperation, limiting the effectiveness of international financial institutions in supporting reconstruction and development efforts. Sanction regimes imposed on countries like Iran and Syria, while aimed at changing political behavior, restrict access to international banking systems and capital markets, hamper efforts to create stable economic environments conducive to investment and growth, undermine the potential for the economic recovery of these countries, and increase the likelihood of humanitarian crises (Moret, 2015). The UN has attempted to mediate peace and coordinate humanitarian assistance, but its role in addressing the financial consequences of these conflicts is limited by geopolitical divisions within the Security Council. This fragmentation contributes to the erosion of global financial governance, as financial flows are increasingly shaped by geopolitical rivalries and unilateral policy measures, rather than collective multilateral management.

Long-standing frustration among developing countries with IMF and World Bank governance and policy prescriptions constitutes a fourth major challenge for the international financial system. Conditionalities attached to IMF loans, often emphasizing austerity and liberalization, have been criticized for exacerbating poverty and limiting policy. Voting power in institutions like the IMF and World Bank remains concentrated in developed countries, often leaving emerging and low-income economies with minimal influence over major decisions. Small and middle-income states are frequently marginalized in IFI[3] boards, reducing their ability to shape global development policy. WTO rules are sometimes seen as favoring developed economies, limiting the ability of developing countries to protect nascent industries or manage trade policies in ways that support economic growth. The IMF's governance structure has been slow to adapt to the growing economic weight of

[3] An IFI is an International Financial Institution, defined as "a financial institution that has been established (or chartered) by more than one country, and hence is subject to international law. Its owners or shareholders are generally national governments, although other international institutions and other organizations occasionally figure as shareholders" (Wikipedia). The World Bank, IMF, and GATT (now WTO) are examples of IFIs.

emerging nations, leading to calls for quota reforms and increased voting power for emerging economies (Mohan & Kapur, 2015). Many Global South countries have reacted to this by forming regional trade blocs and alternative institutions such as the New Development Bank, creating parallel financial and trade governance architectures that further fragment the system. The UN faces the difficult task of bridging these divides, yet its limited mandate in financial governance and the entrenched power of dominant states constrain its influence.

In addition, many developing countries face high debt-to-GDP ratios, exacerbated by volatile interest rates and insufficient concessional financing. Without coordinated restructuring mechanisms, these countries risk prolonged economic instability. The topic of external debt is treated as a separate chapter in this book, and so it is not further discussed here.

A fifth challenge to the international financial system is the rising income inequality in many developed economies (Piketty, 2014), which has generated widespread social discontent and fuelled populist and nationalist movements that oppose globalization and multilateral cooperation. The loss of well-paid manufacturing jobs has particularly affected working-class communities, generating resentment toward international economic institutions perceived as benefiting elites at the expense of ordinary people. These political shifts complicate efforts to pursue international economic cooperation and financial governance reforms, as governments become wary of ceding sovereignty or committing to global agreements that may be unpopular domestically. The UN's ambitious agendas for inclusive development and equitable financial governance face resistance in this environment, where the legitimacy of multilateralism is under question.

The multiple challenges to the international financial system described above are intensified by the risks associated with unrestricted capital flows and excessive deregulation. Whist free capital flows enable risk diversification across countries and access to global financial markets, they are often volatile and can lead to exchange rate volatility (Milne, 2014; Ostry, 2015), creating serious difficulties for monetary policy (see Beck et al., 2023). The volatility and procyclicality of capital flows tend to amplify boom-bust cycles in financial markets. Excess inflows during booms lead to credit expansions and asset price inflation, while sudden stops cause sharp liquidity shortages which can trigger crises. Financial deregulation, such as loosening of capital requirements and reduced oversight, can foster innovation and growth, but can lead to weakening of market discipline, resulting in excessive risk-taking and the build-up of systemic risk through the interconnectedness of markets. When combined with liberalized capital flows, financial deregulation can foster a fragile environment prone to contagion and repeated episodes of crisis.

2 UN Proposals

The United Nations has recently put forward several proposals to reform the international financial system and strengthen multilateral cooperation, most notably through Our Common Agenda (United Nations Secretary-General, 2021) and the Pact for the Future (United Nations, 2023; United Nations General Assembly, 2024).

One of the key areas targeted by the Pact is governance and representation within IFIs. These institutions remain disproportionately influenced by developed countries, with decision-making structures that often marginalize the voices of the Global South. To address this imbalance, the Pact calls for greater voice and representation for developing countries, as well as more inclusive and collaborative approaches with regional development banks, UN agencies, and civil society organizations. Furthermore, the Pact calls for a more inclusive approach to agenda-setting within global financial institutions, ensuring that programs are tailored to local development objectives.

In addressing the issue of sovereign debt, the Pact emphasizes the necessity of robust debt relief mechanisms to support sustainable development. Current structures are often fragmented and lack coordination among stakeholders. The Pact seeks to build upon the G20's Common Framework for Debt Treatments to enable coordinated restructuring processes and to encourage steps that ensure comparability of treatment of sovereign and private creditors. Moreover, it promotes greater use of debt swaps for SDGs, including debt swaps for climate or nature, by developing countries.

Financing sustainable development is a central focus of both the Pact and the international financial architecture reform agenda. The United Nations calls for scaling up long-term, affordable, and stable financing for SDGs, particularly through strengthened global economic governance, improved access to international public finance, and increased domestic resource mobilization (United Nations, 2023; United Nations General Assembly, 2024). Equally important is the effective allocation of Official

Development Assistance (ODA), which should reach the most vulnerable, to ensure impact. Partnerships with the private sector are encouraged as a way to scale investment in infrastructure, climate resilience, and social services. Further, the Pact highlights the need to enhance domestic resource mobilization through institutional capacity, tax systems, and measures to curb illicit financial flows.

The Pact for the Future places emphasis on strengthening the resilience of the international financial system through enhanced international cooperation, improved crisis-response capacity, and efforts to reinforce the global financial safety net, particularly for vulnerable countries (United Nations General Assembly, 2024). It highlights the importance of timely and predictable access to liquidity in times of stress, greater coordination among international financial institutions, and reforms to global financial governance aimed at better reflecting the realities of an increasingly interconnected global economy. In this respect, and building on Our Common Agenda, the UN's recent agenda places greater weight on financial stability, inclusiveness, and long-term sustainability relative to narrow efficiency considerations, pointing toward a more managed and coordinated approach to financial openness and crisis prevention (United Nations General Assembly, 2024; United Nations Secretary-General, 2021).

While the Pact offers a blueprint for structural reform, Our Common Agenda focuses on principles of global governance, promoting solidarity, intergenerational equity, and sustainability. Key proposals under Our Common Agenda include the reform of global economic governance structures to ensure broader representation and coordination. It also seeks to enhance the equity and responsiveness of international public finance mechanisms, particularly in the context of crisis response and recovery (United Nations Secretary-General, 2021; United Nations, 2023; United Nations General Assembly, 2024). This suggests a supportive role for regional development banks in advancing more tailored and inclusive financial solutions, contributing to a more **equitable and decentralized** international financial system aligned with SDGs.

Our Common Agenda, together with its follow-up documents on reforming the international financial architecture, acknowledges that volatile capital flows, financial procyclicality, and regulatory gaps can have destabilizing effects, particularly for developing and emerging economies (United Nations, 2023; United Nations Secretary-General, 2021). These documents support preserving national policy space to use capital flow management measures and macroprudential regulation as part of the regular toolkit for safeguarding financial stability. In this sense, the Our Common Agenda process treats financial openness as a policy choice that must be actively managed within a broader framework of regulation, international coordination, and development- oriented governance, with the aim of reducing systemic risk and protecting macroeconomic stability.

An ambitious element of Our Common Agenda is its call to strengthen international tax cooperation to combat tax evasion and erosion of tax bases in a globalized context, which undermines the ability of governments to mobilize domestic resources for development, especially in the Global South. This reform agenda aligns with broader efforts to reduce dependence on external financing.

3 Assessment

Overall, the UN's reform proposals offer a useful, multidimensional roadmap for reshaping the global financial system, but their impact will depend on whether they can be translated into concrete institutional reforms that reduce volatility, contagion, and recurring crises. In line with the post 2008 crisis re-evaluation of capital flows liberalization, Our Common Agenda and the Pact for the Future place emphasis on the destabilizing effects of volatile capital flows, regulatory erosion, and uneven access to liquidity, signaling a rebalancing toward managed openness and collective risk mitigation. However, the extent of this shift should not be overstated: the proposals largely operate within the existing institutional architecture and stop short of redefining binding global rules on important matters such as capital mobility or financial regulation.

Implementation is inhibited by various challenges, which will need to be addressed for Our Common Agenda and the Pact for the Future to be transformative rather than merely aspirational. First, there is the question of political consensus among major economies. Member states with dominant positions in current IFI structures may resist changes that would dilute their influence, particularly in voting rights, agenda-setting, and access to financial instruments. Second, there is the issue of institutional resistance. The governance structures and operational cultures of institutions like the IMF and World Bank have evolved over decades and are often resistant to rapid transformation (Stiglitz, 2002). Reform efforts will need to navigate these entrenched dynamics carefully while building coalitions for change among member states, civil society, and regional actors. Third, mobilizing sufficient financial resources poses a formidable challenge. Closing the gap in SDG financing, supporting climate mitigation and adaptation, and implementing equitable debt relief programs will require coordinated mobilization of capital from governments and private investors (United Nations, 2023). Without innovative mechanisms and stronger global commitments, these ambitions may remain underfunded. Fourth, perhaps the most complex obstacle is ensuring effective global coordination, which lies at the very heart of multilateralism. Achieving meaningful reform depends on the alignment of diverse actors, namely governments, IFIs, regional development banks, multilateral agencies, and civil society, in contrast with the current international landscape which is marked by fragmentation and geopolitical tension.

References

Beck, R., Berganza, J. C., Brüggemann, A., Cezar, R., Eijking, C., Eller, M., Fuentes, A., Graça Alves, J., Kreitz, L., Marsilli, C., Moder, I., Molina Sánchez, L., Naef, A., Nispi Landi, V., Scheubel, B., Theofilakou, A., Van Den Hove, F., & Wesołowski, G. (2023). *Recent advances in the literature on capital flow management* (ECB occasional paper no. 317). European Central Bank.

Bown, C. P., & Irwin, D. A. (2019). Trump's assault on the global trading system. *Foreign Affairs, 98*(5), 125–137.

Buckley, R. P., & Trzecinski, M. (2022). *Central bank digital currencies and the global financial system: The dollar dethroned?* Oxford Business Law Blog. https://blogs.law.ox.ac.uk/oblb/blog-post/2022/12/central-bank-digital-currencies-and-global-financial-system-dollar-dethroned

Lagarde, C. (2023). *Central banks in a fragmenting world [speech].* European Central Bank. https://www.ecb.europa.eu/press/key/date/2023/html/ecb.sp230417~9f8d34fbd6.en.html

Milne, A. (2014). *The control and management of international capital flows: A review of the literature.* UK Government/Department for International Development.

Mohan, R., & Kapur, M. (2015). Emerging powers and global governance: Whither the IMF? In *IMF working paper* (Vol. No. WP/15/219). International Monetary Fund.

Moret, E. S. (2015). Humanitarian impacts of economic sanctions on Iran and Syria. *European Security, 24*(1), 120–140.

Müller, J., & Kerényi, Á. (2024). The challenges of fragmentation of the international financial system: Towards a brave new world order? *Financial and Economic Review, 23*(2), 131–155.

Ostry, J. D. (2015). Managing capital flows: Capital controls and foreign exchange intervention. In *Taming capital flows: Capital account management in an era of globalization* (IEA conference Volume No. 154, pp. 171–196). Palgrave Macmillan.

Piketty, T. (2014). *Capital in the twenty-first century*. Harvard University Press.

Post, S. C. M., & Tang, F. (2022). China's yuan liquidity reserve pool highlights efforts to loosen U.S. dollar hegemony. *South China Morning Post.*. https://www.scmp.com/economy/china-economy/article/3183242/chinas-yuan-liquidity-reserve-pool-highlights-efforts-loosen

Pozsár, Z. (2023). *January 20*. Great power conflict puts the dollar's exorbitant privilege under threat. https://www.ft.com/content/3e05b491-d781-4865-b0f7-777bc95ebf71

Stiglitz, J. E. (2002). *Globalization and its discontents*. Norton & Company.

UNCTAD. (2025). Generalized system of preferences. United Nations Conference on Trade and Development. https://unctad.org/topic/trade-agreements/generalized-system-of-preferences

United Nations. (2023). Reforms to the international financial architecture. United Nations https://sdgs.un.org/sites/default/files/2023-08/our-common-agenda-policy-brief-international-finance-architecture-en.pdf

United Nations General Assembly. (2024). Pact for the future. Resolution A/RES/79/1. United Nations. https://docs.un.org/en/A/RES/79/1

United Nations Secretary-General. (2021). Our common agenda. *United Nations*. https://www.un.org/en/content/common-agenda-report

World Bank. (2025). Heavily indebted poor countries (HIPC) initiative. *World Bank.*. https://www.worldbank.org/en/topic/debt/brief/hipc

CHAPTER 7

International Monetary System

Juan Francisco Albert

1 The Challenge

The international monetary system (IMS) is currently undergoing a period of structural tensions that highlight both its historical fragilities and new vulnerabilities associated with a changing global environment. One of the main tensions is the hegemony of the US dollar as the principal reserve currency, which exposes countries to fluctuations in the monetary policy of the Federal Reserve and to the increasing use of this currency as an instrument of sanctions and geopolitical pressure. In 2022, for example, 54% of global trade was denominated in dollars, although the United States accounted for only around 10% of global trade (Boocker & Wessel, 2024). The absence of a truly multilateral asset or a diversified set of reserve currencies keeps the global economy disproportionately dependent on shifts in United States policy. When the Federal Reserve adopts a restrictive stance, the dollar appreciates and debts issued in other currencies become more expensive, affecting emerging economies in particular.

J. F. Albert (✉)
University of Valencia, Valencia, Spain
e-mail: juan.f.albert@uv.es

R. de Arriba (ed.), *United Nations Facing Global Economic Disorder: Assessing 20 Policy Proposals*,
https://doi.org/10.1007/978-3-032-21952-7_7

Moreover, this arrangement forces many countries to accumulate substantial dollar reserves as a protective mechanism, which drains resources that could otherwise be allocated to economic and social development (Eichengreen, 2019).

However, despite the historical dominance of the dollar in the IMS, in recent months, particularly since the "Liberation Day" declared by the Trump administration on April 2, 2025, movements have been observed among foreign entities taking measures to reduce their dependence on the dollar in trade, payments, and international investments. In this regard, the elements that have underpinned the dollar's dominance, such as the prudence and predictability of United States economic policy, the safety and liquidity of US Treasury bonds, political and military relations with its traditional partners, and the rule of law and investor protections, have been undermined. In this new context, the dollar's dominance in global markets, which has historically rested on its safety, liquidity, and institutional credibility, could be weakened. Nonetheless, a weakening of the dollar would not necessarily entail an orderly transition toward a more balanced, multipolar monetary system. On the contrary, it could generate greater fragmentation and volatility in international capital flows, increase the cost of trade transactions due to the absence of a clear global reference currency, and hinder the ability to coordinate during international financial crises. Likewise, emerging countries that have relied on the dollar as an anchor of stability would be particularly vulnerable in a scenario without a clear lender of last resort and with higher financing costs. In sum, reducing the hegemony of the dollar may mitigate current asymmetries, but it also threatens to weaken the resilience of the international monetary system if solid and credible alternatives capable of replacing it in a stable manner are not established (Gensler et al., 2025).

To this dependence is added the volatility inherent to flexible exchange rate regimes, widespread since the collapse of the fixed parity system in the 1970s. While they allow the absorption of external shocks, they expose currencies, especially in emerging markets, to abrupt fluctuations driven by international capital flows. Episodes of massive capital inflows followed by sudden outflows, which have been frequent since the Asian crisis of 1997, tend to destabilize local economies and generate recurring cycles of boom and bust (Priewe, 2022). This phenomenon is amplified by financial globalization: the enormous volume and speed of international transactions foster speculative bubbles and systemic contagion. Although market integration facilitates access to financing, it also multiplies the risks of global financial crises, which fall more severely on countries with less developed financial systems (Kharas et al., 2024).

In this context, the International Monetary Fund plays a crucial role as lender of last resort, but its capacity to respond is conditioned both by the limits of its resource base and by a governance framework that favors advanced economies. The distribution of Special Drawing Rights (SDRs) illustrates these inequities: in the extraordinary issuance of 2021, developing countries received barely one third of the total allocated, while Germany obtained amounts equivalent to those assigned to the entire sub-Saharan Africa (United Nations, 2023). This imbalance reflects not only the insufficiency of stable international liquidity, but also the lack of effective redistributive mechanisms. Moreover, IMF programs often entail strict conditionalities and additional surcharges for the most indebted countries, which increases their vulnerability in times of crisis.

The underrepresentation of the Global South in international governance is another persistent weakness of the system. The fact that the United States retains almost 17% of the votes in the IMF grants it veto power, while entire regions such as sub-Saharan Africa maintain a marginal weight in decision-making. This imbalance limits the legitimacy of the system, perpetuates the dependence of developing countries on institutions dominated by the Global North, and restricts the possibility of inclusive reforms (Priewe, 2022). The lack of representation is also linked to a weakening of multilateralism in general: in a context of increasing trade and geopolitical tensions, global institutions—from the IMF to the G20—show a limited capacity to promote broad and lasting consensus, which favors partial and fragmented solutions (United Nations, 2023).

In parallel, sovereign indebtedness has become a central challenge. The external debt of developing countries reached a record of approximately 11.4 trillion dollars in 2023, a historic level equivalent to nearly 99% of their export revenues, which intensifies their financial vulnerability, especially in economies indebted in strong currencies (UNCTAD, 2025). However, the IMF lacks an effective multilateral mechanism for the orderly restructuring of debt. Negotiations are conducted on a case-by-case basis, tend to be prolonged, and involve very high social costs, which amplifies the effects of crises and fuels the perception of injustice in the international financial architecture (Kharas et al., 2024).

Another emerging factor is the climate transition. Climate change not only entails an environmental challenge, but also a financial one. Developing countries face balance of payments pressures associated with natural disasters and the need to finance climate change adaptation and mitigation. However, current mechanisms for the provision of international liquidity do not adequately address these needs, which deepens the gap between global sustainability objectives and the tools available at the IMF (United Nations, 2023).

Finally, the emergence of digital innovations, particularly private cryptocurrencies and central bank digital currencies (CBDCs), opens an uncertain terrain. The digitization of currencies presents significant opportunities and risks for the IMS. Among the benefits are improvements in the efficiency of cross-border payments, reductions in transaction costs, and the potential expansion of financial inclusion, especially for unbanked populations, which can facilitate access to liquidity and strengthen the integration of emerging economies into the global system (United Nations Task Force on Digital Financing of the SDGs, 2020). Likewise, digitization could contribute to diversifying reserve instruments and reducing absolute dependence on the dollar, offering a greater degree of resilience to external shocks. However, risks also exist. The rapid adoption of CBDCs without international coordination could generate fragmentation of the financial system, tensions between monetary blocs, and interoperability challenges. In addition, concerns arise regarding monetary sovereignty, user privacy, and financial stability, as massive shifts toward digital currencies could destabilize traditional banking systems and increase volatility in capital markets (Eichengreen, 2019). Therefore, the net impact of digitization on the IMS will depend on the implementation of robust regulatory frameworks and international cooperation.

In sum, the international monetary system faces a set of interrelated challenges: the hegemony of the dollar and the asymmetries it generates; exchange rate and capital volatility associated with globalized financial markets; governance and liquidity limitations within the IMF; the underrepresentation of the Global South in governance structures and voting rights of major international financial institutions; the increase in sovereign debt without a multilateral restructuring framework; the lack of integration of the climate transition; and the technological uncertainty associated with digital currencies. These factors, far from operating in isolation, reinforce one another, resulting in a system increasingly vulnerable to external pressures and recurrent crises. Hence, the need for deep reforms aimed at building a more inclusive, stable, and resilient system has become one of the major topics on the contemporary international agenda.

2 UN Proposals

To address the structural challenges affecting the international monetary system, the United Nations has developed a set of proposals integrated into *Our Common Agenda*, the associated policy reports, and the Pact for the Future of the 2024 Summit. These reforms aim to transform the global financial architecture to make it more inclusive, resilient, and oriented toward sustainable development, addressing both the historical imbalances of the IMS and the new vulnerabilities arising from globalization, the climate crisis, and the digitization of finance (UNCTAD, 2023; United Nations, 2023; United Nations General Assembly, 2024; United Nations Secretary-General, 2021).

One of the main pillars of these proposals is the reform of international economic governance. The UN and the Group of 24[1] have emphasized the need to expand the voice and representation of developing countries in institutions such as the IMF and the World Bank. The current quota formula, primarily based on financial contributions, limits the influence of emerging economies and perpetuates the disproportionate power of advanced countries. In this regard, it is suggested to incorporate criteria such as population, per capita income, climate vulnerability, and exposure to external shocks, as well as to introduce more equitable voting systems, such as a double majority combining contributions and number of votes (UNCTAD, 2023; United Nations, 2023). Furthermore, it is recommended to modernize the executive boards of these institutions and expand their composition, ensuring that lower-income countries have effective representation in decision-making. This reform aims to reduce the informality of forums such as the G20 and to create a formal global coordination mechanism: the Economic Security Council, which would act as a multilateral space to harmonize macroeconomic, financial, and climate policies, and to reduce the risk of unilateral decisions that affect third parties (High-level Advisory Board on Effective Multilateralism, 2023).

A second block of reforms refers to the strengthening of international liquidity. The United Nations proposes revitalizing the role of

[1] The Group of 24 (G24) is an intergovernmental forum established in 1971 that brings together developing countries and emerging economies with the aim of coordinating common positions on international monetary and financial matters, particularly in discussions within the IMF and the World Bank.

Special Drawing Rights (SDRs) as a countercyclical instrument of global scope. Among the recommendations, the automatic issuance of SDRs in response to systemic crises stands out, as well as allocation based on the real needs of countries rather than on their financial quotas. This measure would allow countries with lower borrowing capacity to gain faster access to international resources in emergency situations, reducing dependence on bilateral lending or conditional aid (UNCTAD, 2023; United Nations, 2023). Likewise, it is suggested to expand the IMF's lending capacity, eliminate regressive surcharges that affect countries with lower creditworthiness, and consider the partial monetization of the Fund's gold reserves as a mechanism to increase resources without the need for new contributions from members. Complementarily, the creation of a multilateral swap mechanism is proposed, which would allow developing countries to access international currencies in a more equitable manner, preventing liquidity from becoming concentrated in bilateral agreements with large countries or specific blocs (UNCTAD, 2023).

The management of sovereign debt is another central pillar of the reform agenda. United Nations (2024) highlights that the current financial architecture lacks agile and equitable multilateral mechanisms for debt restructuring. This forces vulnerable countries to allocate significant resources to the servicing of external obligations, limiting their capacity to invest in social development, infrastructure, or climate mitigation. To address this problem, proposals include sovereign debt markets linked to the Sustainable Development Goals (SDGs), multilateral restructuring processes, and the eventual creation of an international debt authority that would ensure transparency, equity, and speed in renegotiations, thereby reducing systemic financial risks and promoting the sustainability of developing economies (UNCTAD, 2023; United Nations, 2023).

Within the framework of financing for sustainable development, the United Nations has proposed consolidating the multiple existing multilateral climate funds into a World Green Bank, with the capacity to channel resources toward investments in energy transition, climate adaptation, and disaster mitigation. Alongside this, the creation of a global carbon market is proposed, which would provide coherent price signals at the international level and facilitate the mobilization of private capital toward sustainable projects (UNFCCC, 2022; United Nations General Assembly, 2024). In addition, it is recommended to strengthen the capitalization of multilateral development banks, encourage innovative financial instruments such as sustainability-linked bonds or green swaps, and promote long-term investment mechanisms that respond to criteria of climate and social resilience (UNCTAD, 2023).

The regulation of global financial markets constitutes another pillar of the reform. The United Nations and the High-level Advisory Board on Effective Multilateralism (2023) have highlighted the need to apply the principle of "same activity, same risk, same regulation" to banks and non-bank actors, ensuring consistency across the entire financial system. Among the recommendations are taxes on speculative financial transactions, fiscal incentives for sustainable investments, stricter leverage limits, the strengthening of accounting transparency and corporate governance, as well as reforms to the international tax system to combat tax evasion and avoidance. The implementation of these measures seeks to reduce volatility, foster sustainable investment, and increase the resilience of the system in the face of global financial crises (United Nations, 2023; United Nations Secretary-General, 2021).

The United Nations has also addressed the impact of digitalization on the global financial architecture. Recent reports highlight that central bank digital currencies (CBDCs) and private cryptoassets could transform cross-border payments, but they also present risks related to interoperability, privacy, and financial stability. In this context, it is recommended to establish multilateral standards for the issuance and regulation of CBDCs, as well as international coordination frameworks that prevent fragmentation and unfair competition among digital currencies (United Nations, 2023; United Nations Task Force on Digital Financing of the SDGs, 2020).

The Pact for the Future of 2024 partially reflects these recommendations. Among the advances, the rechanneling of 100 billion dollars of the SDRs issued in 2021 toward the countries most in need stands out, with at least half allocated to multilateral development banks, as well as commitments to improve the representativeness of developing countries in the IMF and the World Bank and to convene biennial international coordination summits (United Nations General Assembly, 2024). Nevertheless, the pact does not include binding legal reforms regarding the distribution of IMF voting rights, nor the creation of a multilateral swap system, nor the automatic issuance of SDRs in times of crisis, reflecting the difficulty of reaching consensus in a fragmented geopolitical context.

In sum, the proposals of the United Nations encompass multiple dimensions of the international monetary system: governance, liquidity, sovereign debt, sustainable financing, financial regulation, and digitalization. These measures, if fully implemented, could reduce the dependence of Global South countries on external shocks, increase the effectiveness of international liquidity, promote financial and climate sustainability, and strengthen the legitimacy of the multilateral system. However, political feasibility and international coordination continue to be significant challenges, underscoring the need to maintain a gradual, pragmatic, and sustained approach over time (High-level Advisory Board on Effective Multilateralism, 2023; UNCTAD, 2023; United Nations Secretary-General, 2021).

3 Assessment

The proposals of the United Nations offer a valuable framework to address some structural problems of the international monetary system, although their scope and feasibility present limitations. On the positive side, they recognize the need for a more inclusive system oriented toward sustainable development. Initiatives such as strengthening the voice of emerging countries in the IMF and the World Bank, linking access to quotas to criteria of need, and promoting the use of Special Drawing Rights based on needs seek to rebalance global economic power and reduce dependence on markets dominated by strong creditors. These measures could strengthen confidence in a more transparent and stable financial system and facilitate convergence and inclusive development at the global level.

However, significant obstacles remain. The most ambitious reforms run up against the lack of consensus among the major powers and resistance to transferring power or creating new institutions. Some operational mechanisms proposed in international debates, such as the creation of an automatic system for the issuance of Special Drawing Rights (SDRs), were not incorporated as binding provisions in the final text of the Pact for the Future, adopted at the United Nations Summit of the Future in 2024. This exclusion reflects the political complexity of intergovernmental negotiations and the low priority assigned by the main shareholder countries to reforms that would structurally alter the provision of international liquidity and the balance of power in the international monetary system. Partial measures, such as limited increases in representation in governance bodies or the voluntary rechanneling of SDRs to multilateral development banks, may alleviate some short-term vulnerabilities, but they do not modify structural problems such as the hegemony of the dollar as the principal reserve currency or the voting asymmetries in international financial institutions, derived from quota systems that grant greater decision-making power to advanced economies.

In this context, real progress will likely depend on gradual and pragmatic approaches, through plurilateral agreements in areas where clear interests exist. In conclusion, the United Nations reforms correctly identify the challenges of the IMS and propose relevant courses of action, but their impact will depend on international cooperation and may be limited to partial improvements without transforming the underlying power structures.

References

Boocker, S., & Wessel, D. (2024, August 23). *The Changing Role of the US Dollar*. Brookings Institution. https://www.brookings.edu/articles/the-changing-role-of-the-us-dollar/

Eichengreen, B. (2019). *Globalizing Capital: A History of the International Monetary System* (3rd ed.). Princeton University Press.

Gensler, G., Johnson, S., Panizza, U., & Weder di Mauro, B. (2025). *The Economic Consequences of the Second Trump Administration: A Preliminary Assessment*. CEPR Press.

High-level Advisory Board on Effective Multilateralism. (2023). *A Breakthrough for People and Planet: Effective and Inclusive Global Governance for Today and the Future*. United Nations University. https://unu.edu/sites/default/files/2025-03/highleveladvisoryboard_breakthrough_fullreport.pdf

Kharas, H., Subramanian, A., & Songwe, V. (2024). *Reforms for a 21st-Century Global Financial Architecture*. Brookings Institution. https://www.brookings.edu/articles/reforms-for-a-21st-century-global-financial-architecture

Priewe, J. (2022). Old and New Proposals for Global Monetary Reform. *Review of Keynesian Economics, 10*(4), 533–558. https://doi.org/10.4337/roke.2022.04.05

UNCTAD. (2023). *Trade and Development Report 2023: Growth, Debt, and Climate—Realigning the Global Financial Architecture*. United Nations Conference on Trade and Development. https://unctad.org/publication/trade-and-development-report-2023

UNCTAD. (2025). *Debt Crisis: Developing Countries' External Debt Hits Record $11.4 Trillion*. United Nations Conference on Trade and Development. https://unctad.org/news/debt-crisis-developing-countries-external-debt-hits-record-114-trillion

UNFCCC. (2022). *Report of the Standing Committee on Finance to the Conference of the Parties*. United Nations Framework Convention on Climate Change. https://unfccc.int/documents/620451

United Nations. (2023). *Our Common Agenda Policy Brief 6: Reforms to the International Financial Architecture*. United Nations. https://digitallibrary.un.org/record/4012088?v=pdf

United Nations. (2024). *Financing for Sustainable Development Report 2024*. United Nations. https://unctad.org/publication/financing-sustainable-development-report-2024

United Nations General Assembly. (2024). *Pact for the Future*. Resolution A/RES/79/1. United Nations. https://docs.un.org/en/A/RES/79/1

United Nations Secretary-General. (2021): *Our Common Agenda*. United Nations. https://www.un.org/en/content/common-agenda-report/

United Nations Task Force on Digital Financing of the SDGs. (2020). *People's Money: Harnessing Digitalization to Finance a Sustainable Future*. United Nations. https://unsdg.un.org/resources/peoples-money-harnessing-digitalization-finance-sustainable-future

CHAPTER 8

Taxation

Paula Granell

1 The Challenge

The international tax regime has undergone a profound transformation since its origins in the early twentieth century. Initially, coordination relied almost exclusively on bilateral double taxation treaties negotiated by states on the basis of model conventions produced by the Organisation for Economic Co-operation and Development (OECD) and, to a lesser extent, the United Nations (UN). These models provided a measure of uniformity in allocating taxing rights and mitigating international double taxation, but the system remained essentially bilateral, fragmented, and modest in scope.

Today, the international tax regime consists of a complex set of rules that faces structural challenges arising from the sheer magnitude of tax fraud, aggressive tax planning, and the continued use of tax havens. Recent empirical evidence highlights the scale of the problem. The State of Tax Justice 2023 Report (Tax Justice Network, 2023)

P. Granell (✉)
University of Valencia, Valencia, Spain
e-mail: paula.granell@uv.es

R. de Arriba (ed.), *United Nations Facing Global Economic Disorder: Assessing 20 Policy Proposals*,
https://doi.org/10.1007/978-3-032-21952-7_8

estimated that governments are losing approximately $480 billion annually in tax revenues. Of this amount, around $311 billion results from the profit-shifting practices of multinational enterprises, while an additional $169 billion is lost due to offshore tax evasion involving financial wealth. These figures illustrate that tax avoidance and evasion are not marginal phenomena, but systemic features of the contemporary global economy, deeply embedded in the architecture of international taxation and financial globalisation.

The persistence of tax havens and secrecy jurisdictions plays a central role in facilitating these losses. Jurisdictions offering low or zero taxation, combined with weak transparency standards and preferential regimes, enable both corporations and individuals to artificially relocate profits and wealth to pay less taxes. The Global Tax Evasion Report 2024 (Alstadsæter et al., 2023) underscores that, despite cooperation efforts such as automatic exchange of information, international tax evasion, and profit shifting continue to depress government revenues and widen fiscal deficits, as corporations and high-net-worth individuals succeed in reducing their effective tax burdens. For low and middle-income countries in particular, losses in tax revenue have especially severe welfare implications, as these governments rely heavily on fiscal resources to finance essential public services such as education, healthcare, and infrastructure development.

Over the last three decades, the OECD has progressively expanded its role from a technical forum issuing non-binding reports into the leading actor in global tax governance. Initiatives such as the *Base Erosion and Profit Shifting (BEPS) Project* and the *Two-Pillar Solution* reflect this enhanced influence. These initiatives constitute the OECD's response to the aggressive tax planning challenges described above, while also seeking to adapt traditional concepts of residence and source taxation to the realities of a digitalised and globalised economy.

The projects mentioned above constitute a step in the right direction, as they finally acknowledge that multinational enterprises operate as unitary businesses and recognise the need for a global minimum tax. However, these measures remain insufficient when assessed against the scale of the current challenges (Faccio & Ghosh, 2024). At the same time, new instruments such as the Multilateral Convention to Implement Tax Treaty Related Measures to Prevent BEPS (MLI) demonstrate a shift away from a purely bilateral architecture towards more complex, multi-layered agreements.

The growing reliance on *soft law* has also blurred the contours of the regime. Peer reviews, recommendations, and guidelines, though formally non-binding, exert significant pressure on states and shape domestic legislation. This has produced a system in which bilateral treaties coexist with multilateral conventions, domestic reforms inspired by international standards, and an ever-increasing number of *soft law* mechanisms. The outcome is a highly intricate and sometimes inconsistent architecture. In practice, states may face overlapping obligations, interpretative uncertainties, or even conflicts between treaty provisions and the new multilateral commitments they have endorsed.

The OECD's central role has undoubtedly provided technical expertise and the capacity to mobilise consensus, but its decision-making structures remain dominated by advanced economies. Specifically, the instruments adopted divide the tax base of multinational companies between countries giving a disproportionate share of the tax base to capital-rich states (Hearson, 2018).

On the other hand, many developing countries, whose fiscal interests are directly at stake, participate only peripherally in the Inclusive Framework on BEPS or other OECD-led processes. This imbalance fuels concerns that global tax policy is being shaped by a narrow group of actors, with limited transparency and insufficient regard for distributive equity. The result is a perception—and, for many, a reality—that the OECD-led policies aimed at reforming the international tax regime are OECD impositions onto non-OECD jurisdictions (Allevato & Di Filippo, 2025). Consequently, these policies favour the fiscal priorities of wealthier states while leaving developing economies without meaningful influence over decisions that affect their revenue bases.

The distributive consequences of this imbalance are particularly evident in the allocation of taxing rights. Traditional treaty rules, rooted in the residence principle, tend to privilege developed economies where multinational corporations are headquartered, while restricting the taxing powers of source countries where actual economic activity often occurs. For developing countries that rely heavily on source-based taxation to finance public services, this imbalance has significant implications. The challenges are further amplified by the rise of intangible assets and global value chains, which make it easier for corporations to shift profits away from jurisdictions where value is genuinely created. Although the BEPS project has aimed to address such practices, the reforms have done little to expand taxing rights in favour of lower-income countries, perpetuating structural inequalities.

Unlike other areas of international law, such as trade or environmental protection, there is no single institution with a mandate to coordinate tax policy at the global level. Instead, governance emerges from a patchwork of overlapping treaties, multilateral initiatives, and informal standards.

At the same time, the stakes of tax governance are not merely technical. Taxation lies at the heart of the social contract: it is the means by which states mobilise resources, redistribute wealth, and secure the provision of essential goods and services (Gribnau & Frecknall-Hughes, 2022). The increasing reliance on closed negotiating forums and *soft law* instruments raises normative questions about accountability and sovereignty. If key rules of the global tax order are determined by a limited number of actors without universal representation, the legitimacy of the system is jeopardised. This, in turn, risks eroding compliance and trust, particularly among states that feel excluded from decision-making.

In this context, an alternative venue for international tax cooperation has begun to emerge. The UN, with its universal membership and more transparent procedures, offers a potential platform to rebalance the asymmetries of the current system. While the OECD remains the primary driver of technical reforms, many states—particularly from the Global South—are advocating for a stronger UN role in order to ensure inclusivity, fairness, and greater attention to the needs of developing countries. The ongoing discussions around a potential *UN Framework Convention on International Tax Cooperation* illustrate this shift. Such a convention could provide the governance architecture that the international tax system currently lacks, complementing and potentially reorienting the work undertaken within the OECD framework.

The challenge, therefore, is twofold. On the one hand, there is an urgent need to adapt international tax rules to the realities of a globalised economy, characterised by digital business models, mobile capital, and the persistent use of tax havens. On the other, there is a fundamental question of governance: who should have the authority to shape global tax rules, and through what processes? The OECD has demonstrated leadership in setting international tax standards and has shown a notable capacity to innovate. Yet, its legitimacy deficit—stemming from its limited membership and perceived bias towards advanced economies—remains unresolved. The UN, by contrast, offers universal participation and greater inclusiveness, but still faces the challenge of building the institutional capacity necessary to translate that inclusiveness into effective governance. Reconciling these tensions will be decisive for the future architecture of the international tax regime.

2 UN Proposals

The UN's involvement in international tax cooperation is not entirely new. Since the 1960s, the UN has published its own Model Double Taxation Convention with the stated aim of better reflecting the interests of developing countries in the signature of bilateral tax treaties. Yet, it was only with the adoption of General Assembly Resolution 69/313 of 27 July 2015, endorsing the Addis Ababa Action Agenda, that tax matters were explicitly linked to the global development agenda (United Nations General Assembly, 2015). The Resolution emphasised the need to strengthen international cooperation in tax matters, particularly as a means to mobilise domestic resources for achieving the Sustainable Development Goals (SDGs).

This mandate was subsequently reinforced in Resolution 77/244 of 30 December 2022, which tasked the UN Secretary-General with preparing a report to identify potential measures for enhancing inclusiveness and effectiveness in tax cooperation. Presented in July 2023, the report outlined three possible avenues: a multilateral convention on taxation; a framework convention on tax cooperation; or a flexible framework for tax dialogue and coordination.

Out of these, the General Assembly chose the second option. Through Resolution 78/230 of 22 December 2023, it mandated the drafting of a Framework Convention on International Tax Cooperation and created an Ad Hoc Intergovernmental Committee to develop the Terms of Reference (ToR). This decision was widely interpreted as a turning point, signalling a political willingness to challenge the long-standing OECD dominance in global tax norm-setting.

The Ad Hoc Intergovernmental Committee convened for the first time between 20 and 22 February 2024 in New York. The objective was to launch preliminary discussions on the ToR, which would set the parameters and substantive contours of the future convention. The debates were deliberately process-oriented, focusing on establishing a bureau and ensuring that member states could submit proposals for consideration.

The ToR provided not only a basic architecture for the Convention but also an opportunity for states to influence the structure of subsequent negotiations. For developing countries in particular, this early stage was crucial: it allowed them to place issues such as capacity building, illicit financial flows, and equitable allocation of taxing rights at the heart of the emerging framework. Some authors argue that, in this process, the potential of regional cooperation—exemplified by Africa's push for a unified stance on tax issues—must be recognised (Titus, 2025).

Momentum was further reinforced by the adoption of the "Pact for the Future" on 22 September 2024 (United Nations General Assembly, 2024a, 2024b). The Pact explicitly connected tax cooperation with the broader agenda of sustainable development financing. Action 4 committed member states to closing the SDG financing gap in developing economies, with paragraph 23, letter (i) underscoring the role of inclusive and effective international tax cooperation[1].

This Resolution is significant for at least three reasons:

- It recognises that current governance structures remain insufficient, thereby legitimising the search for alternatives beyond the OECD.
- It stresses the link between taxation and non-fiscal objectives, particularly sustainability and good governance.
- It brings in a dose of reality when considering the complementary role of other relevant forums and institutions (Grau Ruiz, 2025), such as the OECD and regional tax bodies, ensuring that the UN initiative does not emerge in isolation but as part of a broader ecosystem of tax governance.

The Pact for Future also highlighted priority areas for future negotiations, including:

[1] Paragraph 23, letter (i): "Promote inclusive and effective international tax cooperation, which contributes significantly to national efforts to achieve the Sustainable Development Goals, as it enables countries to effectively mobilize their domestic resources, and stress that the current international tax governance structures need improvements. We are committed to strengthening the inclusiveness and effectiveness of tax cooperation at the United Nations, while taking into consideration the work of other relevant forums and institutions, and will continue to engage constructively in the process towards developing a United Nations framework convention on international tax cooperation".

- Creating a more enabling environment for resource mobilisation in developing countries.
- Implementing coherent economic, social, and environmental policies.
- Strengthening efforts against illicit financial flows, money laundering, and tax evasion.
- Exploring cooperation on the taxation of high-net-worth individuals.

Taken together, these commitments provided the political foundation for advancing the negotiations on the UN Framework Convention on International Tax Cooperation.

Subsequently, the General Assembly's Resolution 79/235 of 24 December 2024 marked another milestone. By adopting the negotiated Terms of Reference, the Assembly formally launched the process of drafting the Framework Convention. The Resolution included the establishment of a Member State-led, open-ended intergovernmental negotiating committee, as well as an invitation to civil society and international organisations to contribute to the process.

This inclusive approach was meant to ensure both legitimacy and practical feasibility. By opening the door to multiple stakeholders, the UN sought to demonstrate that its initiative could overcome criticisms often directed at the OECD, namely limited transparency and narrow representation.

Formal negotiations commenced in early 2025 and are expected to continue until 2027. As of the writing of this chapter, two sessions have been held in New York (August 2025), followed by a third session in Nairobi (November 2025).

These sessions have focused on two levels:

- The Framework Convention itself, designed to provide a flexible yet binding structure for cooperation.
- Two initial protocols, addressing specific technical issues of immediate concern: the taxation of cross-border services, highly relevant in the context of digitalization; and mechanisms for dispute prevention and resolution, aimed at reducing costly litigation and uncertainty in the interpretation of tax treaties.

The negotiation dynamics reveal deep tensions between developed and developing countries. While the latter push for stronger commitments on resource mobilisation and equitable allocation of taxing rights, advanced economies remain cautious about ceding fiscal sovereignty. What is clear is that the UN initiative is the only existing tax forum where all states are represented. Consequently, it is also the "only forum that can move away from the power politics that led to the existing divide that threatens the stability of the international tax regime" (Brauner, 2025).

3 Assessment

The path undertaken by the UN to reform the international tax system represents a step forward in the reconfiguration of global tax governance and in the pursuit of more effective and equitable rules, which must be regarded positively. While the challenges to be faced are both significant and urgent, it remains uncertain whether the outcomes of the ongoing negotiation processes within the UN will ultimately prove fruitful and result in truly transformative and concrete proposals.

From a positive perspective, the initiatives undertaken by the United Nations mark a turning point in the evolution of global tax governance. By opening the negotiation process to all member states on an equal footing, the UN has enhanced the legitimacy, transparency, and inclusiveness of international tax cooperation. This institutional shift addresses long-standing criticisms of the OECD-led process, which has often been perceived as privileging advanced economies, and instead offers developing countries a meaningful role in shaping the rules that directly affect their fiscal sovereignty. In any case, the UN Framework Convention represents an "extremely important recognition of the need of counterbalances in the dynamics of powers in international taxation" (Parada, 2024).

Moreover, the UN has placed fiscal resources at the core of its agenda, recognising their essential role in enabling countries to meet the SDGs. In doing so, it has reframed international tax cooperation as not merely a technical exercise, but as a central pillar of global efforts to advance equity, sustainability, and development.

Nevertheless, the process is still subject to considerable strategic uncertainty. An illustrative example is the decision of the United States to withdraw from the UN negotiations in early 2025. Shortly after returning to office, the Trump administration announced that it would neither take part in discussions on a UN tax convention nor recognise any agreements that might emerge from them. In order to achieve the broadest consensus possible—namely, securing the agreement of as many states as possible to the UN Framework Convention—it has been suggested that substantive provisions could be placed in non-mandatory protocols (Hongler & Habich, 2025). In any case, an essential aspect will be the flexibility with which the proposals are articulated, resulting in varying degrees of supranational or international integration or coordination in tax matters (García Prats, 2025).

In pursuit of a more coherent system among international institutions regulating this area, Baistrocchi's (2024) proposal for the establishment of a UN-led platform to standardise international tax agreements is particularly noteworthy. Such a platform would seek to foster institutional integration between the Global North and the Global South within the international tax regime, while ensuring compatibility with both the UN Framework Convention and the Inclusive Framework on BEPS.

Ultimately, the UN Framework Convention's success will depend on whether it can reconcile inclusiveness with effectiveness. Striking a balance between the goal of universal membership and the imperative to preserve momentum towards measures capable of delivering tangible outcomes will be a central challenge (Picciotto, 2024). If the UN process produces only declaratory commitments, its added value will be limited. However, if it manages to set credible standards, foster cooperation, and integrate development concerns into tax governance, it could mark the beginning of a more equitable global tax order.

References

Allevato, G., & Di Filippo, A. E. (2025). Towards Global Tax Justice: An Interdisciplinary Evaluation of the UN Framework Convention on International Tax Cooperation. *The Brown Journal of World Affairs, 31*, 49–70. https://www.proquest.com/magazines/towards-global-tax-justice-interdisciplinary/docview/3224318653/se-2

Alstadsæter, A., Godar, S., Nicolaides, P., Zucman, G. (2023). *Global Tax Evasion Report 2024.* EU Tax Observatory. https://www.taxobservatory.eu//www-site/uploads/2023/10/global_tax_evasion_report_24.pdf

Baistrocchi, E. (2024). How to Restructure the International Tax Regime. *LSE Business Review—Social Sciences for Business, Markets, and Enterprises.* https://blogs.lse.ac.uk/businessreview/2024/06/17/how-to-restructure-the-international-tax-regime/

Brauner, Y. (2025). What Can the UN Do That the OECD Can't or Won't? *Intertax, 53*(1), 44–55. https://doi.org/10.54648/TAXI2025001

Faccio, T., & Ghosh, J. (2024). Guest Editorial: Why Should EU Countries Support a UN Framework Convention on International Tax Cooperation. *Intertax, 52*(5), 358–360. https://doi.org/10.54648/TAXI2024041

García Prats, F. A. (2025). Gobernanza Tributaria Mundial. In *Gobernanza Tributaria Mundial* (pp. 23–54). Aranzadi La Ley. https://www.aranzadilaley.es/tienda/gobernanza-tributaria-mundial?srsltid=AfmBOorf7945JXFIA0yfY9BLJtTm6qcKyUUwdfdrM41J_5NCRKgfD_cp

Grau Ruiz, M. A. (2025). The United Nations Framework Convention on International Tax Cooperation in the Making. Debate and Approval of Its Terms of Reference. *Crónica Tributaria. Nueva Época, 2*(195), 37–65. https://cronicatributaria.ief.es/ief/ct/index.php/cronica-tributaria/article/view/2398

Gribnau, H., & Frecknall-Hughes, J. (2022). The Enlightenment and Influence of Social Contract Theory on Taxation. In *Political Philosophy and Taxation* (pp. 51–101). Springer Nature. https://doi.org/10.1007/978-981-19-1092-0_2

Hearson, M. (2018). The Challenges for Developing Countries in International Tax Justice. *The Journal of Development Studies, 54*(10), 1932–1938. https://doi.org/10.1080/00220388.2017.1309040

Hongler, P., & Habich, S. (2025). Plurilateralism in International Tax Law: A Unique Chance for the UN Framework Convention. *The Journal of World Investment & Trade, 26*(1–2), 247–274. https://doi.org/10.1163/22119000-12340358

Parada, L. (2024). International Cooperation on Tax Matters at the United Nations: A Turning Point in History? *Caribbean Tax Law Journal, 1*, 10–15. https://ssrn.com/abstract=4714506

Picciotto, S. (2024). *The Design of a UN Framework Convention on International Tax Co-operation*. https://papers.ssrn.com/sol3/papers.cfm?abstract_id=4785381

Tax Justice Network. (2023). *The State of Tax Justice 2023*. Tax Justice Network. https://taxjustice.net/reports/the-state-of-tax-justice-2023/

Titus, A. (2025). The Role of the United Nations in Ensuring Equitable Tax Policies for Developing Countries. *Journal of International Economic Law, 27*(4), 624–631. https://doi.org/10.1093/jiel/jgae051

United Nations General Assembly. (2015). *Addis Ababa Action Agenda of the Third International Conference on Financing for Development (Addis Ababa Action Agenda)*. Resolution A/RES/69/313. https://docs.un.org/en/a/res/69/313

United Nations General Assembly. (2023). *Promotion of Inclusive and Effective International Tax Cooperation at the United Nations*. Resolution A/RES/78/230. United Nations. https://docs.un.org/en/a/res/78/230

United Nations General Assembly. (2024a). *Promotion of Inclusive and Effective International Tax Cooperation at the United Nations*. Resolution A/RES/79/235. United Nations. https://docs.un.org/en/a/res/79/235

United Nations General Assembly. (2024b). *Pact for the Future*. Resolution A/RES/79/1. United Nations. https://docs.un.org/en/A/RES/79/1

CHAPTER 9

Intellectual Property and Patents

María Ángeles Tortosa Chuliá

1 The Challenge

One of the public functions to be fulfilled by states is to promote the economic growth and development of their social agents (families, businesses, NGOs, universities). This function takes on greater relevance in the international context of successive crises and changes in the conditions for trade between countries in recent years. The generation of innovation through new technologies and the creation of intellectual property (IP) has become a powerful driver of economic dynamism. Its incorporation into markets and institutions worldwide is an unstoppable activity that generates both benefits and costs.

Competition between countries in this area led some countries to come together long ago (1883) to find solutions to the challenges posed by innovations and new technologies. Initially, this incipient organisation achieved scattered international agreements on patents and technology, trademarks and designs, copyright and creative industries for only a few

M. Á. T. Chuliá (✉)
University of Valencia, Valencia, Spain
e-mail: angeles.tortosa@uv.es

R. de Arriba (ed.), *United Nations Facing Global Economic Disorder: Assessing 20 Policy Proposals*,
https://doi.org/10.1007/978-3-032-21952-7_9

countries. Over time, as processes in this area expanded and improved, the World Intellectual Property Organization (WIPO) was created in 1967, and since 1974 is one of the specialised agencies of the United Nations (UN). WIPO acts as a protector of IP, a catalyst for different actions on patents, and a mediator in risks and conflicts for the development of all countries. WIPO has been working hard to fulfil these functions, and since the UN set the direction for achieving the goals of the 2030 Agenda, WIPO has sought to ensure sustainable consumption and production patterns through new advances in knowledge, technology, and IP. This led WIPO to adopt its own Development Agenda with a commitment to ensure that all UN proposals related to IP, patents, and innovation integrated the development dimension (WIPO, 2007).

The evolution of innovation in recent years has been rapid and continues to grow (analysis of 40 million patent applications; 70 million scientific articles; 300 trillion dollars in exports of goods and services) (WIPO, 2024; 2025a). This demonstrates, as some experts point out, that we are immersed in 'the fourth industrial revolution', with new energy technologies, robotics, and Artificial Intelligence (AI) leading the way.

Globally, innovation is highly concentrated in a few countries and products. China, Japan, South Korea, the United States, Germany, India, France, etc., stand out in terms of innovation (the top eight countries alone account for 50% of exports, 60% of scientific articles and 80% of international patents). The fields with the highest number of technology patent applications are digital communication and information technology, as well as semiconductors, biotechnology and electrical machinery. Therefore, the main areas in which new products are being introduced are: computer technology, health, and others that are being developed, such as renewable energies (with applications in agriculture), transport (motorcycles and cars), video games, etc. (WIPO, 2024; 2025a). It is noteworthy that some areas of innovation continue to be favourites, such as health and information technology, compared to others that require more attention, such as culture. The most developed countries have greater diversification and complexity in innovations and technologies compared to the less developed ones. WIPO seeks diversification, ensuring that all types of innovation are protected equally, regardless of the field in which they occur.

Although countries allocate part of their investments to innovation, little of that effort ends up in IP and patents circulating in the markets. Many factors hinder this process. For this reason, the UN and WIPO are working to generate peaceful, safety and appropriate competition between countries in these areas.

The main challenges faced depend on the stages through which the product to be innovated passes, which are:

- At the origin, when new products are researched and created.
- When the products have already been created, in their integration, dissemination, and commercialisation in the markets.

Taking these phases into account, WIPO identifies and works on various dimensions of innovation capabilities: scientific, technological, and production. The challenges vary depending on the phase of innovation. At the origin, the generation of scientific knowledge is the basis. At this stage, laying the foundations for research and technology creation is essential. A great deal of knowledge and technology is generated by universities, companies, and public institutions, but not all of it ends up becoming IP, let alone a patent for a product that is successfully marketed.

The following are currently key challenges for WIPO:

1. Strengthening local innovation capacities, particularly in small and medium-sized countries and less developed countries.
2. Promoting diversification in innovation so that it is not concentrated in a few areas of the economy.
3. Addressing the complexity of innovation, adapting the conditions for its creation in science, and achieving diversification and improvement in the conditions of production systems.
4. Build innovation ecosystems so that different countries can identify untapped knowledge through scientific results and registered patents, and thus seek out gaps in which to prioritise subsequent investments in innovation and improve competitiveness.
5. Achieve comprehensive and fair regulations through multilateral negotiation. Develop consistent standards that can be applied equally in all countries, including the smallest ones. Given the speed at which innovations occur in the market, standards may not address all social interests and may create injustices. This is one of the most significant obstacles to multilateral negotiation, as it requires more time and leads to international cooperation between only a few countries, or bilateral, regional, or local cooperation, rather than the

signing of global or multilateral treaties. WIPO seeks to extend the various agreements on IP and patents to more countries and to act more quickly.

6. However, apart from the above challenges, it remains a fundamental challenge for WIPO to focus all its efforts on reducing the unequal distribution of IP and patents among countries and individuals, and to expand the number of those who benefit from advances in patent protection, ensuring that access to these advances occurs as quickly as possible.

Unfortunately, the benefits of WIPO‘s actions depend heavily on the responses and capabilities of countries. Hence, the aim is to reduce these ‘insurpassable’ differences in IP between rich and poor, small, medium and large countries[1].

This unequal distribution of the benefits of IP and patents is particularly evident in the field of health. In this area, which is fundamental to human well-being, innovation is constant and there is a strong industry that invests heavily in new technologies for equipment and medicines. Companies that invest and obtain IP and patents acquire exclusive rights to their commercialisation and use. Furthermore, as companies seek a return on their high investment and profits, advances end up being costly and time-consuming. Some products depend on several (or many) patents, as other patents are added throughout the process from research to commercialisation. As a result, for a health advance to reach the relevant population, various barriers must be overcome. Exclusive rights and high prices on one or more patents for a product and/or process complicate, delay, or prevent access to these innovations by countries and individuals with limited resources or who cannot afford to import

[1] The EU response is to launch a major industrial strategy to achieve the 5.0 revolution from latest findings of the Draghi report on the state of European R&D (European Commission, 2025d). The report calls for urgent and priority action in this area (Rua, 2025) through: increasing public investment in R&D; concentrating, streamlining and better coordinating of available resources for innovation; making better use of our IP; removing barriers and bureaucracy to help businesses and integrating their patents into markets; reviewing the single market in terms of innovation and entrepreneurship, allowing for the consolidation of scattered national regulations, as well as improving staff training and retaining talent. Although the European Union has improved its innovation performance since 2018, it remains quite uneven across regions (European Commission, 2025a).

them. The health consequences of these circumstances, and others, are very serious. By way of example, it is worth noting that: one third of the world's population does not have access to essential medicines; in some underdeveloped countries, more than half of the population does not have access to basic medicines and mortality rates are high; of the new drugs that are patented, a very low percentage (1–5%) is allocated to forgotten diseases that still persist in underdeveloped countries (malaria, tuberculosis, diarrhoea diseases, etc.) (Velàsquez, 2025).

It seems that the industry directs its efforts and objectives primarily towards marketing its products to rich countries, but this does not exempt them from problems related to IP and patents in health. The increase in production costs for new products complicates their acquisition and application in developed countries. This leads to shortages/delays in access to products at markets, numerous lawsuits, and complicated negotiations between companies and governments and ultimately, a deterioration in the health of their population.

This leads to an unequal distribution of health progress among populations (especially the most disadvantaged), potential shortages or unequal access to advances even among rich countries, and a serious ethical problem between public health, IP, and patents. We are talking about whether everyone's health takes precedence over the pursuit of profit derived from the commercialisation of patents on products or resources that can save lives (T Hoen, 2023). The UN-WIPO is working to try to reconcile these different views of states and companies through cooperation with other global bodies. This need for collaboration was clearly evident with the COVID-19 pandemic.

2 UN Proposals

WIPO has become an organisation that must ensure that all UN proposals on development incorporate its recommendations on IP and patents adapted to the 2030 Agenda (WIPO, 2007). WIPO has long since expanded its work to promote coordination and deliberation on regulatory proposals, IP and patent management, mediation of conflicts, and expansion of training (experts in data, cybersecurity or robotics, AI, ethics).

In order to address these new challenges, WIPO has launched a series of initiatives (WIPO, 2024; 2025b):

- WIPO as a facilitator and promoter of diversification, and as a key driver of development through the recommendation of new industrial promotion policies in new technologies and sustainability. As well as a creator of a holistic view among industrial and digital innovation in a more creative and digital world.
- Expanding its collaborations with other global organisations (Other UN bodies; international organisations; governments; NGOs; and associations from different business sectors) to solve new challenges.
- The WIPO Dialogue, as an open global forum for discussing the implications of modern technologies for IP (AI, the metaverse, data, etc.). It is now in its tenth edition.
- Creating global WIPO databases on IP and patents to guide decision-makers, providing a platform where communities can debate and publish research in order to translate theory into practice, and using AI to translate IP-related content into as many languages as possible and extend its impact.
- Expanding WIPO‘s technical assistance services to bring IP to all countries and people: the WIPO Centralised Access to Search and Examination (WIPO CASE) system; Digital Access to Priority Documents (WIPO DAS) to increase the efficiency of patent examination. Facilitate public-private collaboration through WIPO Re:Search and the Accessible Books Consortium; WIPO Green: a marketplace to exchange sustainable technologies and IP green inventory (alternative energy production and conservation; transportation; waste management; agriculture/forestry; etc.).
- Development of a policy guide with relevant and successful experiences that countries can emulate[2].

In the field of health, the World Health Organization (WHO) made it very clear in its 2008 *Global Strategy on Public Health. Innovation and*

[2] As example, WIPO influences the EU policies through the New European Innovation Agenda in 2022 that spread to other actions like the EU Strategy for the Creation and Growth of Start-ups, or the European Innovation Act and European Research Area Act (expected in 2026), and finally the European Artificial Intelligence Act and Life Science Strategy (European Commission, 2025b, 2025c). In fact, EU countries already increased their R&D&I budget allocations by 3% in 2024, with universities receiving almost 50% of these budgets (Eurostat, 2025).

Intellectual Property (WHO, 2008) that it would not cease to intervene in matters of IP and health. This Strategy and subsequent ones, extended till 2030 (WHO, 2024), redirected the way all countries implemented policies on pharmaceuticals and new health technologies. With these strategies, basic elements and indicators were established to work on and monitor progress in research and development, innovation, technology transfer, and its application in health promotion, as well as in the management, provision, financing, and access to IP in health for all countries. This made it possible to create: minimum standards for the property rights of pharmaceutical and health technology companies; guidelines for the examination of pharmaceutical patents by countries; transparency in information on R&D costs; guarantees on the health value of products; and solutions to address the different positions of the various stakeholders. In this sense, the WHO is working to grow the health industrial competition and to reduce the monopolistic power of certain companies over IP and patents in the field of health.

Over time, these strategies also led to an unusual development: trilateral cooperation between WIPO, WHO, and the WTO (World Trade Organization) to reach common ground and agreements on these issues. The COVID-19 pandemic left no choice but to collaborate so that access to vaccine patents would be available everywhere in the world (something that did not always happen or arrive on time). WIPO enacted an urgent package of measures and provided a recovery fund for this purpose. However, the most significant development was the creation of a trilateral technical assistance service (WHO-WIPO-WTO, 2020) specifically for Covid-19 to address these IP and COVID-19 issues, which continues to operate today for other public health/IP/patent issues.

This pandemic has shown how important it is to continue innovating in health and collaborating for better organisation and efficient use of IP and patents, especially in medicines, to reduce injustices and inequalities among countries. Currently, the WIPO, WHO, and WTO trilogy has been extended to prevent the effects of future pandemics (Salud y fármacos, 2024).

Given the world is dynamic and constantly changing, WIPO is building a strategic foresight for tomorrow's IP. It is also part of internal review of UN's operating model, with the aim of becoming more agile, responsive and resilient and providing better support to Member States. This means implementing the UN 2.0 Action Plan (United Nations, 2024) for future, in which some transformation areas are now in the hands of WIPO, such as data skills, digital capabilities, and innovation. WIPO will therefore play a key and relevant role in the culture and forward-looking preparedness of the UN.

3 Assessment

Growth and development are among the most important 'mantras' of governments. However, this can no longer be achieved at any cost; these objectives must be pursued in harmony with society and the planet. As never before, social, ethical and human issues, as well as environmental issues, are being considered alongside the purely financial aspects (budgetary, employment, business, etc.) derived from IP and patents.

In this context, the 'dances of power' continue, and with new 'rhythms and music', new ways of living and interacting are established. In these 'races', we hope that the emphasis will not be on who wins the competition, but rather on how best to distribute the 'prize' of growth and development.

The UN/WIPO is concerned that new global industrial policies and the intensification of the race for technological innovation in the consolidation of the '4th industrial revolution' will overlook the above constraints and lead to greater international conflicts and injustices.

WIPO has no choice but to continue to look after creators and innovators by extending the scope of that innovation to new areas, while directing their products towards fair and more humane collective and planetary progress. It will have to take its regulations and negotiations to the multilateral level and at the speed of innovation in order to universalise its benefits.

Evidence of the benefits of adequate expansion and use of IP emerged in the field of health during the COVID-19 pandemic. The financial efforts, concentration and use of available resources, and innovation by governments and social agents worldwide and from the WHO/WIPO enabled unprecedented advances in the field of vaccines and new technologies, public-private cooperation, robotics and AI applied to the operation of health centres, and the scope of more personalised and precise medicine (Omondi, 2025). Despite these efforts, IP and patents could have been better managed and numerous deaths in disadvantaged countries could have been avoided.

In the future, the UN (through WIPO) must continue to seek collaborations to integrate visions and needs that result in agreements that are valuable to all, where the purely commercial interests of IP and patents do not predominate. There is still much room for improvement to achieve global and fair progress.

Despite constant challenges (climate change, SDG targets and a digitalised world), WIPO continues to provide relevant support services for the public-private sector of innovation and creation, ensuring that positive impact on development is generated and accelerated, that the power of IP reaches all parts of the world, and that IP serves as a link between countries. In this sense, WIPO will still have a relevant role in the future to develop the UN 2.0 Action Plan.

References

European Commission. (2025a). *Europe Performs Well in Innovation*. European Commission. Retrieved July 15, 2025, from https://ec.europa.eu/commission/presscorner/detail/en/ip_25_1801

European Commission. (2025b). *Commission Seeks Feedback on the Future European Innovation Act*. Directorate-General for Research and Innovation, European Commission. Retrieved July 9, 2025, from https://research-and-innovation.ec.europa.eu/news/all-research-and-innovation-news/commission-seeks-feedback-future-european-innovation-act-2025-07-09_en.

European Commission. (2025c). *The EU Startup and Scaleup Strategy. Choose Europe to Start and Scale*. European Commission. Retrieved May 28, 2025, from https://research-and-innovation.ec.europa.eu/document/download/2f76a0df-b09b-47c2-949c-800c30e4c530_en?filename=ec_rtd_eu-startup-scaleup-strategy-communication.pdf

European Commission. (2025d). *The Draghi Report on EU Competitiveness*. Publications Office of the European Union. Retrieved September 9, 2025, from https://commission.europa.eu/topics/eu-competitiveness/draghi-report_en

Eurostat. (2025). *EU Governments Increased R&D Allocations by 3% in 2024*. Eurostat News. Retrieved July 29, 2025, from https://ec.europa.eu/eurostat/en/web/products-eurostat-news/w/ddn-20250729-2

Omondi, P. (2025). Unlocking the Power of Intellectual Property in Medical Technology. *WIPO Magazine*. Retrieved February 3, 2025, from https://www.wipo.int/en/web/wipo-magazine/article-details?assetRef=71322&title=unlocking-the-power-of-intellectual-property-in-medical-technology

Rua, C. (2025). *El futur de la innovació a Europa: la resposta a l'informe Draghi*. PierNext. Retrieved February 21, 2025, from https://piernext.portdebarcelona.cat/ca/governanca/el-futur-de-la-innovacio-a-europa-la-resposta-a-linforme-draghi/

Salud y fármacos. (2024). El Tratado de pandemias de la OMS y las obligaciones de la propiedad intelectual. *Boletín Fármacos: Propiedad Intelectual, 27*(2) https://www.saludyfarmacos.org/lang/es/boletin-farmacos/boletines/may202408/44_el/
T Hoen, E. (2023, November 20). *WHO is an Essential Forum for Debates on Intellectual Property and Public Health.* Medicines Law & Policies. https://medicineslawandpolicy.org/2023/11/who-is-an-essential-forum-for-debates-on-intellectual-property-and-public-health/
United Nations. (2024). *UN 2.0 Action Plan.* United Nations. https://www.un.org/two-zero/sites/default/files/2023-09/UN-2.0_Policy-Brief_EN.pdf
Velàsquez, G. (2025). "Pautas de patentabilidad y el acceso a los medicamentos", *Una reflexión sobre el comercio internacional, la propiedad intelectual y el derecho a la salud.* Farmamundi. *https://farmaceuticosmundi.org/wp-content/uploads/2015/12/propiedad-intelectual.pdf*
WHO. (2008). *Global Strategy and Plan of Action on Public Health, Innovation and Intellectual Property (GSPA-PHI).* Resolution WHA61.21. World Health Organization.
WHO. (2024). *Global strategy and plan of action on public health, innovation and intellectual property: implementation plan 2024–2026.* World Health Organization. https://iris.who.int/server/api/core/bitstreams/d0836d28-557e-41d6-b3e7-ab54bb259dee/content
WHO-WIPO-WTO. (2020). *Trilateral Technical Assistance Platform.* World Health Organization, World Intellectual Property Organization and World Trade Organization. https://www.who-wipo-wto-trilateral.org/en
WIPO. (2007). Report Adopted by the Assembly. General Assembly Decision WO/GA/34/16. World Intellectual Property Organization. https://www.wipo.int/edocs/mdocs/govbody/en/wo_ga_34/wo_ga_34_16.pdf
WIPO. (2024). *Making innovation policy work for development. World Intellectual Property Report 2024.* World Intellectual Property Organization. https://www.wipo.int/edocs/pubdocs/en/wipo-pub-944-2024-en-world-intellectual-property-report-2024.pdf
WIPO (2025a). *World Intellectual Property Indicators 2025.* World Intellectual Property Organization. https://tind.wipo.int/record/58959?v=pdf
WIPO. (2025b). *Proposed Program of Work and Budget for 2026/27.* World Intellectual Property Organization. https://www.wipo.int/edocs/mdocs/govbody/en/a_66/a_66_9.pdf

CHAPTER 10

Artificial Intelligence

Olga Blasco-Blasco

1 The Challenge

Zhang and Lu (2021) define AI as a constantly evolving transformative technology that simulates human intelligence in machines. It can be conceptualized as a series of intricate computational systems that possess the capacity to emulate human cognitive abilities, including learning, reasoning, problem-solving, perception and language comprehension (De Fátima Soares et al., 2020).

The advent of new social, cultural, ethical and legal challenges necessitates a re-evaluation of regulatory frameworks and training strategies. This re-evaluation must ensure that changes are managed appropriately and that less technologically developed societies are not adversely affected. In this regard, the UN is addressing the issue of AI from a multidisciplinary perspective, placing special emphasis on human rights, the achievement of SDGs, and the ethical values that should guide international governance and security (United Nations 2025a).

O. Blasco-Blasco (✉)
University of Valencia, Valencia, Spain
e-mail: olga.blasco@uv.es

R. de Arriba (ed.), *United Nations Facing Global Economic Disorder: Assessing 20 Policy Proposals*,
https://doi.org/10.1007/978-3-032-21952-7_10

According to UN Secretary General António Guterres, "AI must benefit everyone, including the one-third of humanity that still does not have access to the Internet" (UNRIC, 2023). He insists that this technology must be harnessed as an engine for inclusive growth and sustainable development, for the benefit of all, particularly developing countries (UN, 2025c). At the July 2023 "AI for Good" Global Summit, the UN highlighted that the use of AI could facilitate the achievement of its SDGs. However, we must not fall into the trap of thinking only about the positive aspects of AI, as issues such as lack of ethical regulation, misinformation, job displacement and the concentration of power must be addressed to prevent AI from exacerbating existing inequalities.

Since the mid-twentieth century, the evolution of AI has brought about a considerable transformation in many aspects of daily life. Booking flights, conducting banking transactions from anywhere, predicting pandemics or promoting inclusion in certain sectors of society have made the use of this technology commonplace in our lives. These are just a few examples of how AI has benefited many areas of life, ranging from public health to agriculture, as well as helping to achieve the SDGs.

Some experts believe that AI can improve and create jobs; however, in certain sectors, professionals are being replaced by automated processes, necessitating caution in its application. In addition, the indiscriminate use of AI, as well as its greater autonomy and decision-making capacity, creates legal, ethical and social challenges. Failure to take account of certain aspects of its use and lack of regulation may increase social and technological inequalities, lead to job losses in specific sectors, and affect individual privacy and security. Therefore, legal and ethical regulation of the use of AI at the international level is necessary (United Nations General Assembly, 2024).

Among the potential challenges of AI currently generating debate at the UN are the following (UNRIC, 2023; UN, 2025a): global governance, increased inequalities, rapid evolution of systems, exclusion of minorities, access to data, environmental impact and misinformation.

The rapid development of AI is a concern for institutions due to the lack of regulations, thus posing potential risks to peace, security and human rights. This has led the UN to consider how to achieve ethical, responsible, global and effective governance. The UN insists on the importance of maintaining human control over society's most important decisions rather than delegating them to uncontrolled algorithm.

The UN identifies increasing inequality as one of the greatest risks posed by AI. The lack of AI regulation, both nationally and internationally, could mean that the opportunities generated by this technology widen the digital divide, concentrating benefits among a privileged few, thus denying equitable access and potentially excluding societies and groups with fewer resources.

The rapid evolution of AI systems poses a significant challenge to the application of traditional regulatory models. This constant evolution, when considered in conjunction with a paucity of transparency in models, inaccessible algorithms and growing autonomy of AI in decision-making, hinders human control and jeopardizes security and equity.

The underrepresentation of minorities in training models has the potential to engender bias in model design, placing women, individuals with disabilities, and gender, ethnic and racial minorities at risk of exclusion. It is important to note that older people may also be excluded due to an absence of digital literacy skills and difficulties in accessing certain services.

Further challenges that must be addressed include unequal access to data, quality and algorithmic bias, misuse and human rights violations. The absence of adequate infrastructure in developing countries poses significant challenges in the generation and storage of substantial volumes of data, thereby hindering the development of AI-related innovation. Concomitantly, the provenance of data must be meticulously examined, as the utilization of incomplete or biased data sources can result in the propagation of biases through algorithmic processes, thereby engendering substantial inequalities. Furthermore, it is imperative to safeguard both data and individual privacy to avert potential violations of human rights.

The environmental impact of AI is significant, due to the substantial amount of energy and water required for model training and the operation of large data centres. These factors have resulted in a considerable increase in carbon footprint, while also engendering tensions due to non-compliance with international commitments on climate change, especially in developing countries.

The dissemination of disinformation or misinformation through campaigns could potentially influence significant issues, including but not limited to climate change and the utilization of renewable energy sources. Furthermore, such campaigns could constitute a violation of human rights, contribute to the proliferation of hate crimes by propagating racist or xenophobic rhetoric, and disseminate content that is deemed to be harmful to sexual well-being. The dissemination of such content could also compromise the safety and integrity of humanitarian and peace operations. It is important to note that such campaigns have the potential to undermine the very foundations of democracy.

2 The Proposals

In 2021, as part of the commemoration of the 75th anniversary of the UN, a series of proposals was submitted with the aim of fulfilling 12 commitments, all of which are aligned with the SDGs. Commitment 7, "Improve digital cooperation", explicitly mentions the Global Digital Compact, as it is a proposal that insists on the need to promote the regulation of AI (UN, 2021). The commitment seeks to improve digital cooperation by carrying out various actions, including the promotion of AI regulation. In this regard, the UN has convened numerous international meetings and forums to address concerns regarding the integration of AI. These deliberations aim to ascertain the extent to which the incorporation of AI can be guaranteed, the implications of this technology for economic development, the measures to be implemented to ensure that it does not infringe on human rights, invade privacy, exacerbate discrimination or the digital divide, and how to implement AI in a manner that benefits all segments of society, reduces inequalities and enhances quality of life for all, including the most disadvantaged.

The Global Digital Compact, an annex to the Pact for the Future, seeks to establish an inclusive, open, responsible and sustainable digital environment. It underscores the necessity to fortify international data governance, govern AI for the benefit of humanity and cultivate international collaborations to enhance AI capabilities. This is particularly salient in the context of emerging technologies, including AI, which present novel opportunities to propel development. Furthermore, efforts to bridge the digital divide and accelerate progress on all SDGs will serve to mitigate the risks associated with AI, while also harnessing its benefits and directing them towards the achievement of these goals. The UN asserts that these objectives can be achieved through the following means: the development, dissemination and maintenance of open, secure AI collaborations and models that benefit the entire society; the support of the development of national data governance frameworks to ensure accountability, equitability and interoperability; and the improvement of international AI governance, especially in developing countries (United Nations General Assembly, 2024).

The primary lines of action of the UN in the field of AI are outlined below, grouped into the following categories: ethics and human rights; sustainable development; global governance and regulation; peace and security; and inclusion and equity.

The Recommendation of the United Nations Educational, Scientific and Cultural Organization (UNESCO, 2021) on the Ethics of Artificial Intelligence establishes the first universal regulatory framework for AI ethics, requiring an inclusive approach based on human rights, justice, sustainability and inclusive governance. This approach is further defined by the necessity for data management that respects the privacy, transparency and protection of all individuals. Member states are encouraged to voluntarily implement the provisions, through legislation or other actions, ensuring that the principles and standards established respect international law and human rights while remaining compatible with national legal systems. It is further recommended that companies, authorities, academic institutions and civil society be involved in the implementation of the Recommendation, ensuring rigorous scientific research and appropriate ethical criteria, while promoting the use of open and secure data with guarantees of responsible use.

The positive impact of AI could represent a step forward in achieving the SDGs, with a particular impact on health, the environment, humanitarian aid, education, agriculture and peacebuilding, ensuring an ethical, inclusive and respectful approach to human rights. To achieve this objective, it is recommended that international cooperation be strengthened, access to data and technologies be promoted, and that developing countries be supported in their efforts to reduce inequalities and promote global well-being. However, it should be noted that, in order to reduce emissions produced by the increased use of AI, it is necessary to promote the use of renewable energies that reduce emissions related to the AI life cycle and to advance the development of more efficient infrastructures.

The international governance of AI needs to be enhanced. This can be achieved by means of adoption of a balanced and inclusive approach that fully and equally incorporates all countries, especially developing countries. It is imperative to advocate for the establishment of inclusive international regulatory frameworks that ensure universal access to technology and contribute to the reduction of inequalities. Moreover, the private sector must not be overlooked. In the event that companies guarantee the safe, reliable and transparent development of AI, it will be possible to promote the coordination and compatibility of international AI governance standards and effective mechanisms for their implementation (UNCTAD, 2025). At this juncture, it is pertinent to cite the proposal set forth in the "Governing AI for Humanity" report (UN, 2024), which calls for the establishment of a global framework to regulate the availability, interoperability, security and equitable access to data, in addition to a global network through which resources, data and technology are shared to promote access in developing countries.

At the BRICS+ Summit in July 2025, the UN Secretary General once again articulated concerns regarding the utilization of AI as a military instrumentation, coinciding with a period of profound transformation in warfare brought about by AI-powered drones. This has given rise to a plethora of ethical dilemmas concerning the potential consequences of algorithmic determination of military outcomes, including the fate of soldiers, geographical areas and targeted objectives (UN, 2025c). Consequently, the UN and several non-governmental organizations are advocating for the establishment of international regulatory frameworks to prevent automated systems from making decisions regarding the selection of targets for attack. Human Rights Watch has drawn attention to the fact that autonomous land and sea weapons represent the most recent and serious example of "digital dehumanization" (UN, 2025b). The utilization of AI in law enforcement, particularly in the domains of police surveillance and border control, signifies the delegation of decision-making authority to algorithms, thereby conferring upon them the capacity to exert a profound influence upon the lives of individuals. The UN has expressed its conviction that this practice should be prohibited by international law (UN, 2025b). Izumi Nakamitsu of the UN Office for Disarmament Affairs further asserts that "there is an emerging agreement that weapon systems that are fully autonomous should be prohibited" (UN, 2025b). This has prompted the UN Secretary General to call upon member states to achieve a legally binding agreement that would prohibit the use of autonomous weapons by 2026 (UN, 2025b).

Artificial intelligence has significant potential to benefit individuals living with disabilities. However, this potential can only be realized if AI systems are designed to facilitate this technology are constructed with the explicit intention of eliminating barriers and creating new opportunities for inclusion. Consequently, member states are strongly encouraged to regulate the utilization of AI in a manner that safeguards the rights of persons with disabilities, in accordance with the principles established in the Convention on the Rights of Persons with Disabilities (UNRIC, 2024). Conversely, the use of algorithms derived from statistical averages, the training of algorithms on specific combinations of characteristics, and the identification of pre-programmed behaviour patterns can exclude persons with disabilities, thereby exacerbating their marginalization. A range of universal connectivity programmes under the Pact for the Future, in conjunction with various global human rights protection frameworks, international ethical regulations, digital training strategies and gender equality policies, have the potential to mitigate the risks of AI-driven exclusion of gender, ethnic and racial minorities, older persons and migrants.

Regarding key recommendations for global AI governance, aimed at improving and strengthening global cooperation and establishing a global, networked, agile and flexible vision that allows AI to be governed for the benefit of humanity, the United Nations Final Report on the Governance of Artificial Intelligence for the Benefit of Humanity (2024) presents seven recommendations:

- The establishment of an international group of multidisciplinary and independent AI expert scientists with the objective of providing support to the UN in the assessment of opportunities, risks and advances in the field. The group will also be responsible to produce timely reports.
- The creation of inclusive political forums to facilitate dialogue on AI governance policies, and for states and stakeholders to share best practices and regulations, and to collaborate on the international governance of AI. A UN report (The Guardian, 2024) recommends that governments and the private sector should contribute to a global AI fund that would allow developing nations to benefit from advances in AI technology.
- The founding of an entity to facilitate the exchange of AI standards, including the coordination and harmonization of AI technical, ethical and governance standards at the global level, to promote interoperability and prevent fragmentation.
- The establishment of an AI capacity-building network to facilitate the sharing of resources, data, training and technology. This network

will focus on the development of resources in under-resourced countries.

- The establishment of a global AI fund to finance infrastructure, data, research and projects designed to reduce the digital divide and promote the inclusive use of this technology.
- The development of a global AI data framework to regulate availability, interoperability, data protection and equitable access to training systems.
- The creation of an AI office within the UN Secretariat to coordinate global governance initiatives, support the implementation of recommendations and promote international cooperation (UN, 2024).

In conclusion, given the profound transformations that AI is generating in society, it is essential to advance the analysis and implementation of mechanisms that minimize the associated risks while maximizing the potential of this technology. In addition, it is imperative to establish a comprehensive global legal framework that governs the use of AI and prevents its misuse.

3 Assessment

The AI proposals set forth by the UN constitute a multifaceted endeavour, with a focus on the common good, ethics, security, inclusion, global governance, sustainable development and respect for human rights. The UN has demonstrated its commitment to leveraging AI as a catalyst for achieving the SDGs. This approach signifies a strategic utilization of technological innovations to promote global progress, while emphasizing the necessity for international regulatory frameworks that prioritize the well-being of all humanity. The UN has advocated for measures to mitigate inequalities, foster inclusivity and prohibit the unrestrained deployment of autonomous weapons systems, thereby ensuring that the benefits of technological advancement are equitably distributed and the interests of vulnerable populations are safeguarded.

While these proposals are ambitious and ethical, the achievement of the objectives they set out will depend, to a large extent: on collaboration between states and transnational corporations; on the ability of institutional and regulatory frameworks to adapt to rapidly evolving technology, which makes it difficult to formulate appropriate regulations; and on the political will of member states to establish and enforce rules governing AI. It is imperative to acknowledge that these recommendations are not legally binding and that the UN does not possess the legal mechanisms to enforce compliance.

Consequently, the geopolitical interests of developed countries may impede the establishment of international agreements, hinder compliance with legislation and the ethical utilization of AI, and exacerbate the digital divide with developing countries. It is imperative that international governance mechanisms incorporate the perspectives and concerns of the Global South, ensuring that the AI development benefits all and does not exacerbate existing inequalities and ethical concerns.

References

De Fátima Soares Borges, A., Laurindo, F., Spínola, M., Gonçalves, R., & Mattos, C. (2020). The Strategic Use of Artificial Intelligence in the Digital Era: Systematic Literature Review and Future Research Directions. *International Journal of Information Management, 57*, 102225. https://doi.org/10.1016/J.IJINFOMGT.2020.102225

The Guardian. (2024, September 19). Global AI Fund Needed to Help Developing Nations Tap Tech Benefits, UN says. *The Guardian*. https://www.theguardian.com/business/2024/sep/19/global-ai-fund-needed-to-help-developing-nations-tap-tech-benefits-un-says

UNCTAD. (2025). Technology and Innovation Report: Inclusive Artificial Intelligence for Development: Overview (UNCTAD/TIR/2025/Overview). *United Nations Conference on Trade and Development*. https://unctad.org/system/files/official-document/tir2025overview_en.pdf

UNESCO. (2021). Recommendation on the Ethics of Artificial Intelligence (41st session, General Conference Resolution, Annex VII). *United Nations Educational, Scientific and Cultural Organization*. https://unesdoc.unesco.org/ark:/48223/pf0000380455?locale=en

United Nations. (2024). Governing AI for Humanity: Final Report. High-level Advisory Body on Artificial Intelligence. *United Nations*. https://www.un.org/sites/un2.un.org/files/governing_ai_for_humanity_final_report_en.pdf

United Nations. (2025a, June 1). As AI evolves, pressure mounts to regulate 'killer robots'. UN News. *United Nations*. https://news.un.org/en/story/2025a/06/1163891

United Nations. (2025b). Artificial Intelligence (AI). *United Nations*. https://www.un.org/en/global-issues/artificial-intelligence

United Nations. (2025c, July 6). Artificial Intelligence Needs a Multilateral Response Grounded in Equity, Human Rights Press Release. *United Nations*. https://press.un.org/en/2025b/sgsm22717.doc.htm

United Nations General Assembly. (2024). Pact for the Future. Resolution A/RES/79/1. *United Nations*. https://docs.un.org/en/A/RES/79/1 (27/12/2025).

United Nations Secretary-General. (2021). Our Common Agenda: Report of the Secretary-General. *United Nations*. https://www.un.org/en/content/common-agenda-report/assets/pdf/Common_Agenda_Report_English.pdf

UNRIC. (2023). AI: Transformative Power and Governance Challenges. *United Nations Regional Information Centre for Western Europe*. https://unric.org/en/ai-transformative-power-and-governance-challenges/

UNRIC. (2024). Building an Accessible Future for All: AI and the Inclusion of Persons with Disabilities. *United Nations Regional Information Centre for Western Europe*. https://unric.org/en/building-an-accessible-future-for-all-ai-and-the-inclusion-of-persons-with-disabilities/

Zhang, C., & Lu, Y. (2021). Study on Artificial Intelligence: The State of the Art and Future Prospects. *Journal of Industrial Information Integration, 23*, 100224. https://doi.org/10.1016/J.JII.2021.100224

CHAPTER 11

Climate Change

Marta R. Casanova

1 The Challenge

Since the Industrial Revolution, the global average temperature has risen by more than 1.2 °C. The main reason for this change is the increase in greenhouse gas and aerosol emissions. Every three seconds, the world loses an area of forest equivalent to a football field, and in the past century alone, half of all wetlands have been destroyed. Furthermore, 50% of coral reefs have already disappeared, and by 2050, up to 90% could vanish—even if global warming is limited to 1.5 °C, the target set by the Paris Agreement (Masson-Delmotte et al., 2018).

Climate change is affecting all countries across all continents and is becoming one of the greatest challenges facing humanity. It is disrupting national and global economies, altering weather systems, causing sea levels to rise, and increasing the frequency and intensity of extreme weather events (Masson-Delmotte et al., 2019). These impacts disproportionately affect low-income populations and developing countries, reinforcing global inequities and complicating international relations. Thus, climate

M. R. Casanova (✉)
University of Valencia, Valencia, Spain
e-mail: marta.roig-casanova@uv.es

R. de Arriba (ed.), *United Nations Facing Global Economic Disorder: Assessing 20 Policy Proposals*,
https://doi.org/10.1007/978-3-032-21952-7_11

change also has profound socio-political implications that extend beyond environmental degradation to affect governance, security, and social stability. These pressures can undermine livelihoods, contribute to food insecurity, and increase the likelihood of forced migration and displacement, especially in climate-vulnerable regions. As a result, governments face growing challenges in managing population movements, maintaining social cohesion, and ensuring equitable access to resources.

Scientific robustness in assessing this global phenomenon is being achieved thanks to the work of the 'Intergovernmental Panel on Climate Change' (IPCC)[1]. Its reports have played a key role in placing climate change at the forefront of the international political agenda. This United Nations body was established in 1988 to provide policymakers with regular scientific assessments of climate change, including its causes, implications, potential future risks, and to offer strategies for adaptation, mitigation, and response.

IPCC reports are developed and reviewed through a multi-stage process, ensuring both objectivity and transparency. These documents are policy-relevant and globally neutral, but not policy-prescriptive. As such, they serve as a vital contribution to international negotiations aimed at addressing climate change.

All of this has led to broad consensus regarding the recognition of climate change and its devastating consequences, both within the scientific literature (Cook et al., 2013) and among the majority of political leaders. Nevertheless, some countries continue to foster debate over its acknowledgment and anthropogenic origin (Boykoff, 2013; Fernández-Reyes, 2018). This is particularly evident in the case of the United States. On July 31, 2025, following his return to office after the latest elections, U.S. President Donald Trump—well-known for his climate change denialism and scepticism—made headlines once again. According to a controversial report covered by The Washington Post[2], the U.S. Department of Energy released a document authored by scientists within the Trump administration, claiming that United Nations reports distort the state of climate science.

[1] https://www.ipcc.ch/reports/

[2] https://www.washingtonpost.com/climate-environment/2025/07/31/endangerment-repeal-climate-science-report/

Therefore, even in times of geopolitical complexity, cooperation remains the only viable path forward. It is essential to transcend borders and overcome differences between nations and interests, with the shared goal of protecting our planet. This is precisely the mission of the United Nations, as reaffirmed by Inger Andersen, Executive Director of the 'United Nations Environment Programme' (UNEP)[3], in her official statement.

2 UN Proposals

The United Nations took more than two decades since its founding in 1945 to begin addressing environmental issues and climate change. These matters did not become a significant concern for the UN until 1968, when its main bodies began to seriously consider environmental challenges. From that point onward, the organization started to recognize the magnitude of the problem and took action. In what follows, we review, chronologically, the main treaties, protocols, and agreements promoted by the United Nations in support of environmental protection.

Over the course of more than five decades, the United Nations has acted on solid scientific foundations and has progressively developed a growing legal framework—from regional treaties to universal global agreements. Throughout this process, three distinct phases can be identified. The first phase, spanning the 1970s and early 1980s, marks a period of global environmental awakening, characterized by increased awareness and the emergence of an initial institutional framework. The second phase, from the late 1980s through the 2000s, reflects a period of scientific institutionalization, the formalization of environmental norms, and the establishment of the first binding actions and global conventions. Finally, the third phase, covering the past two decades, has been marked by the expansion of integrated goals and environmental justice principles, alongside the consolidation of regulatory frameworks, aiming to achieve genuine global environmental governance.

This process began in 1972, during the United Nations Conference on the Human Environment, held in Stockholm—the first major environmental summit organized by the UN. In this conference, the Stockholm Declaration was adopted. The declaration set out 26 principles aimed

[3] https://www.unep.org/

at guiding states in the preservation and improvement of the human environment, emphasizing the links between environmental protection, human rights, and economic development. The Declaration addressed the issue of climate change for the first time, warning governments to consider activities that could lead to climate change and to assess the likelihood and magnitude of their potential impacts on the climate. The conference also led to the establishment of the 'United Nations Environment Programme' (UNEP), which became the world's leading environmental authority. Since then, this UN body has worked in collaboration with governments, civil society, the private sector, and other UN entities to address the most pressing environmental challenges facing humanity - from restoring the ozone layer and protecting the world's oceans, to promoting an inclusive and green economy (Citaristi, 2022; WHO, UNEP & WOAH, 2022).

The second phase marked the beginning of major binding international agreements and the scientific institutionalization of environmental governance. In 1987, the United Nations negotiated its first major environmental agreement, which actively and unanimously engaged all countries around the world. The Montreal Protocol was a landmark treaty with universal ratification, aimed at regulating the production and consumption of substances that deplete the ozone layer. Its central objective was the elimination of chlorofluorocarbons (CFCs), the primary agents responsible for ozone depletion. The implementation of the protocol helped prevent millions of cases of skin cancer, making it one of the most important and successful environmental agreements to date, achieving widespread commitment from its signatories (Fröhlich, 2007).

In 1988, the 'Intergovernmental Panel on Climate Change' (IPCC) was established[4]. Its main objective is the preparation of comprehensive scientific reports on climate change and its possible causes, the assessment of its social and economic impacts, and the formulation of response strategies. The IPCC's First Assessment Report, published in 1990, highlighted climate change as a challenge requiring international cooperation. It contributed directly to the creation of the 'United Nations Framework Convention on Climate Change' (UNFCCC)[5], which was adopted

[4] In 2007, the IPCC was awarded the Nobel Peace Prize for its efforts to advance and disseminate greater knowledge about human-induced climate change and for laying the foundations for the measures needed to counteract it.

[5] https://www.ipcc.ch/report/ar1/syr/

in 1992, at the Earth Summit in Rio de Janeiro, and entered into force in 1994. This legal framework seeks to stabilize greenhouse gas concentrations and introduced the principle of 'common but differentiated responsibilities,' meaning that developed countries must take greater action to address emissions, as they have historically been the largest contributors to global greenhouse gas levels.

In 1995, the first meeting of world leaders to address global warming - known as the 'Conference of the Parties'(COP1) - was held in Berlin. During this summit, discussions began on the development of a protocol that would include stronger and binding commitments for developed countries and those in economic transition. As a result, in 1997, the Kyoto Protocol was adopted, the most influential climate policy measure at the time (Jackson, 2007). Its primary objective was to reduce total emissions of carbon dioxide and other greenhouse gases from industrialized countries by at least 5% below 1990 levels, during the commitment period of 2008 to 2012 (the first commitment period of the Protocol). The European Union signed the Kyoto Protocol in 2002, although it did not enter into force until 2005, following Russia's ratification. In fact, for the Protocol to come into effect, it required ratification or approval by at least 55 countries, which together accounted for at least 55% of global greenhouse gas emissions. Subsequently, additional agreements were adopted, which introduced amendments, improvements, and extensions to the Kyoto Protocol[6]. However, in the end, the Kyoto Protocol failed to meet its agreed objectives. One of the reasons was its short-term vision, but more critically, the lack of participation by key countries such as the United States and China significantly undermined its effectiveness.

[6] The Marrakech Agreement, adopted in 2001 (COP7), detailed the rules for the implementation of the Kyoto Protocol, established new financial and planning instruments for adaptation, and set a framework for technology transfer. In 2007 (COP13), the Bali Road Map was agreed upon, laying out the path toward a post-2012 outcome and introducing the Ad Hoc Working Group on Long-term Cooperative Action. In 2010, the Cancun Agreements (COP16) were accepted, through which countries formalized their emissions reduction commitments. In 2011, the Durban Platform (COP17) clearly acknowledged the need to develop a new universal and legally binding agreement to address climate change beyond 2020, as the existing frameworks were falling short of their goals in terms of participation and emissions reductions. Finally, in 2012, the Doha Amendment to the Kyoto Protocol was adopted. It introduced new commitments for the Parties, who agreed to assume them during a second commitment period (2013–2020), enhanced transparency measures, and amendments to several articles of the original Kyoto Protocol.

In the most recent phase, efforts have focused on consolidating existing frameworks with the aim of achieving environmental justice and establishing a new model of global environmental governance. At the 2015 Climate Summit (COP21), the Paris Agreement was adopted - a pact that would replace the Kyoto Protocol after its expiration in 2020 and which remains in force today. Its central commitment is to strengthen the global response to the threat of climate change by keeping global temperature rise this century well below 2 degrees Celsius above pre-industrial levels, while pursuing efforts to limit the increase to 1.5 degrees Celsius. The Agreement also establishes progressively ambitious emission reduction commitments and climate adaptation financing obligations. According to several European Union representatives—as environment ministers or commissioners speaking on behalf of the Council of the EU or the European Commission—the Paris Agreement is 'the first universal and legally binding agreement on climate change' (Miralles-Quirós & Miralles-Quirós, 2022).

Also in 2015, during the Sustainable Development Summit in New York, the UN General Assembly and its Member States endorsed the Sustainable Development Goals (SDGs) and adopted the 2030 Agenda—a global action plan grounded in planetary sustainability. The 2030 Agenda addresses the three core dimensions of sustainable development: social, economic, and environmental. Among the 17 Sustainable Development Goals, Goal 13 is directly linked to climate action, while Goals 14 and 15 address the protection of marine and terrestrial ecosystems, respectively.[7]

In 2022, the IPCC warned that the world is at risk of catastrophic and irreversible climate change (Parmesan et al., 2022)[8]. Later that same year, at COP27 in Sharm El-Sheikh, Egypt, countries agreed to establish a Loss and Damage Fund to address the financial impacts of climate-related disasters. Nevertheless, the summit did little to directly address the emissions that drive those disasters. In 2023, at COP28, in the United Arab

[7] SDG 13—Take urgent action to combat climate change and its impacts (acknowledging the decisions adopted by the Conference of the Parties to the United Nations Framework Convention on Climate Change). SDG 14—Conserve and sustainably use the oceans, seas, and marine resources for sustainable development. SDG 15—Protect, restore, and promote sustainable use of terrestrial ecosystems, sustainably manage forests, combat desertification, and halt and reverse land degradation and halt biodiversity loss.

[8] https://www.ipcc.ch/report/sixth-assessment-report-working-group-ii/

Emirates—a major oil-producing nation—countries reached a landmark agreement to transition away from fossil fuels. These new commitments represent a step forward in global climate ambition, although implementation remains insufficient. That same year, the 2023 SDG Summit was held in New York. The Summit adopted a political declaration that provides a roadmap to get the world back on track toward achieving the Sustainable Development Goals (SDGs) by their 2030 deadline. This renewed commitment comes in light of the alarming fact that only 15 percent of the SDG targets are currently on track to be achieved globally by 2030.

3 Assessment

The United Nations has been at the forefront of global environmental governance for more than five decades (UNEP, 2025). However, despite its efforts, significant challenges remain that hinder its ability to effectively address environmental concerns and implement cohesive and effective environmental governance.

An analysis of the limitations of international environmental treaties reveals that they often fall short of achieving their objectives due to a combination of factors—such as institutional weaknesses, lack of national commitment, insufficient financial resources, and multiple challenges in monitoring and evaluation, among others. These limitations, deeply embedded in the socio-political structure of international environmental governance itself, give rise to systemic issues that hinder both the enforcement and the rigorous assessment of treaty implementation.

Firstly, we can speak about limitations due to political and institutional interests. Environmental treaties are often influenced by political considerations, institutional biases, and power dynamics. The effectiveness of their implementation can be affected by the political priorities of countries or their leaders, as well as by the willingness of the parties involved to act accordingly. If member states lack the authority or political will to implement the recommendations outlined in the treaties, their impact may be significantly limited, as we will detail below. In this sense, the political and institutional context of each country becomes a decisive factor in achieving both national and global objectives, with the latter being of paramount importance.

As the ultimate goal is the global implementation of environmental treaties, collective action is essential to address global environmental problems—often framed as a 'tragedy of the commons.' Nonetheless, geopolitical shifts, changes in global power balances, and the evolution of national interests significantly affect the effectiveness of environmental treaties. A treaty may lose effectiveness if key nations withdraw their commitments due to changes in domestic political priorities or international relations. A clear example is the United States, which has disengaged from key treaties - such as the Paris Agreement- depending on the interests of its Administration. Shortly after President Donald Trump took office in 2017, during his first term, the U.S. announced its withdrawal from the agreement. However, under the Biden Administration, starting in 2021, the country promptly re-joined the treaty. In 2025, the United States announced once again, during Donald Trump's second presidency, the withdrawal from the Paris Agreement—a cornerstone in the global fight against climate change—with the exit becoming effective on January 27, 2026.[9]

To minimize the vulnerability of international treaties to shifts in national political agendas, it is essential to develop treaty frameworks that are adaptable to geopolitical fluctuations and political cycles. Moreover, sustained and cross-partisan consensus would be key to ensuring the long-term effectiveness of these treaties.

Referring to institutional limitations, one of the major obstacles to effective environmental governance within the United Nations is the fragmentation among its various agencies and bodies. While the existence of multiple agencies allows for specialized expertise, it can also lead to inefficiencies and confusion, particularly when it comes to coordinating policies and actions at the global level. The United Nations Environment Programme (UNEP) is the main body responsible for coordinating global environmental efforts. However, other entities, such as the Commission on Sustainable Development (CSD) and the UN Framework Convention on Climate Change (UNFCCC), often have overlapping mandates. This lack of coordination and collaboration among different agencies contributes to confusion and inefficiencies in environmental governance.

Another aspect that creates inefficiency is the normative ambiguity of the treaties, since they are often negotiated through complex political processes, involving numerous states with diverse interests and priorities, as previously discussed. This can lead to deliberately vague agreements

[9] https://efe.com/medio-ambiente/2025-01-28/ee-uu-acuerdo-paris-onu-trump/

regarding key obligations, lacking concrete and measurable targets, or including loopholes and escape clauses. Consequently, if treaty obligations are poorly defined, it becomes extremely difficult to objectively assess compliance or effectiveness. Therefore, treaty design must be robust, with clear obligations and sanctions, as well as transparent monitoring and enforcement mechanisms. The most effective environmental treaties are those founded on solid and enforceable legal pillars.

Secondly, financial constraints and limited resources prevent achieving a good ecological transition and the ambitious goals of the United Nations environmental agreements and treaties. The United Nations Environment Programme (UNEP) provides funding; however, this is insufficient (Weiss, 2016). UN environmental initiatives often require substantial financing, but Member States' financial contributions remain inconsistent.

At the 2024 United Nations Climate Change Conference (COP29) held in Baku, Azerbaijan, countries pledged to triple funding in support of developing nations affected by climate change. Nevertheless, this commitment fell short of the amounts requested by many countries.

In developing countries, the impacts of climate change and environmental degradation are often felt more acutely; however, local governments in these nations typically lack the resources to implement their own environmental policies. Therefore, it is imperative that countries begin to provide the necessary funding for climate adaptation and the ecological transition, and commit to the level of financial support required for effective global environmental governance.

Thirdly, we find challenges in the evaluation of environmental treaties and agreements. It is of vital importance to assess the effectiveness of international environmental agreements by identifying their achievements and highlighting the shortcomings that hinder their intended purpose. The goal of such evaluation is to ensure that the environmental treaties proposed by the United Nations are not merely symbolic documents, but active instruments that drive real change on our planet and in our lives.

However, environmental systems are extremely complex and involve numerous interacting and feedback-driven components. Attributing specific environmental changes solely to a treaty is often a significant and scientifically unrealistic challenge. Pollution, for instance, is rarely caused by a single factor; rather, it is typically the result of a complex interplay of industrial activities, agricultural practices, urbanization, and natural processes. External factors—such as economic shifts, technological advancements, and unforeseen natural disasters—can also significantly influence environmental outcomes, making it difficult to isolate the specific impact of a given treaty.

Accordingly, the evaluation of environmental treaties faces numerous limitations that may compromise their ability to provide accurate and actionable information. A key limitation is the lack of data control and transparency—an issue the United Nations has sought to address through the Paris Agreement. The United Nations Environment Programme provided technical support to 64 countries in the preparation of their first biennial transparency reports, which reflect the degree of compliance with their national emission reduction commitments. In recent years, UNEP's work on transparency has supported countries in improving the use of national climate data, building the capacity of national staff involved in climate reporting, and establishing systems aimed at strengthening national reporting bodies.

Finally, we must highlight the limited scope of the treaties. Indeed, environmental issues are deeply interconnected with social challenges such as poverty and lack of resources, and the effectiveness of treaties often depends on addressing these broader contexts. If these wider dimensions are not incorporated into the treaties, there is a risk of presenting an incomplete and potentially misleading picture of their effectiveness. Expanding the scope of environmental treaties to include social, economic, and governance aspects can provide a more comprehensive understanding of their performance and inform more effective policymaking.

References

Boykoff, M. T. (2013). Public Enemy no. 1? Understanding Media Representations of Outlier Views on Climate Change. *American Behavioral Scientist, 57*(6), 796–817.

Citaristi, I. (2022). United Nations Environment Programme—UNEP. In *The Europa Directory of International Organizations* (pp. 193–199). Routledge.

Cook, J., Nuccitelli, D., Green, S. A., Richardson, M., Winkler, B., & Painting, R., et al. (2013). Quantifying the Consensus on Anthropogenic Global Warming in the Scientific Literature. *Environmental Research Letters, 8*(2), 024024.

Fernández-Reyes, R. (2018). Trump, eventos extremos y cumbres internacionales en la cobertura mediática del cambio climático. *La comunicación de la mitigación y la adaptación al cambio climático*, 13–47.

Fröhlich, M. (2007). *Political Ethics and the United Nations: Dag Hammarskjöld as secretary-general*. Routledge.

Jackson, P. (2007). From Stockholm to Kyoto: A Brief History of Climate Change. *UN Chronicle, 44*(2).

Masson-Delmotte, V., Pörtner, H. O., Skea, J., Buendía, E. C., Zhai, P., & Roberts, D. (2019). Climate Change and Land. *IPCC Special Report*.

Masson-Delmotte, V., Zhai, P., Pörtner, H. O., Roberts, D., Skea, J., & Shukla, P. R., et al. (2018). Global Warming of 1.5 C. *An IPCC Special Report on the Impacts of Global Warming, 1*(5), 43–50.

Miralles-Quirós, M. M., & Miralles-Quirós, J. L. (2022). Decarbonization and the Benefits of Tackling Climate Change. *International Journal of Environmental Research and Public Health, 19*(13), 7776.

Parmesan, C., Morecroft, M. D., & Trisurat, Y. (2022). *Climate Change 2022: Impacts, Adaptation and Vulnerability* (Doctoral dissertation). GIEC.

UNEP. (2025). We Are All in This Together—Annual Report 2024. *United Nations Environment Programme*. https://wedocs.unep.org/20.500.11822/47082.

Weiss, T. G. (2016). *What's Wrong with the United Nations and How to Fix It*. John Wiley & Sons.

WHO, UNEP and WOAH. (2022). One Health Joint Plan of Action (2022–2026): Working Together for the Health of Humans, Animals, Plants and the Environment. *World Health Organization, United Nations Environment Programme and World Organisation for Animal Health*.

CHAPTER 12

Water and Sanitation

Spartak Keremidchiev

1 The Challenge

Despite sustained international commitments, global water security remains off-track across the SDG 6 chain—from household services to basin-scale resource integrity. Recent UN reporting indicates that 2.2 billion people still lack safely managed drinking water services, while 3.4 billion lack safely managed sanitation and 1.7 billion lack basic hygiene services at home, underscoring that deficits persist not only in access but also in the safety and management conditions that determine public-health outcomes (UN DESA, 2025a). Open defecation remains a severe manifestation of these gaps (e.g., 419 million in 2022; estimates for 2024 indicate a further decline), reflecting enduring exclusion in the hardest-to-reach and often poorest contexts (WHO/UNICEF, n.d.).

Beyond households, weak pollution control and monitoring continue to constrain progress in water quality. Globally, 58% of household wastewater was estimated to be safely treated in 2022, leaving a substantial

S. Keremidchiev (✉)
Economic Research Institute at the Bulgarian Academy Of Sciences, Sofia, Bulgaria
e-mail: keremidas@gmail.com

R. de Arriba (ed.), *United Nations Facing Global Economic Disorder: Assessing 20 Policy Proposals*,
https://doi.org/10.1007/978-3-032-21952-7_12

share discharged without safe treatment and contributing to downstream environmental and health risks (UN DESA, 2025b). Consistent with this, global assessments of ambient water quality show that only roughly 56% of monitored water bodies are classified as having good water quality, while data gaps remain particularly pronounced in lower-capacity settings—suggesting that risks may be underestimated where monitoring is weakest (Heinle, 2024). Resource pressure is also rising: UN SDG 6 reporting places global water stress at 18.6% (2021), masking strong regional hotspots where withdrawals approach or exceed sustainable availability (UN-Water, 2024a). In parallel, freshwater ecosystems—critical for natural storage, filtration, and resilience—are deteriorating in many countries; roughly half of reporting countries show degradation in at least one freshwater ecosystem type, and river flow has decreased in 402 (out of 12,572) river basins worldwide (UN-Water, 2024a).

Climate change amplifies these challenges by altering hydrological regimes and increasing extremes: extreme events are making water scarcer, more unpredictable, and more polluted, thereby compounding risks to service reliability, water quality, and ecosystem stability. This risk clustering is echoed in global risk outlooks. The World Economic Forum's *Global Risks Report 2025* identifies environmental risks as dominant over the long-term horizon, including critical change to Earth systems, biodiversity loss and ecosystem collapse, and pollution—all tightly coupled to water quantity and quality (World Economic Forum, 2025).

To tackle these challenges, the UN undertakes global initiatives and actions.

2 UN Proposals

The United Nations (UN) has acknowledged the problem of water and sanitation as central to human dignity, health, and sustainable development. It has built a framework of legal recognition, dedicated action decades, global goals, monitoring systems, and high-level conferences to mobilize political will and accelerate progress. Over the decades, the UN has progressively elevated the issue through binding treaties, political declarations, dedicated decades of action, and global monitoring frameworks.

The United Nations has developed several landmark documents and initiatives to address problems related to water supply, sanitation, and hygiene.

In the Universal Declaration of Human Rights, adopted in 1948 (United Nations General Assembly, "General Assembly (UN General Assembly)", 1948) water is not explicitly mentioned, but it lays the foundation for recognizing access to basic services as a human right.

Although the International Covenant on Economic, Social and Cultural Rights does not explicitly recognize a right to water, the Committee on Economic, Social and Cultural Rights subsequently affirmed it as implicit in the right to an adequate standard of living (United Nations General Assembly, "General Assembly (UN General Assembly)", 1966; OHCHR, 2002). This recognition was reinforced by UN General Assembly Resolution 64/292 (2010), which explicitly acknowledged safe and clean drinking water and sanitation as a human right essential to life and the enjoyment of all other rights.

The human right to water, formulated in the UN Resolution A/RES/64/292, establishes that every person is entitled to sufficient, continuous, safe, acceptable, physically accessible, and affordable water for personal and domestic use, enabling them to live with dignity and good health (United Nations General Assembly, "General Assembly (UN General Assembly)", 2010; Leal Filho et al., 2021).

The 2030 Agenda for Sustainable Development (United Nations, 2015) sets Sustainable Development Goal 6 (SDG 6): ensure availability and sustainable management of water and sanitation for all by 2030. To achieve SDG 6, six outcome targets and two implementation targets have been developed. An appropriate system of monitoring indicators was set up as well.

The outcome targets and indicators are:

- 6.1 Universal access to drinking water aims by 2030 to achieve universal and equitable access to safe and affordable drinking water for all. Progress is measured by Indicator 6.1.1, "Proportion of population using safely managed drinking water services."
- 6.2 Sanitation and hygiene for all aims by 2030 to achieve access to adequate and equitable sanitation and hygiene for all, end open defecation, paying special attention to women, girls, and vulnerable groups. Progress is measured by Indicator 6.2.1, "Proportion of population using (a) safely managed sanitation services and (b) a hand-washing facility with soap and water."
- 6.3 Improve water quality aims by 2030 to improve water quality by reducing pollution, eliminating dumping, minimizing the release of

hazardous chemicals, halving the proportion of untreated wastewater, and increasing recycling and safe reuse globally. Progress is measured by Indicator 6.3.1, "Proportion of domestic and industrial wastewater flow safely treated," and Indicator 6.3.2, "Proportion of bodies of water with good ambient water quality."

- 6.4 Increase water-use efficiency and ensure sustainable withdrawals aims by 2030 substantially to increase water-use efficiency across all sectors and ensure sustainable withdrawals and supply to address water scarcity and reduce the number of people suffering from it. Progress is measured by Indicator 6.4.1, "Change in water use efficiency over time," and Indicator 6.4.2, "Level of water stress: freshwater withdrawal as a proportion of available freshwater resources."
- 6.5 Implement integrated water resources management aims by 2030 to implement integrated water resources management at all levels, including through transboundary cooperation as appropriate. Progress is measured by Indicator 6.5.1, "Degree of integrated water resources management implementation (0–100)"; Indicator 6.5.2, "Proportion of transboundary basin area with an operational arrangement for water cooperation."
- 6.6 Protect and restore water-related ecosystems aims by 2020 to protect and restore water-related ecosystems (rivers, wetlands, aquifers, lakes). Regardless of timing, this action extends beyond 2020. Progress is measured by Indicator 6.6.1, "Change in the extent of water-related ecosystems over time."

The implementation targets are:

- 6.a International cooperation and capacity-building aims by 2030 to expand international cooperation and strengthen capacity-building support to developing countries in water- and sanitation-related activities and programs, including water harvesting, desalination, efficiency, wastewater treatment, recycling, and reuse. Progress is measured by Indicator 6.a.1, "Amount of water- and sanitation-related official development assistance that is part of a government-coordinated spending plan."
- 6.b Community participation aims to support and strengthen local communities' participation in improving water and sanitation

management. Progress is measured by Indicator 6.b.1, "Proportion of local administrative units with established and operational policies and procedures for participation of local communities in water and sanitation management."

Accordingly, the UN engages in major initiatives aimed at enhancing strategic planning, strengthening institutions, improving communication, and ensuring accountability. In 2003, the special UN inter-agency was established as a coordination mechanism for water-related issues—the UN-Water. It brings together more than 30 UN entities including programs, agencies, funds, and regional commissions working on freshwater and sanitation. Its mission is to ensure coherence, coordination, and joint action within the UN system on water-related matters.

The International Decade for Action "Water for Life" (2005–2015) aimed to mobilize and intensify efforts to meet international commitments related to water and water-related issues by 2015. The initiative was aligned with, and designed to support, Millennium Development Goal 7 on ensuring environmental sustainability.

The International Decade for Action "Water for Life" (2005–2015) sought to advance implementation of international commitments on water through its contribution to Millennium Development Goal 7. In particular, it emphasized halving—by 2015—the proportion of the population without sustainable access to safe drinking water and basic sanitation, while also promoting strengthened global action to advance integrated water resources management.

The International Decade for Action "Water for Sustainable Development" (2018–2028) builds on the achievements and lessons of the previous "Water for Life" Decade (2005–2015), while aligning with the 2030 Agenda for Sustainable Development.

The Decade recognizes that water is not only a basic human right but also a prerequisite for achieving peace, sustainable development, and climate resilience. It points out that water challenges require innovation, political commitment, and cooperation across sectors and borders.

The Decade aims to galvanize global efforts to achieve SDG 6, promote sustainable water management, strengthen partnerships, and raise awareness of water's central role in health, climate, ecosystems, and peacebuilding.

The UN 2023 Water Conference was the first UN water conference in nearly 50 years and served as the mid-term comprehensive review of the implementation of the International Decade for Action "Water for Sustainable Development" (2018–2028), assessing progress and reaffirming water-related goals, including those in the 2030 Agenda for Sustainable Development (Ovink et al., 2023; United Nations, 2023).

The conference sought to identify obstacles and scaling-up opportunities, exchange best practices, and mobilize innovative actions to drive momentum in the second half of the decade. Also, it raises the global awareness of the water crisis, stimulate concerted action across sectors, and advance policy through solution-oriented dialogues.

The UN System-wide Strategy for Water and Sanitation (2024) was launched to follow up on the UN 2023 Water Conference and its Water Action Agenda, positioning water as a core UN priority. It aims to unite the entire UN system's work around a shared vision: a world where water and sanitation are accessible, available, and sustainably managed for all people and the planet. It shifts from siloed approaches to a holistic, coordinated framework across UN entities.

The UN-Water Collaborative Implementation Plan 2025–2028 (UN-Water, 2025) was set up as an operational roadmap for the UN System-wide Strategy for Water and Sanitation. It ensures that the UN system acts together, efficiently and accountably to accelerate progress on SDG 6 and related development goals between 2025 and 2028.

The most important tool for tracking progress toward SDG 6 is a dedicated, integrated monitoring system established by the UN. It is built around UN-Water's Integrated Monitoring Initiative, supported by specialized custodian agencies, and delivered through the WHO/UNICEF Joint Monitoring Programme for Water Supply, Sanitation and Hygiene, UN-Water Global Analysis and Assessment of Sanitation and Drinking-Water, country-led data collection, and the global SDG 6 Data Portal (https://sdg6data.org). The purpose of this system is to ensure coherent, reliable, and comparable data to track progress and guide policy and investment.

Each of the eight SDG 6 targets has at least one global indicator (11 in total, presented above). These indicators are used for regular data collection and reporting (Takane et al., 2025).

3 Assessment

The main progress in achieving SDG 6, "ensure availability and sustainable management of water and sanitation for all by 2030," has been observed in the share of the population using safely managed drinking water, which rose from 68% to 74%; in safely managed sanitation coverage, which increased from 48% to 58%; and in basic hygiene services, whose coverage expanded from 66% to 71% (UN-Water, 2025). However, the main findings of the latest evaluation report (UN-Water, 2024b) are that, although some progress is visible, the global trajectory toward achieving SDG 6 by 2030 is alarmingly insufficient.

Multiple indicators are stagnating or regressing, highlighting the urgent need for accelerated, coordinated action across financing, institutional strengthening, technology, and local engagement. At the midpoint of the 2030 Agenda, the world is far off-track to achieve SDG 6. While data collection has improved, progress remains uneven and insufficient, with billions of people still lacking basic water services. Therefore, António Guterres, Secretary-General of the United Nations, urged that "with just five years to reach the Sustainable Development Goals, we need to shift into overdrive" (UN DESA, 2025a).

The next in-depth review of SDG 6 is expected to take place at the UN High-level Political Forum on Sustainable Development in 2026, at the UN Water Conferences in 2026 and 2028, and during the follow-up to the Pact for the Future in 2027.

Nevertheless, within the remaining years, the full achievement of all SDG 6 indicators appears unlikely. Rather, it is more plausible to expect progress, or at least improvements, in those indicators that do not require large-scale investments, complex technologies, or extended time frames for the completion of construction activities.

References

UN DESA. (2025a). *The sustainable development goals report 2025.* United Nations Department of Economic and Social Affairs.

UN DESA. (2025b). The sustainable development goals extended report 2025: Goal 6 (clean water and sanitation). United Nations Department of Economic and Social Affairs https://unstats.un.org/sdgs/report/2025/extended-report/Extended-Report-2025_Goal-6.pdf

Heinle, M. (2024, August 30). New Report on UN SDG Indicator 6.3.2 Released. *GEMStat*. https://gemstat.org/2024-sdg-632

Leal Filho, W., Azul, A. M., Brandli, L., Salvia, A. L., & Wall, T. (Eds.). (2021). Clean water and sanitation. *Spring*. https://doi.org/10.1007/978-3-319-70061-8

OHCHR (2002). *General Comment No. 15: The Right to Water (arts. 11 and 12 of the International Covenant on Economic, Social and Cultural Rights)*. United Nations Committee on Economic, Social and Cultural Rights. https://www.ohchr.org/en/documents/general-comments-and-recommendations/general-comment-no-15-right-water-arts-11-and-12

Ovink, H., Rahimzoda, S., Cullman, J., & Imperiale, A. J. (2023). The UN 2023 water conference and pathways towards sustainability transformation for a water-secure world. *Nature Water, 1*, 212–215. https://doi.org/10.1038/s44221-023-00052-1

Takane, M., Naylor, K. A., Gore, F., Harlin, J., Glennie, P., Crane, S., et al. (2025). Rethinking monitoring of the means of implementation for SDG 6 up to 2030 and beyond. *PLOS. Water, 4*(12). https://doi.org/10.1371/journal.pwat.0000495

United Nations. (2015). *Transforming Our World: The 2030 Agenda for Sustainable Development*. Resolution A/RES/70/1. United Nations. https://sdgs.un.org/2030agenda

United Nations. (2023). *United Nations 2023 Water Conference: Water Action Agenda*. United Nations. https://sdgs.un.org/conferences/water2023

United Nations. (2024). *United Nations System-wide Strategy for Water and Sanitation*. United Nations. https://unsceb.org/united-nations-system-wide-strategy-water-and-sanitation

United Nations General Assembly. (1948). *Universal Declaration of Human Rights*. Resolution 217 A (III). United Nations.

United Nations General Assembly (1966). *International Covenant on Economic, Social and Cultural Rights*. Resolution 2200 A (XXI). United Nations.

United Nations General Assembly. (2010). *The Human Right to Water and Sanitation*. Resolution A/RES/64/292. United Nations. https://digitallibrary.un.org/record/687002

United Nations General Assembly(2018). *International Decade for Action "Water for Sustainable Development" 2018–2028*. Resolution A/RES/71/222. United Nations. https://docs.un.org/en/a/res/71/222

UN-Water. (2024a). *Progress on the Level of Water Stress: Mid-Term Status of SDG Indicator 6.4.2 and Acceleration Needs, with Special Focus on Food Security (SDG 6 Progress Update Series: Visual Summary)* UN-Water. https://www.unwater.org/sites/default/files/2025-09/SDG6_Visual_Summary_Indicator_Report_642_Progress-on-water-stress_2024_EN.pdf

UN-Water. (2024b). *Summary Brief: Mid-Term Status of SDG 6 Global Indicators and Acceleration Needs*. UN-Water https://www.unwater.org/publications/summary-brief-mid-term-status-sdg-6-global-indicators-and-acceleration-needs

UN-Water. (2025). *Collaborative Implementation Plan 2025–2028*. UN-Water. https://www.unwater.org/publications/collaborative-implementation-plan

WHO/UNICEF (n.d.). *Open Defecation*. World Health Organization and United Nations Children's Fund Joint Monitoring Programme. Retrieved January 4, 2026, from https://washdata.org/topics/sanitation/open-defecation

World Economic Forum. (2025). *Global Risks Report 2025*. World Economic Forum https://www.weforum.org/publications/global-risks-report-2025/

CHAPTER 13

Transport

Julián Martinez-Moya

1 The Challenge

In recent decades, maritime transport has constituted the cornerstone of international trade, being responsible for carrying more than 80% of the global trade volume measured in tonnes (UNCTAD, 2021). The transport network articulated through merchant vessels and ports, as strategic infrastructures within this process, enables the worldwide exchange of manufactured goods, raw materials, foodstuffs, and energy (Martinez-Moya et al., 2024). This system of maritime routes, which interconnects continents and facilitates trade among countries, has historically been a key driver of economic globalisation and of the dynamism of national economies integrated into global value chains (del Rosal & Moura, 2022; Fugazza & Hoffmann, 2017).

Indeed, the critical importance of maritime transport for the supply, provisioning, and production activities of firms has recently become evident through disruptions that, for diverse reasons, have generated tensions in global production. The blockage of the Suez Canal, the

J. Martinez-Moya (✉)
University of Valencia, Valencia, Spain
e-mail: julian.martinez-moya@uv.es

R. de Arriba (ed.), *United Nations Facing Global Economic Disorder: Assessing 20 Policy Proposals*,
https://doi.org/10.1007/978-3-032-21952-7_13

COVID-19 pandemic, and the ongoing Red Sea crisis (Bedoya-Maya et al., 2025) stand as salient examples of shocks that have profoundly affected companies and countries, resulting in higher transportation costs, delivery delays, and increased emissions of polluting gases.

In this regard, maritime transport faces a number of structural challenges that shape its current and future development. These include the increasing concentration of shipping services in a small number of large global operators, the growing need for investment in port and logistics infrastructure to accommodate ever-larger vessels in an efficient and reliable manner, and the rapid digitalisation of maritime and port operations. While all of these issues are of major economic and strategic relevance, this chapter focuses on a challenge of a different order: the urgent need to decarbonise international maritime transport, a global problem whose scale and transboundary nature require coordinated international action.

This structural dependence on maritime transport, therefore, entails profound global challenges that transcend the economic domain, raising serious concerns about the planet's environmental health. While it is true that maritime transport is among the most efficient modes in terms of emissions per tonne-kilometre, the sheer scale of activity renders it a significant source of atmospheric pollution. International shipping is estimated to be responsible for approximately 3% of global greenhouse gas (GHG) emissions, primarily carbon dioxide (CO_2), methane (CH_4), and nitrogen oxides (NO_x) (UNCTAD, 2023). Although this percentage may appear modest compared to other sectors, the absolute volume is alarming. Even more concerning is that, between 2012 and 2023, the sector's emissions increased by 20% (UNCTAD, 2023), and projections indicate that, absent decisive measures, they could continue to rise in the coming decades.

It is important to note that maritime transport has historically been excluded from binding commitments under major international climate agreements, such as the Kyoto Protocol and the Paris Agreement. This is due in part to the regulatory complexity of a sector that is inherently transnational, where vessels often operate under flags of convenience, with owners, operators, and crews dispersed across the globe. Such fragmentation has hindered the implementation of coordinated and effective policies to address the sector's environmental impact. Consequently, the challenge of designing a global system that provides the necessary incentives and penalties to reduce emissions from maritime transport is formidable.

Therefore, maritime transport stands simultaneously as a vital force for the global economy and a significant source of environmental pressure. The search for solutions to reconcile these two realities is not optional but imperative. The international community, through the IMO, faces a historic opportunity to establish a global regulatory framework that enables progress towards a truly sustainable model of trade, one in which the environmental impact of economic activity is internalised and equitably shared.

2 UN Proposals

The United Nations has promoted a coordinated global response through the International Maritime Organization (IMO), the specialised agency responsible for regulating safety and environmental protection in maritime navigation (IMO, 2025a). Established in 1948, the IMO currently comprises 176 Member States. In recent years, the IMO has adopted the IMO 2023 GHG Strategy to reduce greenhouse gas emissions from ships (IMO, 2023). This strategy includes intermediate targets of a 20–30% reduction in GHG emissions by 2030 and a 70–80% reduction by 2040, ultimately reaching net-zero emissions by 2050, relative to 2008 levels. The strategy is framed within the IMO's broader commitment to advancing the United Nations Sustainable Development Goals, in particular Goal 13: Climate Action.

In April 2025, the International Maritime Organization's Marine Environment Protection Committee (MEPC 83) approved the draft IMO Net-Zero Framework, a comprehensive set of proposed amendments to MARPOL Annex VI aimed at reducing greenhouse gas emissions from international shipping. These amendments, which would introduce a global fuel standard and a pricing mechanism for carbon emissions, were expected to be formally adopted in October 2025 and to enter into force in 2028. However, during the extraordinary MEPC session held in London from 14 to 17 October 2025, Member States voted to adjourn the session and postpone the formal vote on adoption for 12 months (IMO, 2025b), with discussions scheduled to resume in 2026 and work continuing on implementation guidelines. International Maritime Organization has stated that Member States will continue to work towards consensus on the Framework during the interim period.

It must be emphasised that the implementation of such a system requires broad consensus among IMO Member States, many of which hold divergent interests concerning the costs, benefits, and responsibilities associated with the decarbonisation of maritime transport. The proposal may represent a turning point for the environmental governance of international trade.

Grounded in the "polluter pays" principle, the system seeks to place a price on the carbon emissions generated by ships, thereby incentivising the transition towards cleaner technologies, alternative fuels, and sustainable operational practices. The rationale underpinning this measure is twofold. On the one hand, it seeks to internalise the environmental costs of shipping through a carbon levy. On the other hand, through the establishment of the Net-Zero Fund, it aims to mobilise sufficient financial resources to support the energy transition of countries—particularly developing and least-developed countries—ensuring that new regulations do not exacerbate existing inequalities.

A key aspect of the framework concerns the determination of which actors should pay and to what extent. Vessels subject to the levy are those with a gross tonnage (GT) greater than 5000, which, according to IMO estimates, account for approximately 97% of global tonnage and represent 85% of total emissions. Regarding the monetary contribution, vessels must comply with an emission threshold that sets a maximum carbon intensity limit (Greenhouse Gas Fuel Intensity, GFI) per tonne-kilometre, benchmarked against the average GFI of the fleet in 2008. GFI emissions are calculated from a full life-cycle perspective (well-to-wake), encompassing emissions from fuel extraction, cultivation, production, and transport, as well as those from combustion or energy conversion and any methane leakage on board.

Ships exceeding the established GFI thresholds—reviewed annually—will be subject to a fee. The magnitude of the fee will vary depending on the degree of non-compliance, with two key measures established:

- Base Target. This sets a basic efficiency benchmark, understood as the deviation of a ship's emissions from the sector's overall progress, thereby allowing performance comparisons with the average of the existing fleet. Exceeding this threshold entails a levy of USD 100 per tonne of excess CO_2 equivalent.
- Direct Compliance Target. This stricter threshold corresponds to the annual regulatory objectives for ship decarbonisation. Failure to meet this target results in a higher penalty: if the ship exceeds this

limit, the levy increases to USD 380 per tonne of additional CO_2 equivalent.

What happens if a vessel meets the established thresholds? In this case, the framework provides a positive incentive through the allocation of Surplus Units (SU) to ships operating below the Direct Compliance Target. These units may be accumulated or transferred to non-compliant vessels through a central registry managed by the IMO.

What happens if a vessel fails to meet the thresholds? Two options are available. First, surplus units may be transferred from compliant vessels to the non-compliant vessel. Second, shipowners may purchase Remedial Units (RU) through the newly created financial mechanism—the Net-Zero Fund—whose purpose is to facilitate regulatory compliance when technical reductions are not feasible. Ultimately, every vessel must meet the Direct Compliance Target, whether by reducing its GFI, purchasing RUs from the IMO's Net-Zero Fund, or transferring SUs from compliant vessels.

Within this system, one of the critical components is the creation of the Net-Zero Fund. This fund will play a central role in enabling the transition towards sustainable maritime transport. Its financial resources will derive from the fees paid for the acquisition of remedial units due to excess emissions. These resources will be allocated to support the shift towards alternative fuels (such as methanol, green hydrogen, or ammonia) and the development of clean technologies. They will also finance the necessary infrastructure for supplying these fuels in ports. In addition, the fund's resources will be directed to ensuring that the transition remains just for developing countries by facilitating the investments required to meet the environmental objectives established under the IMO strategy.

3 Assessment

Beyond the technical and economic weaknesses identified above, the recent postponement of the formal adoption of the IMO Net-Zero Framework adds a further and equally critical dimension: political and institutional fragility. The decision taken in October to defer the vote, due to the inability of Member States to reach a sufficiently broad majority, signals that the agreement remains politically contested and therefore uncertain. This new scenario of instability is not neutral. The costs of international disagreement are particularly high in a capital-intensive and technologically complex sector such as maritime transport, where long investment cycles require a clear, credible, and predictable regulatory framework. Without binding rules and stable policy signals, shipowners, fuel suppliers, and companies face strong incentives to delay or redirect investments, slowing down the deployment of zero- and near-zero-carbon technologies and fuels. As a result, the postponement of the agreement effectively delays the industry's transition by at least one additional year and moves the sector further away from the decarbonisation pathway established in the IMO's 2023 GHG Strategy, thereby increasing both the environmental and the economic costs of inaction.

The system designed by the IMO has not yet entered into force (it is expected to do so in early 2028), which represents a limitation for conducting an in-depth evaluation of the proposal. In its current state, it does not allow for an assessment of market reactions to the new regulatory framework, nor does it enable predictions regarding how shipping companies will adapt in terms of strategies and investments aimed at reducing their emissions. Nevertheless, based on the current design of the measures, there are several points that may prove critical for achieving the environmental objectives established under the IMO Net-Zero Framework. This section focuses on two particularly important aspects.

First, the system establishes a "tolerated" emissions threshold, below which no levy will be applied, and consequently, such emissions will not be subject to economic penalties. A major concern here is that this could ultimately legitimise a level of pollution that, although reduced, remains incompatible with the net-zero target. This dynamic may generate two effects. The first is the potential incentive for investment in intermediate or medium-term technologies that allow emissions to fall just below the established threshold, while still remaining polluting. In other words, the measure could create perverse incentives for investment in fuels that do not represent the desired solution, such as liquefied natural gas (LNG) or biofuels, as their lower costs render them attractive alternatives to avoid levies. Moreover, in the case of biofuels, production entails additional environmental challenges, including the substitution of crops to obtain the necessary inputs. Although the life-cycle approach to emissions accounting formally incorporates these effects into the energy calculation, it remains to be seen whether the economic calculus will still favour their use within the industry.

The other effect concerns the fact that a portion of emissions will not be covered by the system (despite being polluting), effectively granting the industry “free” emissions. This, in turn, will reduce the revenues generated for the Fund, thereby limiting its capacity to finance the transition. It should be recalled that the Fund plays a vital role in ensuring a just transition by financing the development of clean fuels and technologies and facilitating access for the industry at large. Without sufficient resources to fulfil this critical mission, the transition may be significantly delayed and rendered costlier, thereby jeopardising the achievement of the stated objectives.

Second, the sequencing of economic policy instruments employed is decisive in determining both the effectiveness of the environmental objectives and the extent to which firms invest in the desired eco-innovations (Tchorzewska et al., 2025). The limited empirical evidence available to date suggests that better outcomes are achieved when economic incentives for the adoption of eco-innovations are introduced first, followed by penalties for polluting emissions (Tchorzewska et al., 2025). The barriers are not exclusively financial: firms also face administrative and operational obstacles to adopting sustainable alternatives that could improve environmental performance. In the case of maritime transport, penalties have preceded the incentives designed to facilitate the transition. Moreover, they have done so in a context in which the options available to companies for reducing emissions remain highly limited, and considerable uncertainty persists. To date, there is still no green alternative that inspires investor confidence: technologies are under development, and clean fuels are not yet widely available in the market. As a result, operational barriers are substantial, hindering the voluntary transition of the industry, even as firms are penalised for their emissions.

The solution to accelerate the process and shorten the time horizon for the availability of clean fuels and technologies partially depends on channelling greater financial resources into their development. These resources should be provided through the Net-Zero Fund, as this is one of its core functions. Consequently, the Fund must be capable of accumulating substantial resources—though significant uncertainty and concern remain as to whether it will be sufficient to successfully carry out this critical task.

References

Bedoya-Maya, F., Beckers, J., Cant, J., Martínez-Moya, J., van Hassel, E., & Vanelslander, T. (2025). Container Port Competitiveness Amid Disruptions: Insights from the European Maritime Network During the Red Sea Crisis. *Journal of Transport Geography, 128*, 104304.

Del Rosal, I., & Moura, T. G. Z. (2022). The Effect of Shipping Connectivity on Seaborne Containerised Export Flows. *Transport Policy, 118*, 143–151.

Fugazza, M., & Hoffmann, J. (2017). Liner Shipping Connectivity as Determinant of Trade. *Journal of Shipping and trade, 2*(1), 1.

IMO. (2023). *2023 IMO Strategy on Reduction of GHG Emissions from Ships* (MEPC.377(80) Annex 15). *International Maritime Organisation.*

IMO. (2025a). IMO Approves Net-Zero Framework for Shipping Emissions. International Maritime Organisation. https://www.imo.org/en/MediaCentre/PressBriefings/pages/IMO-approves-netzero-regulations.aspx

IMO. (2025b). IMO Net-Zero Shipping Talks to Resume in 2026. *International Maritime Organisation.* https://www.imo.org/en/mediacentre/pressbriefings/pages/imo-net-zero-shipping-talks-to-resume-in-2026.aspx

Martinez-Moya, J., Mestre-Alcover, A., & Sala-Garrido, R. (2024). Connectivity and Competitiveness of the Major Mediterranean Container Ports Using 'Benefit-of-the-Doubt' and 'Common Sets of Weights' Methods in Data Envelopment Analysis. *Maritime Economics & Logistics, 26*(2), 261–282.

Tchorzewska, K. B., del Rio, P., Garcia-Quevedo, J., & Martinez-Ros, E. (2025). Carrot First, Stick Second? Environmental Policy-Mix Sequencing and Green Technologies. *Technological Forecasting and Social Change, 210*, 123835.

UNCTAD. (2021). *Review of Maritime Transport*. United Nations Conference on Trade and Development.

UNCTAD. (2023). *Review of Maritime Transport. Chapter 3 Decarbonizing Shipping*. United Nations Conference on Trade and Development.

CHAPTER 14

Development Cooperation

Marta Pedrajas Herrero

1 The Challenge

In 1945, "we the peoples" gathered at the San Francisco Conference, established the Charter of the United Nations, which shaped an international order based on peace, cooperation, and universal respect for human rights. Member States also assumed the commitment to "promote social progress and better standards of life in larger freedom" and, for these ends, to employ an "international machinery for the promotion of the economic and social advancement of all peoples" (United Nations, 1945).

Since then, this international mechanism has given rise to a multilateral system for development cooperation, providing a common framework for addressing global challenges and advancing development. Over recent

The opinions in this article are those of the author and do not necessarily represent the views of the Ministry of Foreign Affairs, EU and Cooperation of Spain.

M. Pedrajas Herrero (✉)
Ministry of Foreign Affairs, European Union and Cooperation, Madrid, Spain
e-mail: marta.pedrajas@maec.es

R. de Arriba (ed.), *United Nations Facing Global Economic Disorder: Assessing 20 Policy Proposals*,
https://doi.org/10.1007/978-3-032-21952-7_14

decades, priorities such as the fight against hunger and poverty, the promotion of education and health, gender equality, and environmental sustainability, among others, have shaped the international cooperation agenda.

Today, on the 80th anniversary of the United Nations, this system stands at a crossroads. Multilateralism is going through a crisis of confidence and financing, driven by fragmentation and polarization, and reflected in growing unilateralism and dynamics of confrontation rather than cooperation. This context constrains the capacity of international institutions not only to forge consensus, but also to implement it in an agile and effective manner. Addressing these challenges is one of the core objectives of the recent UN80 reform (discussed later), which seeks to reverse these trends and make cooperation more effective and impactful. As the *Human Development Report 2023–2024* warns, "we need to dial down the temperature and push back on polarization, which poisons practically everything it touches and impedes international cooperation" (UNDP, 2024).

The development paradigm has evolved since the middle of the last century. After decades dominated by models centred on economic growth—from trickle-down to Latin American structuralism or dependency theory—it was from the 1980s onwards that Amartya Sen, drawing on economics and philosophy and building on the capabilities approach, began to articulate a people-centred model. This is the human development approach (Sen, 2000), adopted by the United Nations Development Programme (UNDP) from 1990 onwards, and further developed and refined over the past three decades. In its 2010 formulation, this model integrates the core of Amartya Sen's theoretical contribution with the practical implementation driven by Mahbub ul Haq and UNDP itself: "Human development is the expansion of people's freedoms to live long, healthy and creative lives; to advance other goals they have reason to value; and to engage actively in shaping development equitably and sustainably on a shared planet" (UNDP, 2010).

This model was consolidated in parallel with the major development summits of the 1990s: the Earth Summit (Rio 1992), the International Conference on Population and Development (Cairo 1994), the World Summit for Social Development (Copenhagen 1995), and the Fourth World Conference on Women (Beijing 1995), which led to the first major development agenda agreed by the 193 countries at the United

Nations: the Millennium Declaration and the eight Millennium Development Goals, adopted in 2000 (United Nations General Assembly, 2000). For the first time, the Declaration included the fundamental values on which international cooperation is based: "freedom, equality, solidarity, tolerance, respect for nature and shared responsibility", and put them into practice through concrete objectives. The MDGs promoted a global agenda, with a strong focus on social issues: reducing extreme poverty, hunger, health, education, equality, and sustainability. In 2002, this agenda was reinforced by the first Conference on Financing for Development (Monterrey), although it was not until the 2005 Summit that the MDG targets and indicators were fully agreed. By 2010, results had already been achieved: the share of the world's population living in extreme poverty declined from 47 per cent in 1990 to 22 per cent in 2010 (United Nations, 2010; World Bank, 2012). The world began to realize that agreeing on common objectives makes it possible to coordinate efforts, avoid fragmentation and duplication, and increase collective impact.

This optimistic and hopeful context paved the way for the 2030 Agenda and the SDGs, negotiated through a highly participatory and open process between 2012 and 2015. Indeed, recent scholarship highlights the role of actors from the Global South in shaping the normative foundations of the SDGs through broad negotiation (Fukuda-Parr & Muchhala, 2020). This openness resulted in a complex and comprehensive agenda, carefully balanced across the 17 SDGs and 169 targets, accompanied by a political declaration, means of implementation, and a follow-up and review framework.

This agenda represented a qualitative leap compared to the MDGs: a universal, inclusive, and transformative agenda that addresses the root causes of development challenges and integrates the three dimensions of development: social, economic and environmental. Its political declaration included an ethical principle of profound significance, which has served as a guiding compass for the international system: "we promise that no one will be left behind and that we will reach the furthest behind first" (United Nations General Assembly, 2015).

This broadening of multidimensional approaches to development and poverty measurement has been further developed in the recent literature, which emphasizes the relevance of metrics beyond GDP for policy design and implementation in the context of the 2030 Agenda (Alkire et al., 2023).

Nevertheless, despite this robust conceptual framework, implementation is significantly delayed. According to the *SDG Progress Report 2025* (United Nations Secretary-General, 2025), only 35 per cent of the targets assessed show an adequate level of progress (18 per cent are on track and 17 per cent show moderate progress), while 47 per cent display insufficient progress and 18 per cent have regressed compared to 2015. In an increasingly complex global context, still marked by the pandemic in 2020, followed by several years of record levels of international conflict, the environment for achieving these objectives has become highly unfavourable. Nearly 800 million people continue to live in extreme poverty, hunger is once again on the rise (affecting 757 million people today, almost 9 per cent of the world's population, a setback compared to 2015), food insecurity already affects more than 2.3 billion people and child malnutrition remains at critical levels. Global inequalities continue to increase, and conflicts have multiplied the number of refugees, reaching 38 million people. These interconnected crises not only slow progress but are reversing achievements made in the first decade of the 2030 Agenda, highlighting the magnitude of the challenge currently facing development cooperation within the United Nations system. This assessment is further supported by recent research showing that multiple, overlapping global crises have significantly slowed progress towards key SDG targets (Beltramo et al., 2025).

Since the adoption of the 2030 Agenda and the Paris Agreement, multiple estimates have been produced regarding the financial needs required to meet the SDGs and climate objectives. In preparation for the Fourth International Conference on Financing for Development in Sevilla, and as reflected in its final consensus document, the *Sevilla Commitment* estimates an annual financing gap of 4 trillion US dollars (United Nations, 2025).

The financing gap is further compounded by a worrying trend in official development assistance (ODA): several traditional donors have announced significant cuts. For 2025, a reduction of up to 31 billion US dollars is projected, driven by severe cuts in the United States, with additional, though less pronounced reductions in other donors, such as Germany. The United Kingdom has confirmed that it will also reduce its ODA by 2027, and the Netherlands has set out additional multi-year cuts.

Alongside declining ODA, the growing debt crisis further exacerbates the situation. UNCTAD data show an increasingly alarming reality: in 48 developing countries, more resources are allocated to debt servicing than to guaranteeing basic rights for their populations. An estimated 3.3 billion people live in countries that spend more on debt service than on health, while 2.1 billion people live in countries that spend more on debt service than on education (UNCTAD, 2023).

In response to this situation, the Fourth International Conference on Financing for Development, held in Sevilla (FfD4), focused on domestic resource mobilization, strengthening tax administrations, international tax cooperation, and the fight against corruption as immediate levers to increase revenues and reduce financing gaps.

2 UN Proposals

In an international context marked by multiple, interconnected crises, polarization and a loss of confidence in multilateralism, the renewal of development cooperation at the United Nations is structured around three main pillars: renewed multilateralism, accelerating the sustainable development agenda, and financing for development.

Within this framework, the reform of the United Nations Development System initiated by the Secretary-General in 2018, the SDG review summits held in 2019 and 2023, the *Our Common Agenda* initiative launched in 2021, the *Pact for the Future* in 2024 and the current "reform of the reform" under the UN80 initiative in 2025, all reflect a clear commitment to a more renewed, effective and results-oriented multilateralism. Together, these processes lay the foundations for a system that is more coherent in its instruments and strategies, further complemented by the outcomes of the FfD4 Conference in Sevilla. Between 2015 and 2025, a relatively comprehensive set of proposals agreed by Member States for the future of cooperation at the United Nations has taken shape. The renewal of the system can be organized around three interconnected pillars: acceleration of the SDGs, reform of the UN Development System, and financing for development.

With regard to accelerating progress on the SDGs, in September 2019, Heads of State and Government met for the first time since 2015 to review implementation of the 2030 Agenda under the theme "Gearing up for a decade of action and delivery for sustainable development". A political declaration was adopted, and more than 100 voluntary commitments were announced by countries and organizations to accelerate SDG implementation.

In 2021, the Secretary-General presented the "Our Common Agenda" initiative, conceived to renew political momentum for the 2030 Agenda after the pandemic. The report set out a series of reforms aimed at strengthening multilateralism and accelerating progress towards the SDGs, by anticipating structural transformations in areas such as food systems, energy, digital connectivity, education, employment, and climate action. These transformations were later articulated through the six transitions agreed in 2023 (United Nations General Assembly, 2023; United Nations Secretary-General, 2021).

The 2023 SDG Summit, held in New York, marked the midpoint between the adoption of the 2030 Agenda in 2015 and its target date in 2030. It represented a critical moment to take stock of progress and obstacles, including the impacts of the pandemic, a health crisis, a socio-economic crisis, and the multiplication of conflicts, as well as to relaunch action. A political declaration was adopted committing States to adopt transformative, fair, and ambitious actions, with particular attention to financing, data, innovation, equity, and the principle of "leaving no one behind".

Within this framework, six key transitions were identified as strategic investment pathways with a multiplier effect to accelerate progress towards the SDGs:

1. Food systems
2. Energy access and affordability
3. Digital connectivity
4. Education
5. Jobs and social protection
6. Climate change, biodiversity loss, and pollution

With regard to reforming multilateralism for development, the 2024 Summit of the Future represented an attempt to update the global social contract. The *Pact for the Future*, adopted by consensus, included key commitments: a *Declaration on Future Generations*, which underscores collective responsibility towards those who will inherit the planet, and a *Global Digital Compact*, which seeks to reduce the technological divide and regulate the use of new technologies, including artificial intelligence. Together, these components reflect the UN's determination to provide global responses to global challenges that directly affect sustainable development and equity (United Nations General Assembly, 2024).

Political and programmatic in nature, the *Pact* is complemented by a more technical and institutional process: the UN80 initiative, launched in 2025 by the Secretary-General. This initiative can be understood as a "reform of the reform" and, specifically in the area of development cooperation, it proposes the following measures:

1. Institutional efficiency, avoiding duplication and improving the division of functions among agencies, funds, and programmes.
2. Rationalization of mandates, whose proliferation has generated overlaps, disproportionate expectations and a lack of coherence between objectives and resources. Proposed measures include the creation of a single register of mandates, the introduction of sunset clauses and periodic collective reviews.
3. Deep structural changes, including the possible reorganization of entities within the UN development system to strengthen coherence, accountability, and results orientation.

In practical terms, these reforms seek to shorten and simplify resolutions, reduce the proliferation of reports and meetings, optimize financing modalities, and strengthen evaluation and results frameworks. Ultimately, the objective is to ensure that the UN does not become trapped in a dynamic of expanding mandates and shrinking resources.

Finally, the third pillar concerns financing for development, beyond official development assistance (ODA). Over the past two decades, the financing debate has evolved from an approach focused almost exclusively on ODA to a broader and more comprehensive framework, which includes domestic resource mobilization, sustainable private investment, international cooperation on tax matters, and the provision of global public goods. In this framework, the International Conferences on Financing for Development have constituted key milestones along this path: Monterrey (2002), Doha (2008), Addis Ababa (2015), and, more recently, Sevilla (2025).

The Fourth International Conference on Financing for Development (FfD4), held in Sevilla from 30 June to 3 July 2025, marked a turning point. With only five years remaining until the 2030 Agenda deadline, the Conference achieved what many considered unlikely: the adoption of the *Sevilla Commitment*, a new global framework for financing for development that builds on the Addis Ababa Action Agenda while adapting to today's challenges (United Nations, 2025). Among its main areas of consensus, the following stand out:

1. Domestic resource mobilization: measures to advance tax justice, support developing countries in expanding their fiscal space, combat tax evasion, and strengthen revenue mobilization. The emphasis is placed on national ownership, the establishment of national coordination platforms, and a strengthened role for public development banks, including their support for the expansion of social protection systems.
2. Private finance: a renewed push to mobilize impact investment and the social and solidarity economy, supported by instruments designed to facilitate the channelling of private capital flows towards sustainable development priorities.
3. Development cooperation: reaffirmation of the commitment to ODA targets (0.7 per cent), recognition of its catalytic role within a broader financing ecosystem, and the promotion of new metrics beyond GDP, as well as new approaches to measuring financing for development, including the complementary use of multidimensional indicators and Total Official Support for Sustainable Development (TOSSD[1]).
4. Debt and debt sustainability: actions to respond to the debt crisis, including proposals such as the establishment of a global debt registry, the use of suspension clauses, debt swaps, and the strengthening of the G20 Common Framework[2].
5. Reform of international financial architecture, including proposals to increase the lending capacity of multilateral development banks and

[1] TOSSD: The Total Official Support for Sustainable Development (TOSSD) statistical framework includes all officially supported resource flows to promote sustainable development in developing countries and to support development enablers and address global challenges at regional and global levels, thereby going beyond the narrower scope of Official Development Assistance (ODA).

[2] The G20 Common Framework for Debt Treatments is an initiative agreed by the G20 in 2020, together with the Paris Club, to co-ordinate debt restructuring processes for low-income countries in an orderly and transparent manner. Its aim is to co-ordinate all creditors (official bilateral, private and multilateral) and restore debt sustainability, while at the same time supporting macroeconomic stability and development.

to improve the representation of developing countries within these institutions.

6. Enhanced follow-up, with an expanded mandate for the ECOSOC Forum on Financing for Development to strengthen monitoring and ensure greater accountability.

In addition, the Sevilla Platform of Action (SPA) was launched, bringing together more than 130 concrete initiatives aimed at implementing these commitments. Its main innovation lies in moving beyond the traditional North–South logic, favouring voluntary and flexible coalitions built around shared priorities, ranging from global health, hunger and poverty, and debt swaps, to progress towards metrics beyond GDP.

Ultimately, the Sevilla Conference represents one of the United Nations' most ambitious efforts in recent years to link multilateralism, sustainability, and financing. While some debates, such as debt restructuring or climate finance, revealed persistent divisions, the agreement reached in Sevilla provides a renewed basis for action over the next five years. The challenge ahead will be to translate commitments into effective resources and ensure that the multilateral development system has the coherence, legitimacy, and capacity required to accompany countries on their path towards the achievement of the 2030 Agenda.

3 Assessment

Development cooperation is one of the fundamental pillars that give meaning to the creation of the United Nations, alongside peace and security, and human rights. Over the decades, very significant progress has been made in building broad consensus, reducing poverty and hunger, advancing gender equality, inclusive economic growth, decent work, and the integration of the entire sustainability agenda, including biodiversity and the fight against climate change. However, in recent years a serious stagnation has emerged. This is reflected not only in increasingly worrying data, but also in a growing crisis of confidence affecting the system itself. Today's world, still struck by the pandemic, and above all by recent conflicts, has called into question the value of the multilateral system in all areas, especially that of the United Nations, and development cooperation is no exception.

For this reason, revisiting in this chapter how consensus has been achieved, how global development agendas have evolved, and above all the improvement in people's lives in the most disadvantaged countries, helps to reaffirm a central lesson: development is indeed possible when there is political will.

The recent Conference on Financing for Development in Sevilla provides further evidence of this: it demonstrated that it is still possible to move forward together and has given renewed momentum to the system. Together with the reforms under way, particularly the UN80 initiative, this opens a decisive window of opportunity for the SDGs on the horizon of 2030. It is likely that the goals will not be fully achieved, or not all of them everywhere; the world may indeed require more time. Yet this is not the moment to debate deadlines or to seek excuses. Rather, it is a moment to renew commitments to accelerate development, strengthen cooperation in times of growing suspicion and competition, fulfil financial commitments, and move forward without leaving anyone behind. The coming years will be decisive, and we must approach them with all our strength and with the unity of the multilateral development system, demonstrating that true cooperation is indeed necessary and possible.

References

Alkire, S., Kövesdi, F., Scheja, E., & Nogales, R. (2023). Moderate Multidimensional Poverty Index: Paving the Way Out of Poverty. *Social Indicators Research, 168*, 409–445.

Beltramo, T., de Giorgi, G., & Sarr, I. (2025). Tracking SDG Achievements in the Age of Polycrisis. *Journal of Human Development and Capabilities, 26*(1), 9–32.

Fukuda-Parr, S., & Muchhala, B. (2020). The Southern Origins of Sustainable Development Goals: Ideas, Actors, Aspirations. *World Development, 126*, 104706.

Sen, A. (2000). *Development as Freedom*. Anchor Books.

United Nations. (1945). *Charter of the United Nations*. United Nations.

United Nations. (2010). *The Millennium Development Goals Report 2010*. United Nations.

UNCTAD. (2023). *A Debt Report*. United Nations Conference on Trade and Development.

UNDP. (2010). *Human Development Report 2010: The Real Wealth of Nations—Pathways to Human Development*. United Nations Development Programme.

UNDP. (2024). *Human Development Report 2023–2024: Breaking the Gridlock—Reimagining Cooperation in a Polarized World*. United Nations Development Programme.

United Nations. (2025). *Sevilla Commitment. Final Outcome Document of the Fourth International Conference on Financing for Development*. A/CONF.227/2025/L.1. https://docs.un.org/en/A/CONF.227/2025/L.1

United Nations General Assembly. (2000). United Nations Millennium Declaration. Resolution A/RES/55/2. United Nations.

United Nations General Assembly. (2015). Transforming Our World: The 2030 Agenda for Sustainable Development. Resolution A/RES/70/1. United Nations.

United Nations General Assembly. (2023). Political Declaration of the High-Level Political Forum on Sustainable Development Convened Under the Auspices of the General Assembly: SDG Summit 2023. Resolution A/HLPF/2023/L.1. United Nations.

United Nations General Assembly. (2024). Pact for the Future. Resolution A/RES/78/1. United Nations.

United Nations Secretary-General. (2021). Our Common Agenda: Report of the Secretary-General.

United Nations Secretary-General. (2025). *The Sustainable Development Goals Report 2025*. United Nations.

World Bank. (2012, February 29). World Bank Says World Has Reached Millennium Development Goal on Poverty Ahead of 2015 Deadline (Press Release No. 2012/297/DEC). World Bank.

CHAPTER 15

External Debt

Jordi Sanjuán

1 The Challenge

External debt is a commonly used tool as a source of financing when a country's domestic savings and foreign exchange reserves prove insufficient to achieve its development objectives or other policy priorities. However, this desirable resource can be a hindrance and a major obstacle to development when its burden becomes excessive and the increasingly difficult repayment of debt takes precedence and compromises the achievement of other goals of national interest.

At present, external debt represents a profound and multifaceted challenge, especially for countries in the Global South. According to the United Nations Conference on Trade and Development (UNCTAD), 3400 million people (i.e., more than 40% of the world's population) live in countries that spend more on debt interest than on education or health (UNCTAD, 2025). In 2024, 54 countries were in a debt crisis, mainly on the African continent, but also in Asia, Latin America and, to a lesser extent, Europe, according to data from Debt Justice (2024).

J. Sanjuán (✉)
University of Valencia, Valencia, Spain
e-mail: jordi.sanjuan@uv.es

R. de Arriba (ed.), *United Nations Facing Global Economic Disorder: Assessing 20 Policy Proposals*,
https://doi.org/10.1007/978-3-032-21952-7_15

This situation, far from improving, has worsened in recent years. After the harsh consequences of the Great Recession in the previous decade, the new situation characterised by the COVID-19 pandemic, inflation, rising interest rates and a continuum of international conflicts have led to an escalation in external debt levels that has put many countries in a position of extreme fragility (United Nations, 2025a). In just over a decade, from 2011 to 2021, countries eligible for the Debt Service Suspension Initiative[1] had increased their total external debt stock by 2.6 times (Cohen & Harnoys-Vannier, 2023). Naturally, this translates into a higher interest outlay. Among countries eligible to apply for loans from the International Development Association (IDA)—that is, particularly vulnerable countries with low incomes and difficulty accessing international financial markets—interest payments on external debt doubled from 2015 to 2022, a situation that does not seem likely to be reversed in the near future given the rising prospects of global interest rates. In addition, in the last decade, a growing part of loans from multilateral banks such as the World Bank or the IMF has been replaced by financing from private markets, especially in the form of bonds (Arrieta de Armas, 2024). This diversification of creditor profiles, in addition to making access to credit more expensive and causing negative net flows, also increases the vulnerability of indebted countries, given their greater volatility and difficulty in negotiating debt restructurings in the event of a crisis (Cohen & Harnoys-Vannier, 2023). As for the total debt service that low- and middle-income countries had to face, it stood at record levels in 2023, reaching $1.4 trillion (United Nations, 2025a).

Beyond the overwhelming list of figures, it is clear that this situation can act for the countries that suffer from it as an anchor that perpetuates their conditions of underdevelopment. Many studies show a negative association between external debt and economic growth, both in the short and long term (Mumba & Li, 2020; Siddique et al., 2016). Other studies go further and not only point to debt as a brake on growth, but also as a cause of social inequality and unemployment (Ayoub et al., 2024; Nguyen, 2025).

[1] Temporary initiative promoted by the G20 in 2020 to postpone the payment of official bilateral debt of lower-income countries, with the aim of freeing up resources during the COVID-19 crisis. It was aimed at countries eligible for the International Development Association and/or classified as least developed countries by the United Nations.

Furthermore, an excessive cost of debt servicing monopolises the usually scarce public resources and diverts them from more pressing development needs such as poverty reduction, health, or education, and prevents investments in key infrastructure for the future, such as those aimed at tackling the ecological transition and reducing dependence on fossil fuels (Vasic-Lalovic et al., 2023). Besides, the current architecture of the international financial system enables and contributes to irresponsible lending, while hindering transparency and public control over the management of state debt (Eurodad, 2024).

Finally, in response to dominant discourses that attribute full responsibility for indebtedness to debtor countries (thereby legitimising the consequences they endure), it should be noted that, in many cases, the debt of Global South countries has historical roots in the colonial legacy and continues to reproduce and reinforce neo-colonial and extractive economic relations (Debt Justice, 2024). At the beginning of the century and before the Great Recession, some authors were already arguing that countries in the Global South had more than repaid the debt they had acquired, but they continued to be trapped by abusive and self-perpetuating payment systems (Nakatani & Herrera, 2007). In interest alone, the amount transferred from the Global South to the countries of the Global North between 1970 and 2022 amounts to 2.5 trillion dollars (Debt Justice, 2024).

In short, the central challenge is to guarantee the right to development without jeopardising access to finance for Global South countries, generating orderly, predictable and, above all, fair mechanisms. Such mechanisms should ensure that the resolution of eventual crises does not depend on fragmented negotiations characterised by pronounced asymmetries of power between creditors and debtors.

2 UN Proposals

The United Nations' concern about foreign debt is made explicit in the formulation of the Sustainable Development Goals (SDGs), in which it occupies a discreet position, but not absent. Specifically in the latest SDG, number 17, 'Partnerships for the goals'. Although this title, a priori generic, does not seem to indicate any relationship with debt, it includes five targets framed in this SDG on finance-related issues. In particular, target 17.4 reads: 'Assist developing countries in attaining long-term debt sustainability through coordinated policies aimed at fostering debt financing, debt relief and debt restructuring, as appropriate, and address the external debt of highly indebted poor countries to reduce debt distress'. This target includes debt service (as a proportion of exports of goods, services, and primary income) as a tracking indicator. Currently, not only has it failed to meet its targets, but it is also in regression (United Nations, 2025a).

The UN, through UNCTAD and other bodies, has promoted the adoption of development financing and debt cancellation instruments, although its role has been considerably more limited than that of the major international financial institutions (IMF and World Bank). On numerous occasions since its creation, the United Nations General Assembly has advocated the creation of low-interest loan funds and has recognised the debt crisis as a matter of global concern (Hardy, 1987).

Since the debt crisis of the 1980s, UNCTAD has insisted on the need to establish orderly debt workout procedures. Since the Asian financial crises, the member states of the United Nations insisted on this idea of articulating an international mechanism for the restructuring of unsustainable debts (Eurodad, 2024). In 2012, following the aftermath of the Great Recession, UNCTAD published its voluntary 'Principles on Promoting Responsible Sovereign Lending and Borrowing'.

The real turning point came in September 2014, when the United Nations General Assembly adopted Resolution 68/304, entitled 'Towards the establishment of a multilateral legal framework for sovereign debt restructuring processes'. This resolution recognised the sovereign right of every State to restructure its debt, and called for an orderly, predictable, and durable solution to the debt problem in developing countries through the adoption of a multilateral legal framework for sovereign debt restructuring processes. Despite being approved with a significant majority of 124 votes in favour, it was opposed or abstained by a large part of creditor countries.

Shortly afterwards, in December of the same year, the Assembly passed another resolution (69/247) to form the special committee that was to draw up such a legal framework, open to all member states. Unfortunately, the process to establish a binding framework did not bear fruit due to the lack of consensus and its blocking by creditor countries (Arrieta de Armas, 2024). As a result, the most ambitious approaches were abandoned. In 2015, the Addis Ababa Action Agenda was adopted as a general framework of commitments for financing development (Resolution 69/313). Shortly after, in a new resolution (69/319), the 'Basic Principles on

Sovereign Debt Restructuring Processes' were introduced, reducing the initial claims to guidelines of voluntary application and with little success (Eurodad, 2024).

Since then, there have been successive calls for the improvement of international financial and debt mechanisms and for commitments to avoid unsustainable debt, through annual UN General Assembly resolutions on debt and debt sustainability, and the outcome documents of the United Nations Economic and Social Council's Financing for Development Forums.

The last major event in which this issue was addressed was the Fourth International Conference on Financing for Development, which was held in Sevilla in July 2025. Some voices saw it as a historic opportunity for member states to reach an international consensus to develop a United Nations Framework Convention on Sovereign Debt, addressing the prevention and resolution of unsustainable and illegitimate debts, creating the necessary rules and structures to do so (Eurodad, 2024). These expectations have not been met due to the adoption of no binding agreements. Despite this, some commitments expressed in the so-called 'Sevilla Commitment' (United Nations, 2025b) have been reiterated. A selection of some of the most relevant proposals is highlighted below:

- The IMF and the World Bank are requested to take into account sustainable development priorities in debt sustainability assessments, and especially spending needs for climate action and long-term investments.
- The streamlining and consolidation of existing debt databases into a single global central registry, hosted by the World Bank, is encouraged to improve transparency.
- The UN Secretary-General is urged to convene a working group with the IMF and the World Bank to propose a set of voluntary guiding principles on responsible sovereign lending.
- The need to broaden the representation of countries of the Global South in the decision-making processes of international economic and financial institutions is underscored, through reviews of quotas, shareholding structures, and composition of executive boards.
- The inclusion of state-contingent clauses is promoted, in order to suspend debt servicing in contexts of crisis and natural disasters.

- Commitment to strengthening the global financial safety net, particularly through the issuance of special drawing rights by the IMF to provide liquidity to countries with development needs.
- The establishment of a platform for borrowing countries is proposed, with the participation of different institutions and under the coordination of the United Nations, to strengthen the voice of debtor countries.

In sum, after the adoption of a binding legal framework failed in 2014, the UN's emphasis shifted to reconfiguring the development finance architecture from a more holistic point of view. There was an increasing focus on crisis prevention through the promotion of sustainable finance, improving existing debt instruments and greater international cooperation to ensure that countries had the fiscal space and tools to achieve their SDGs (UNEP & WBG, 2017). Nevertheless, these are non-binding soft law instruments that, although they may have certain effects due to the reputational costs of non-compliance (Guisado et al., 2021), have not managed to tackle the problem.

3 Assessment

While it cannot be denied that the United Nations has paid attention to the problem of over-indebtedness in the countries of the Global South and has played a role in denouncing it, little progress has certainly been made in a solution. This is especially true when it comes to permanent solutions through the articulation of a specific institutional mechanism that rethinks and transforms international financial relations. Even though some interesting proposals have been made, in the face of the lack of will on the part of creditor states and the limited executive capacity of the United Nations, they have remained little more than a declaration of intent.

The frameworks of the international financial architecture have proven dysfunctional and biased in favour of creditors. In particular, debt restructuring processes continue to be fragmented, uncoordinated, and unfair, driven mainly by the preservation of creditors' interests—who have the capacity to block legitimate restructurings—and with profound power asymmetries (Arrieta de Armas, 2024; Eurodad, 2024).

The various initiatives promoted by the World Bank, the IMF (the HIPC: Heavily Indebted Poor Countries Initiative in 1996; or the

Multilateral Debt Relief Initiative in 2005), the G20 (the Debt Service Suspension Initiative or the Common Framework[2], in 2020), and forums such as the Paris Club, have proved insufficient and have been characterised by imposing conditionality requirements on debtor countries, which has implied a reduction in economic sovereignty and social well-being. In the face of these biased and ineffective measures, the UN should position itself as the truly appropriate and democratic forum to address this challenge, given its mandate to address major international challenges, and its non-identification with either the debtor or creditor party (Eurodad, 2024).

The solution inevitably lies in the creation of a binding multilateral mechanism for sovereign debt restructuring with balanced and transparent arbitration under the auspices of the United Nations, accompanied by profound reforms of international law based on the right to development as a legal shield. In the absence of this, debtor countries are in a very weak legal position, which perpetuates the relationship of dependency and slows down their development.

To this end, it is imperative to regain greater ambition and promote an international treaty on sovereign debt to pursue global financial justice, starting by recognising the historical responsibility of Global North countries in the over-indebtedness situation of many countries. Beyond the will of the majority of the countries in the General Assembly, the main stumbling block is probably to be found in issues related to United Nations governance itself and its real capacity to influence the international financial architecture. It is no coincidence that this challenge is included in SDG 17 'partnerships for the goals', since it is essential to involve different actors to achieve an effective, lasting and just solution.

[2] The Common Framework emerges as the permanent successor to the Debt Service Suspension Initiative, which was proposed as a temporary instrument in the context of the COVID-19 crisis. Unlike the latter, it contemplates debt restructuring (not just deferrals of service) and seeks to coordinate all official bilateral creditors, including those not belonging to the Paris Club. However, only four countries have formally signed up to this framework until 2025 (Chad, Ethiopia, Zambia and Ghana), given its significant limitations, mainly due to prolonged exclusion from financial markets during the process and the absence of legally binding mechanisms to compel the effective participation of private creditors.

References

Arrieta de Armas, C. (2024). Necesidad de un mecanismo multilateral para la negociación de la deuda soberana (2019-2024). *Política Internacional, 7*(1), 143–159. https://doi.org/10.5281/zenodo.14472956

Ayoub, A., Wani, T. A., & Sultan, A. (2024). External debt crisis & socio-economic fallout: Evidence from the BRICS nations. *Regional Science Policy & Practice, 16*(6), 100029. https://doi.org/10.1016/j.rspp.2024.100029

Cohen, D. & Harnoys-Vannier, B. (2023). *The resistible rise of external debt in the global south (2011–2021)*. Finance for Development Lab, Working Paper 3. https://findevlab.org/working-paper-3-the-resistible-rise-of-external-debt-in-the-global-south-2011-2021/

Eurodad. (2024). UN framework convention on sovereign debt - building a new debt architecture for economic justice. A reform agenda for the fourth international financing for development conference. *European Network on Debt and Development.*. https://www.eurodad.org/un_framework_convention_on_sovereign_debt

Guisado, T. M., Llano, M. M., Lucero, L., & Zanarello, E. E. (2021). Deuda Pública y principios de la ONU: Análisis jurídico económico de los principios básicos de reestructuración de deuda pública de la Organización de las Naciones Unidas. *Revista de la Escuela del Cuerpo de Abogados y Abogadas del Estado, 6*, 355–374.

Hardy, C. (1987). Debt negotiations and the north-south dialogue, 1974–1980. In I. W. Zartman (Ed.), *Positive sum: Improving north-south negotiations* (pp. 259–277). Routledge. https://doi.org/10.4324/9781351317924

Debt Justice. (2024). *The colonial roots of global south debt: A tale of plunder, exploitation and resistance.* https://debtjustice.org.UK/wp-content/uploads/2023/09/The-colonial-roots-of-global-south-debt. Pdf.

Mumba, C. S., & Li, J. H. (2020). The impact of external debt on economic growth: Evidence from southern Africa. *Journal of Finance and Economics, 8*(3), 135–141. https://doi.org/10.12691/jfe-8-3-6

Nakatani, P., & Herrera, R. (2007). The south has already repaid its external debt to the north: But the north denies its debt to the south. *Monthly Review, 59*(2), 31–36. https://doi.org/10.14452/MR-059-02-2007-06_3

Nguyen, V. B. (2025). The relationship between public debt and income inequality in advanced and developing economies: Empirical evidence on the difference. *Panoeconomicus, 72*(1), 71–90. https://doi.org/10.2298/PAN211221001N

Siddique, A., Selvanathan, E. A., & Selvanathan, S. (2016). The impact of external debt on growth: Evidence from highly indebted poor countries. *Journal of Policy Modeling, 38*(5), 874–894. https://doi.org/10.1016/j.jpolmod.2016.03.011

UNCTAD. (2025). *A world of debt' Report 2025,*. United Nations Trade and Development. https://unctad.org/publication/world-of-debt

UNEP, & WBG. (2017). Roadmap for a sustainable financial system. United Nations Environment Programme & World Bank Group. http://documents.worldbank.org/curated/en/903601510548466486

United Nations. (2025a). The sustainable development goals report 2025. United Nations. https://unstats.un.org/sdgs/report/2025/.

United Nations. (2025b). *Sevilla commitment.* Fourth international conference on financing for development - draft resolution submitted by the president of the conference. A/CONF.227/2025/L.1. https://docs.un.org/en/A/CONF.227/2025/L.1

Vasic-Lalovic, I., Merling, L., & Wu, A. (2023). *The growing debt burdens of global south countries: Standing in the way of climate and development goals.* Center for Economic and Policy. *Research.* https://cepr.net/publications/the-growing-debt-burdens-of-global-south-countries-standing-in-the-way-of-climate-and-development-goals/

CHAPTER 16

Food Security

Victòria Soldevila-Lafon

1 The Challenge

The UN's challenge regarding food is embodied in Sustainable Development Goal 2 (SDG2) of the 2030 Agenda, known as the "Zero Hunger" goal. SDG2 contains five targets to be achieved by 2030, which are summarized below: SDG 2.1: End hunger and ensure access to safe, nutritious, and sufficient food all year round. SDG 2.2: End all forms of malnutrition. SDG 2.3: Double the agricultural productivity and incomes of small-scale food producers. SDG 2.4: Ensure sustainable food production systems. SDG 2.5: Maintain the genetic diversity of seeds, cultivated plants, and farmed and domesticated animals. Additional targets without

This work was supported by the Ministry of Science and Innovation (MCIN) of the Spanish Government [Grant PID2020-119152GB-I00, 10.13039/501100011033].

V. Soldevila-Lafon (✉)
University Rovira i Virgili, Tarragona, Spain
e-mail: mariavictoria.soldevila@urv.cat

R. de Arriba (ed.), *United Nations Facing Global Economic Disorder: Assessing 20 Policy Proposals*,
https://doi.org/10.1007/978-3-032-21952-7_16

a defined timeline include: SDG 2a: Increase investment in rural infrastructure and agriculture research. SDG 2b: Prevent and correct trade restrictions and distortions in world agricultural markets. SDG 2c: Ensure the proper functioning of food commodity markets (United Nations, 2015).

Data from the latest report on *The State of Food Security and Nutrition in the World* indicate that between 638 and 720 million people experienced hunger in 2024, 28% of the global population (over 2.3 billion people) faced food insecurity, and more than one-third of the world's population (2.6 billion people) cannot afford a healthy diet. Additionally, obesity is rising: 5.5% of children under five and 15.8% of adults are obese. Achieving SDG2 appears unattainable, with an estimated 512 million people suffering chronic undernourishment by the end of the decade (FAO et al., 2025).

FAO identifies the main drivers of food insecurity and malnutrition nowadays as conflict, extreme climate events, and economic crises, exacerbated by growing inequality (FAO et al., 2021). These factors have intensified in recent years. The situation may worsen in the medium and long term: global population projections suggest 9.7 billion people by 2050, and FAO estimates that, in order to feed this population, agriculture will need to produce nearly 50% more food than in 2012, in a context of climate change that could severely impact agricultural productivity (FAO, 2017).

2 UN Proposals

The most widely accepted definition of food security was coined at the 1996 FAO Summit: "Food security exists when all people, at all times, have physical and economic access to sufficient, safe and nutritious food which meets their dietary needs and food preferences for an active and healthy life" (FAO, 1996). Food security is a multidimensional concept. Therefore, policies and interventions in this field involve different institutions and actors, often with conflicting visions and ideologies. This proliferation of actors is also evident within the UN itself. According to Fillol (2020), three main UN bodies can address food security: the

General Assembly, the Economic and Social Council (ECOSOC)[1], and the Security Council[2]. Other agencies like the World Health Organization (WHO) and UN Development Program (UNDP) are also involved. However, the UN bodies statutorily engaged in food security are the so-called "Rome-based agencies":

- The Food and Agriculture Organization (FAO) plays the leading role, with one of its founding goals being the eradication of hunger[3]. Within FAO, the Committee on World Food Security (CFS) advises the Council (FAO's executive body) and has established itself as an international forum on food security, including participation from social movements, institutional actors, private sector, jointly with States. The CFS is actively developing (voluntary) guidelines to assist States in formulating food security policies[4].
- The World Food Programme (WFP) focuses on emergency food aid.
- The International Fund for Agricultural Development (IFAD) provides funding (loans or grants) to governments in impoverished countries for agricultural and rural development projects.

Among the UN's proposals to advance food security, the transformation of agri-food systems has gained prominence in recent years. This was the theme of the 2021 Summit and features prominently in recent FAO reports. The 2021 UN Food Systems Summit (UNFSS) was promoted as

[1] ECOSOC is the United Nations body responsible for coordinating the organization's efforts in economic, social, cultural, health-related, and other issues. Food-related issues have significant economic, social, and health dimensions, which fall within the scope of ECOSOC's mandate.

[2] The Security Council may intervene to safeguard food security when its absence poses a threat to international peace and security.

[3] The FAO was established in 1945 with the following main objectives: to raise nutrition levels, enhance the efficiency and productivity of food production and distribution, improve living conditions of rural populations (See the FAO Constitution for more details).

[4] Some examples are: *Voluntary Guidelines to Support the Progressive Realization of the Right to Adequate Food in the Context of National Food Security* (2004); *Voluntary Guidelines on the Responsible Governance of Tenure of Land, Fisheries and Forests in the Context of National Food Security* (2012, revised version in 2022); *Principles for Responsible Investment in Agriculture and Food Systems* (2014); *Framework for Action for Food Security and Nutrition in Protracted Crises* (2015); and *Voluntary Guidelines on Food Systems and Nutrition* (2021).

inclusive and "open to all," involving not only States but also civil society, social movements, the private sector (companies, financial institutions), philanthropic organizations, etc.[5].

The Summit's main goal was to define policies and actions to transform the global agri-food system to meet the SDGs. Five action tracks were established:

1. Ensure access to safe and nutritious food for all.
2. Shift to sustainable consumption patterns.
3. Boost nature-positive production.
4. Advance equitable livelihoods.
5. Build resilience to vulnerabilities, shocks, and stress.

As a result of the national dialogues, 103 countries presented national pathways for the transformation of the food systems (FAO, 2021). A Coordination Hub was also established to provide technical and policy support and monitor Summit outcomes. The Summit produced over 2000 "transformative solutions," covering diverse and disparate issues—from "mobilizing private capital" to "increasing gender equality." On technical issues, it combined biotechnology and agroecology under the argument of needing "all tools in the toolbox."

This profusion and diversity reflect conflicting visions of how to transform food systems and combat food insecurity. These discrepancies can be broadly categorized into two approaches:

- A productivist, market-oriented vision, favoring free trade and a globalized agri-food system, emphasizing technological change (biotechnology, "sustainable intensification"), supported by major producing countries and private sector actors (producers and traders).
- A rights-based approach, prioritizing short supply chains and local markets, aligned with agroecology and food sovereignty, supported by small farmers, indigenous communities, and some civil society representatives.

[5] The World Economic Forum (WEF) played a prominent role in organising the Summit, which raised widespread concerns due to its close ties with major corporations

There is some consensus that the productivist, pro-market vision dominated the Summit, with resulting proposals being mostly technical, sidelining political and transformative elements.

Recent FAO reports on *The State of Food Security and Nutrition in the World* and *The State of Food and Agriculture* also emphasize food system transformation. The 2021 report proposed six pathways to transform food systems for improved food security, nutrition, and affordable healthy diets (FAO et al., 2021):

1. Integrating humanitarian, development, and peacebuilding policies in conflict-affected areas.
2. Increasing climate resilience of food systems.
3. Strengthening resilience of vulnerable populations to economic shocks.
4. Intervening throughout food supply chains to reduce the cost of nutritious foods.
5. Combating poverty and inequality through inclusive interventions.
6. Improving food environments and consumer behavior to promote healthy and sustainable diets.

The report also stresses the need for a systemic approach and greater coherence in investments and policies (FAO et al., 2021). The 2024 report highlights that lack of funding or access to funding has hindered implementation of necessary policies and investments. It estimates that achieving SDG 2.1 and 2.2 requires over $15.4 trillion (FAO et al., 2024).

3 Assessment

The UN and FAO cannot transform global agri-food governance without first transforming their own governance structures. As Pons (2013) points out, FAO was founded with functions limited to scientific-technical aspects, without effective political capacity. There has been no political will to strengthen its authority (Elver, 2024). Plans, directives, and agreements on food security are non-binding; they are merely political in nature and have not led to enforceable policies. There is no international convention or treaty providing legal security and compelling compliance. Full and effective recognition of the "right to food" could be a powerful legal tool for enforcing obligations on States. This right is included in the *UN's International Covenant on Economic, Social and Cultural Rights*[6], but as Elver notes, there is little interest in fully implementing it or safeguarding its provisions (Elver, 2024)[7].

Budget constraints and excessive bureaucracy also hinder FAO's effectiveness. WFP and IFAD rely on voluntary contributions, creating financial instability and limiting independence, as donor countries largely determine the allocation of funds.

Nonetheless, some governance reforms have occurred. The 2009 reform of the Committee on World Food Security (CFS) is a positive example, contrasting with the UNFSS. The Committee opened participation to private sector and civil society organizations, but decision-making power remains with States, allowing accountability—what McKeon calls "inclusive multilateralism," as opposed to the "multi-stakeholderism" of the Summit, where private sector and governments are equated and accountability is lacking (McKeon, 2021). In fact, the Summit and its institutionalization via the Coordination Hub (which excludes governments) are seen as corporate-driven efforts to undermine the CFS and fracture multilateralism (McMichael, 2023, Montenegro de Wit et al., 2021). As the International Panel of Experts on Sustainable Food Systems—IPES FOOD—denounces, the UNFSS has brought major agribusiness associations to the UN governance table (IPES FOOD, 2023).

Regarding food security proposals analyzed through Summit resolutions and recent reports, the focus is shifting toward reforming the global agri-food system, marginalizing the defense of the "right to food," which had previously been more prominent. Even when focusing on system reform, two crucial issues are overlooked: power relations in the global agri-food system and the role of trade.

[6] Following the drafting of the Universal Declaration of Human Rights, the United Nations adopted two convenant instruments for the protection of Human Rights: the International Covenant on Civil and Political Rights and the International Covenant on Economic, Social and Cultural Rights. The right to food appears in the latter Covenant and is therefore considered a "social, economic and cultural human right" (Fillol, 2020).

[7] Although the Optional Protocol to the International Covenant on Economic, Social and Cultural Rights came into force in 2013, which should allow violations of economic, social, and cultural rights to be reported to international bodies, the protocol remains virtually inactive due to the reluctance of States to implement it (Elver, 2024).

On power concentration and transnational food corporations' behavior, FAO has made timid calls for responsible business conduct and due diligence. But this issue is unlikely to be addressed if corporate participation in UN governance increases. Civil society boycotts of the UNFSS emerged in response to this growing corporate influence and the Summit's omission of corporate power issues—also absent from FAO reports.

Regarding trade, FAO does not question free trade and aligns with WTO positions, criticizing producer subsidies and tariffs. SDG 2b itself calls for "Correct and prevent trade restrictions and distortions in world agricultural markets, including through the parallel elimination of all forms of agricultural export subsidies and all export measures with equivalent effect." FAO argues that open global markets improve agricultural efficiency and offer lower prices to consumers. While acknowledging potential environmental and social impacts, these are seen as affecting only low-productivity countries, which should be compensated through complementary policies (e.g., improving small farmers' access to technology) (FAO, 2022).

Again, without capacity or will to address these issues, transforming the global agri-food system and eradicating hunger remains unlikely.

The current global governance structure cannot solve hunger, and food security is becoming increasingly politicized (Elver, 2024). The two visions discussed are difficult to reconcile and hinder progress in hunger eradication. Therefore, despite its limitations, preserving the UN framework (avoiding its "corporate capture" (McMichael, 2023)) is more necessary than ever, as UN should be the appropriate framework to discuss these issues through democracy and cooperation.

References

Elver, H. (2024). Global food systems in crisis: A human rights approach. In R. Falk & A. Lopez-Claros (Eds.), *Global governance and international cooperation: Managing global catastrophic risks in the 21st century* (pp. 332–347). Routledge. https://doi.org/10.4324/9781032699028-24

FAO. (1996). Rome declaration on world food security. Food and Agriculture Organization of the United Nations. https://www.fao.org/4/w3613e/w3613e00.htm

FAO. (2017). The future of food and agriculture: Trends and challenges (short version). *Food and Agriculture Organization of the United Nations..* https://openknowledge.fao.org/server/api/core/bitstreams/2e90c833-8e84-46f2-a675-ea2d7afa4e24/content

FAO. (2021). Outcomes of the United Nations food systems summit. Food and Agriculture Organization of the United Nationshttps://openknowledge.fao.org/handle/20.500.14283/nh659en.

FAO. (2022). *The state of agricultural commodity markets 2022: The geography of food and agricultural trade*. Food and Agriculture Organization of the United Nations. https://doi.org/10.4060/cc0471en

FAO, IFAD, UNICEF, WFP & WHO. (2021). The state of food security and nutrition in the world 2021: Transforming food systems for food security, improved nutrition and affordable healthy diets for all. *Food and Agriculture Organization of the United Nations, International Fund for Agricultural Development, United Nations Children's Fund, World Food Programme, & World Health Organization.* https://doi.org/10.4060/cb4474en

FAO, IFAD, UNICEF, WFP & WHO. (2024). The state of food security and nutrition in the world 2024: Financing to end hunger, food insecurity and malnutrition in all its forms. *Food and Agriculture Organization of the United Nations, International Fund for Agricultural Development, United Nations Children's Fund, World Food Programme, & World Health Organization.* https://doi.org/10.4060/cd1254en

FAO, IFAD, UNICEF, WFP & WHO. (2025). The state of food security and nutrition in the world 2025: –addressing high food price inflation for food security and nutrition. *Food and Agriculture Organization of the United Nations, International Fund for Agricultural Development, United Nations Children's Fund, World Food Programme, & World Health Organization.* https://doi.org/10.4060/cd6008en

Fillol Mazo, A. (2020). Seguridad alimentaria y derecho internacional. *Dykinson.*

IPES-FOOD. (2023). Who's tipping the scales? The growing influence of corporations on the governance of food systems, and how to counter it. International Panel of Experts on Sustainable Food Systems https://ipes-food.org/wp-content/uploads/2024/03/tippingthescales.pdf

McKeon, N. (2021). *Global food governance. Development, 64*(3), 172–180. https://doi.org/10.1057/s41301-021-00326-9

McMichael, P. (2023). Food regime dynamics. *Revista de Economía Crítica, 36*, 78–93. https://www.revistaeconomiacritica.org/index.php/rec/article/view/737

Montenegro de Wit, M., Canfield, M., Iles, A., Anderson, M., McKeon, N., Guttal, S., & Prato, S. (2021). Resetting power in global food governance: The UN food systems summit. *Development, 64*(3), 153–161. https://doi.org/10.1057/s41301-021-00316-x

Pons, X. (2013). *Alimentación y derecho internacional: Armas, instituciones y procesos*. Marcial Pons.

United Nations. (2015). Transforming our world: The 2030 agenda for sustainable development. In *UN general assembly resolution a/RES/70/1*. Nations. https://www.un.org/sustainabledevelopment

CHAPTER 17

Poverty

Carlos H. Ramirez

1 The Challenge

From 1990 to 2015, extreme poverty—defined then as income of US$1.25 per day—fell from 47% of the developing world's population to 14%. Undernourishment in these same countries also dropped from 23.3% in 1990–1992 to 12.9% in 2014–2016. During that period, the number of people in extreme poverty fell by more than half, from 1.9 billion to 836 million, about 11.3% of the global population (UNDP, 2015). The UN can certainly take some credit for these achievements, as they coincided with the Millennium Development Goals (MDGs) adopted in 2000. The poverty trends were a cause for celebration and inspired the Sustainable Development Goals (SDGs) that replaced the MDGs in 2016.

However, beginning in 2013 and accelerating during COVID-19, progress stalled. Between 2014 and 2019, poverty reduction slowed to 0.6 percentage points per year, the weakest rate in three decades (UN, n.d.). World poverty rose from 689 million in 2019 to 712 million

C. H. Ramirez (✉)
Kindai University, Osaka, Japan
e-mail: cramirez@intl.kindai.ac.jp

R. de Arriba (ed.), *United Nations Facing Global Economic Disorder: Assessing 20 Policy Proposals*,
https://doi.org/10.1007/978-3-032-21952-7_17

in 2022 under a new $2.15/day line (UN DESA, 2024). SDG 1 on ending extreme poverty by 2030 is now projected as unattainable. The $3.00/day line adopted in 2025 worsens the picture, with an estimated 808 million still in poverty by 2030 (UN DESA, 2025). Two caveats apply: poverty decreased slightly from 10.5% in 2022 to 9.9% in 2025, and incomes of the poorest have risen (World Bank, 2025). Still, 1 in 10 people—9.9% of the world—remain in extreme poverty (UN DESA, 2025).

More importantly, the UN recognizes that extreme poverty is only the most basic measurement of human livelihood and thus also incorporated other components than solely income to assess human well-being. Among the most important is the Multidimensional Poverty Index (MPI) that helps monitor the progress toward poverty elimination in *all of its aspects*. The MPI measures acute deprivations in multiple dimensions of health, education, and living standards. While MPI is not an official benchmark of the SDGs, it is recognized as a tool to measure outcomes, particularly for SDG 1.2, which has the stated goal of reducing global poverty in 2030 by 50% in every dimension.

Based on MPI measurements, similar to the progress in reducing extreme poverty, results have been mixed depending on the timeframe. From 2010 to 2020 (MPI data available only after 2010), substantial progress was made in reducing MPI. However, after 2020, partly due to the COVID pandemic, advancement slowed considerably. In 2010, the number of people in poverty measured by MPI in 104 countries was 1.75 billion out of 5.2 billion (OPHI & UNDP, 2022). In 2022, this decreased to 1.2 billion out of 6.1 billion in 111 countries (OPHI & UNDP, 2022). Progress slowed further in 2024: across 112 countries and 6.3 billion people, MPI measured 1.1 billion (OPHI, 2024). These trends suggest SDG poverty targets are unattainable without accelerated progress. The World Bank (WB) reports that under current trends, it will take over three decades to lift humanity above $2.15/day (World Bank, 2024), and logically even longer under the revised $3.00 threshold. While improvements in MPI are moderately positive as investment in health, education, and welfare continues, results remain underwhelming. In sum, significant MPI reduction will be prolonged, comparable in duration to eliminating extreme poverty.

Debt and its servicing costs are one of the main exogenous factors impeding the UN's efforts in reducing poverty. Indeed, the trade-off between debt servicing and development is increasingly retarding poverty reduction efforts. Debt servicing costs reached a total of $1.4 trillion among developing economies in 2023. The poorest countries have tripled their servicing of debt and quadrupled their interest payments over the past decade (Jensen, 2025). In 56 developing nations, interest payments now account for more than 10% of total government income, which is almost twice as much as they were ten years ago. Seventeen of these nations spend more than 20% of their income on interest payments, a level that is closely associated with default risk (Jensen, 2025). Pope Francis' mandated Jubilee Commission (2025) notes the particularly harsh consequences in Africa, where debt distress is most acute: 57% of the population—751 million people, including 288 million in extreme poverty—lives in countries spending more on debt than on education or healthcare. According to Jensen (2025), in general many developing countries risk long-term solvency crises under current circumstances and jeopardize progress, especially MPI, as public funds are redirected from health, education, and social welfare to pay onerous debt servicing costs.

The reduction of global poverty is primarily dependent on the local and international political economy context. The UN's strategy is to contend with poverty at a micro level via projects aligned with a national strategy for development. However, broad poverty reduction requires both state-initiated solutions and supportive global conditions.

On the one hand, the internal political context and institutional capabilities of developing countries are critical for the success of both UN-sponsored projects and, more importantly, sustainable development. Weak institutional regimes are at the core of the development failure and poverty issue (Acemoglu & Robinson, 2012). This institutional fragility drives poor macroeconomic management and is reflective of insufficient institutional capacity to foster investments into productive transformation. The rent-seeking behavior and infiltration of vested interests into policy formulation are at the root of poor governance and corruption manifested in fragile institutions. At an extreme, weak and failed states suffering from conflict and civil war make the UN quest to reduce poverty via targeted projects a herculean task.

On the other hand, the international geopolitical environment facing developing countries has cycled through favorable and unfavorable economic periods during the past 70 years, coinciding with success and retreat in the battle against poverty. In the 1990s, for example, East and Southeast Asia exploited the favorable trade conditions to reduce poverty dramatically. The start of the twenty-first century has also witnessed numerous peaks and valleys: global economic expansion in the early 2000s, then the global economic crisis of 2008, the brief recovery from 2013 to 2019, and finally the calamity of Covid beginning in 2019. Poverty figures rose and fell with these events.

The current period of intense great-power competition between the USA and China, which began under the first Trump administration (2016–2020) and moderated under Biden (2020–2024), coincided with a slowdown in poverty reduction. Under the second Trump (2025) presidency, this competition has escalated as the administration seeks to deepen its unilateralist America-first agenda, opposing multilateralism, promoting economic nationalism, withdrawing from international agreements, imposing trade barriers, and cutting aid. In response, China has redirected its manufacturing overcapacity from the USA to other countries, harming their industrial production and employment. Whether China–USA relations reach a modus vivendi or break down into spheres of influence, reduced trade, and GDP will undermine poverty reduction and development.

2 UN Proposals

The UN's vision on poverty is grouped into three categories here: *modeling poverty; the debt crisis and finance; and the domestic and international political economy context. First, t*he UN models for a world without poverty rest on broad definitions of poverty and development. Drawing from Amartya Sen's concept of capability as freedom, the UN has built a model that extends beyond income or GDP growth. Like Sen's vision, the UN's approach to human development—including poverty eradication— coincides with the attainment of minimal standards and levels of education, health, and social welfare. Subsequently, Sen's ideas were explicitly embedded within the UN mindset by economist Mahbub ul-Haq, who operationalized Sen's ideas through the creation of the Human Development Index (HDI). HDI shifted the focus from GDP growth as the sole metric of progress to a human-centered approach measuring a country's average achievements in three basic dimensions of human development directly echoing Sen's ideas: health, education, and standard of living. The MPI grew directly from HDI, and the MDGs and SDGs similarly derive from these frameworks.

Sen and ul-Haq's theories continue to guide UN programs, as evidenced in their reliance on HDI and MPI as benchmarks. These indexes in turn are intimately related to the SDGs and underpin the UN's 3 × 6 × 3 Framework, the primary roadmap to achieving the SDGs. This roadmap envisions three directions of change—transforming systems, tackling inequality, and boosting resilience—using six solution areas and driven by three key enablers (UNDP, 2021). The six principal areas requiring solutions are poverty, governance, resilience, environment, energy and gender inequality. They are to be enabled or resolved via three tools: strategic innovations, digitization, and development financing. Moreover, together with the 3 × 6 × 3 Framework, the UN's formal Theory of Change (ToC) operationalizes development by mapping inputs to expected outcomes (UNSDG, 2017).

Second, at the UN Fourth Conference on Financing for Development in Sevilla, Spain, in summer 2025, participants reached agreements on a number of important issues related to the debt crisis, formulated in a document called the *Compromiso de Sevilla*. Many of the resolutions called for convening new forums or working groups to further study issues and for the strengthening of dialogue at the UN or G20 level (Pham, 2025). A concrete outcome was the creation of a Global Hub for Debt Swaps for Development aimed at redirecting debt servicing costs to development investment. Nevertheless, the UN is emphasizing the role of private capital as the main conduit to finance development (Tooze & Abadi, 2025), more commonly known as blended finance (Suzman, 2025). It entails grants or funds from a development entity such as the Gates Foundation and governmental aid acting as a guarantee to lower risk, reduce interest rates, and ensure project viability in order to attract private capital. Over time, the goal is self-sustaining credit markets requiring less aid while crowding in private capital (Suzman, 2025).

Finally, recognizing the dual challenges of domestic and international political-economic dysfunction, the UN has posited strategies to address both in order to tackle poverty. On the domestic front, the Sevilla Conference launched two main initiatives to confront financial corruption and malpractice. First, the establishment of a UN Working Group on responsible lending and borrowing that also includes the WB and IMF (Pham, 2025). Its aim is to foster principles and practices that should guide both creditors and sovereigns to avoid unsustainable debt, opaque deals, and misuse of funds. Second, the creation of a UN-backed Global Debt Register with the objective of increasing financial transparency by recognizing corruption risks in sovereign lending and borrowing. It is meant to be a new database of all government debts, open to oversight.

On the international front, other than wielding its moral authority to promote and cajole for global solidarity, collective action, and member commitment to a rules-based order, the UN is determined to focus on its own much-needed reform in the expectation that a more efficient and functional body will be more attractive to its membership. Key concerns are bureaucratic excess and financial waste. The reform proposal consolidates and streamlines organizations and mandates, addressing inefficiencies that create resentment and backlash among UN member countries.

3 Assessment

The assessment is organized around the same issues of modeling poverty, the debt crisis, and the domestic and international political economy context. At the project level, the UN's poverty models provide useful tools to set goals, measure progress, and deliver results. However, the 3 × 6 × 3 Framework and the ToC are not full-fledged strategies of developmental change. They simply outline causal pathways without specifying preconditions for success. For example, improved access to education may lead to better jobs and poverty reduction. Essentially, they explain pathways to success but do not elicit the necessary preconditions—i.e., they fail to outline the requirements to embark on change. Questions such as these go unanswered: do local institutions, communities, or governments actually have the ability or resources to carry out the project? Or, how do you build political support and legitimacy needed to induce change? In the above example of education, success first requires schools, teachers, and educational resources (e.g., books, computers). To have these items in place, a broader theory or strategy of development is necessary.

Thus, project-based frameworks should not be viewed independently of grander theories of development. To be sure, the UN is mindful of grounding country- or micro-level programs in broader strategies of development. Indeed, the UN incorporates elements from various well-known theories and strategies. This is consistent with Rodrik's argument for "one economics, many recipes" of tailored policy solutions to specific local political and economic conditions (Rodrik, 2008). Examples include UNIDO's industrial parks in Ethiopia, sustainable agriculture in Rwanda, and trade development programs in Egypt. These reflect grander development strategies such as import substitution industrialization, agriculture-driven industrialization, and export promotion strategies respectively.

The UN's eclectic application of various development theories in accordance with Rodrik's logic to modify policy to local context has had positive outcomes (see above programs in Rwanda, Ethiopia, and Egypt). Nevertheless, as Smith (2024) argues, there should be a bias toward manufacturing, particularly for exports, in the design of specific projects that ultimately should tie into a national strategy of industrial transformation. The large employment-producing effects of manufacturing in a developing country context, both inside and outside of industry, also feed into general rising living standards (Smith, 2024).

Another omission in the UN's toolkit is the role of domestic savings and investment. While the UN prioritizes international capital, long-term growth requires mobilizing domestic resources (Tooze & Abadi, 2025; Suzman, 2025). Although local funding is undoubtedly insufficient to ensure robust development, it is important to fully understand the mechanisms that generate significant domestic savings, which should then be directed toward investment. Klein and Pettis (2020) argue in the Chinese context that high domestic savings rates were at the root of its economic success. More generally, this model was at the center of East Asia's extraordinary economic growth.

Whether Sevilla's commitments on providing debt relief will be honored remains uncertain. However, history does not augur well. The Jubilee Commission (2025) emphasizes the cyclical nature of global finance: during global expansion investment flows to developing nations but retreats to advanced economies in downturns. This countercyclical movement enhances the safe haven status of developed markets, thereby economically strengthening them, and inversely, impoverishing developing countries. The UN has had little to offer in solutions for these types of dysfunctional global financial flows.

During boom periods, private creditors often engage in excessive and risky lending behavior, expecting bailouts in case of defaults, as has happened in the past. Developing countries, in turn, taking advantage of periods of rapid economic expansion, sometimes engaged in reckless borrowing—often too many loans at too high rates—as a result of short-term political or vested interests and then failed to invest in growth-sustaining projects (Jubilee Commission, 2025). This recurring dynamic has created a moral hazard for both creditors and borrowers. Sevilla initiatives like the Global Debt Register seek to address these problems, but earlier efforts, such as the 2012 UNCTAD Principles, achieved little without enforcement mechanisms.

According to Tooze and Abadi (2025), an estimated $4 trillion per year of investment is required to lift the world out of poverty. These sums are unlikely to materialize for two reasons. First, financial aid commitments from developed countries have significantly declined since the pandemic (OECD, 2025). For example, the Trump administration cut bilateral global health funding by two-thirds (OECD, 2025). Much of the remaining aid has been diverted from long-term development (education, health, infrastructure) to refugee assistance or crisis funding (wars, earthquakes, droughts). Second, aid retrenchment has left the private sector unwilling to provide additional funding. Even under ideal circumstances, blended finance has been "oversold" (Suzman, 2025), as the private sector has been unable to supply sufficient complementary investments. Real progress will require a triad of domestic savings, international aid, and private capital—with the first two leading.

At a domestic level, the UN is largely reduced to an advisory role, encouraging national governments to pursue policies serving their own interests. Yet it must manage individual projects within weak institutional environments. The capture of state policy and finance by vested interests, leading to mismanagement and corruption in developing countries, is a complex issue. The Sevilla conference initiatives are important steps forward but insufficient on their own. Ultimately, a comprehensive country-wide approach where economic growth strengthens governing institutions and competent governance is imperative. In conflict zones, such as Congo and Sudan, where the state is absent or semi-functioning, sustained long-term poverty reduction is unlikely. However, in countries with some institutional autonomy, micro-level projects may foster a virtuous cycle of poverty alleviation and economic development. In this context, the 3 x 6 x 3 Framework and ToC will have the most impact.

On the international level, the UN's laudable efforts to reform and revitalize itself will not be enough to confront the chaotic and high-tension filled diplomatic landscape with ongoing wars in Europe, the Middle East, and Africa. The UN has not been spared from the USA's undermining of global institutions, losing $1 billion in funding from the administration, its largest donor (Better World Campaign, 2025). The funding crisis will only hinder the UN's reform initiatives, casting doubt on the organization's efficacy and credibility. It leaves the UN in a weakened position, unable to address the current fraught state of international affairs.

The United States, which spearheaded the creation of the UN, has abandoned multilateralism under President Trump. The Trump administration‘s attempts to weaken international organizations have created major obstacles for the UN and developing nations. Indeed, the administration has incredulously repudiated and disassociated itself from the SDGs (Suzman, 2025). This subversion of the global order will be primarily manifested in the slowdown of international trade, investment, and global economic growth. Moreover, the UN's work in developing countries is threatened by great-power competition between the USA and China. The result will be the narrowing of diplomatic and commercial space, and its concomitant negative economic impact, as nations are forced to choose allegiance in a divided world. In this rivalry, China is not a benign actor. It is also a contributor to global tensions through its problematic lending practices; its political weaponizing of trade; and its excessive exporting capacity. All are detrimental to industrial transformation, development, and poverty alleviation.

The unbearably slow progress of economic development and poverty reduction stems not from a lack of UN theoretical rigor or faulty concepts. Rather, it is the consequence of dysfunctional financing, global and local corruption, fragile states, and a contentious global political economy inconducive to development. Indeed, when robust domestic institutions exist and deliver enlightened economic policy matched with a fortuitous global political economy, then UN programs can produce maximum impact. This was true between 1990 and 2013, when poverty reduction achieved noteworthy outcomes, particularly in East Asia, Chile, Turkey, and elsewhere. Absent the political will of nations in both the developed and developing world to agree to work collectively, poverty will remain with us for the foreseeable future.

References

Acemoglu, D., & Robinson, J. A. (2012). *Why nations fail: The origins of power, prosperity, and poverty*. Crown Publishers.

Better World Campaign. (2025, July 18). *Congress just clawed back $1 billion in foreign assistance: Here's where the cuts are hitting* [Blog post]. Better

World Campaign. https://betterworldcampaign.org/budget/congress-just-clawed-back-1-billion-in-foreign-assistance-heres-where-the-cuts-are-hitting

Jensen, L. (2025, February). *Development Futures Series: Debt Update—Development gives way to debt (UNDP Debt Update).* United Nations Development Programme. https://www.undp.org/publications/dfs-undp-debt-update-development-gives-way-debt

Jubilee Commission. (2025). *The Jubilee Report: A blueprint for tackling the debt and development crises and creating the financial foundations for a sustainable, people-centered global economy.* Pontifical Academy of Social Sciences. https://ipdcolumbia.org/publication/jubilee-debt-development-blueprint/

Klein, M. C., & Pettis, M. (2020). *Trade wars are class wars: How rising inequality distorts the global economy and threatens international peace.* Yale University Press.

OECD (2025, June 26). *Cuts in official development assistance: OECD projections for 2025 and the near term* (OECD Policy Briefs). Organisation for Economic Co-operation and Development. https://www.oecd.org/en/publications/2025/06/cuts-in-official-development-assistance_e161f0c5.html

OPHI. (2024, October 17). *Global Multidimensional Poverty Index 2024: Poverty amid conflict* (OPHI Report No. 15). Oxford Poverty and Human Development Initiative https://ophi.org.uk/global-mpi/2024

OPHI & UNDP. (2022). *Global Multidimensional Poverty Index 2022: Unpacking deprivation bundles to reduce multidimensional poverty.* Oxford Poverty and Human Development Initiative & United Nations Development Programme https://ophi.org.uk/2022-global-mpi-report

Pham, M. T. (2025, July 16). *The Compromiso de Sevilla marks a new path for development finance.* Carnegie Endowment for International Peace. https://carnegieendowment.org/research/2025/07/sevilla-development-finance-conference-multilateralism?lang=en

Rodrik, D. (2008). *One economics, many recipes: Globalization, institutions, and economic growth.* Princeton University Press. https://muse.jhu.edu/pub/267/monograph/book/64825

Smith, N. (2024, February 8). *Do poor countries need a new development strategy?* Noahpinion. https://www.noahpinion.blog/p/do-poor-countries-need-a-new-development

Suzman, M. (2025, August 5). Development funding is in crisis. What now? With Mark Suzman [Interview] *The Economics Show.* Financial Times. https://www.ft.com/content/e417ab0e-97f9-40d4-82ff-1d61b2f59718

Tooze, A., & Abadi, C. (Hosts). (2025, August 1). Whither global development? (Season 1, #96) [Audio podcast episode]. In *Ones and Tooze Foreign Policy Magazine Podcast.* https://foreignpolicy.com/podcasts/ones-and-tooze/whither-global-development/

UN DESA. (2024). *The Sustainable Development Goals Report 2024*. United Nations Department of Economic and Social Affairs. https://unstats.un.org/sdgs/report/2024/

UN DESA. (2025). *The Sustainable Development Goals Report 2025*. United Nations Department of Economic and Social Affairs. https://unstats.un.org/sdgs/report/2025/

United Nations. (n.d.). *Ending poverty*. United Nations. https://www.un.org/en/global-issues/ending-poverty

UNDP. (2015). *The Millennium Development Goals Report 2015*. United Nations Development Programme. https://www.undp.org/publications/millennium-development-goals-report-2015

UNDP. (2021). *UNDP strategic plan 2022–2025*. United Nations Development Programme. https://www.undp.org/sites/g/files/zskgke326/files/2021-09/UNDP-Strategic-Plan-2022-2025_1.pdf

UNSDG. (2017). *UNDG-UNDAF companion pieces 7: Theory of change*. United Nations Sustainable Development Group. https://unsdg.un.org/sites/default/files/UNDG-UNDAF-Companion-Pieces-7-Theory-of-Change.pdf

World Bank. (2024, October 15). *Poverty, prosperity, and planet report 2024: Pathways out of the polycrisis*. https://www.worldbank.org/en/publication/poverty-prosperity-and-planet

World Bank. (2025, June 5). *June 2025 update to global poverty lines*. https://www.worldbank.org/en/news/factsheet/2025/06/05/june-2025-update-to-global-poverty-lines

CHAPTER 18

Inequality

Néstor Vercher

1 The Challenge

Economic inequality among individuals remains one of the most pressing and persistent challenges on the global agenda. Far from being a merely distributive problem, inequality is a structural reality that shapes the boundaries of human development, political stability, and ecological sustainability. The figures are stark: in 2023, 1.5% of the world's population owned more than 47% of global wealth, while the poorest 39% held just 0.5%. Meanwhile, over 82% of humanity controlled only around 13% of total wealth (UBS, 2024). The concentration is even more striking at the top of the wealth pyramid. Fourteen individuals together own close to two trillion US dollars, equivalent to more than 14% of global wealth. Below them, twelve people hold between USD 50 and 100 billion, while a larger group of about 2600 individuals controls fortunes ranging from USD 1 to 50 billion, together accounting for 79% of the wealth in these upper tiers (UBS, 2024).

N. Vercher (✉)
University of Valencia, Valencia, Spain
e-mail: nestor.vercher@uv.es

R. de Arriba (ed.), *United Nations Facing Global Economic Disorder: Assessing 20 Policy Proposals*,
https://doi.org/10.1007/978-3-032-21952-7_18

Recent evidence further reinforces this picture of extreme concentration. According to the World Inequality Report 2026 (Chancel et al., 2026), the richest 10% of earners receive more income than the remaining 90% taken together, while the bottom half of the global population accounts for less than 10% of total earnings. When viewed through the lens of wealth rather than income, disparities appear even more acute, with the top decile owning approximately three quarters of global wealth, compared to a mere 2% held by the poorest 50%. Moreover, a group of roughly 60,000 individuals—representing just 0.001% of the global population—now holds a volume of wealth equivalent to three times that owned by the poorest half of humanity combined.

The spatial dimension is equally evident: 68% of billionaires reside in the Global North, where nearly 70% of wealth is located, despite this region representing only 20% of the world's population (Oxfam, 2025). In 2023, 38% of millionaires were based in the United States, followed by the EU and Western Europe (23%), China (13%), Southeast Asia (10%), the United Kingdom (5%), and Japan (5%) (UBS, 2024). Over the past three decades, inequality has increased in the world's most populated countries—notably China and India—as well as in most high-income economies. Latin America and Africa continue to record the highest levels of income inequality, although many Latin American countries have managed to reduce their Gini coefficients. Overall, countries where inequality has grown most sharply are home to two-thirds of the global population (UN DESA, 2025).

This spatial concentration goes hand in hand to a historically upward trajectory, marked by notable fluctuations. According to Milanovic (2024), historically, global inequality can be understood in three broad phases. From the early nineteenth century until the mid-twentieth century, income disparities widened both within and between countries. For example, at the beginning of the nineteenth century the average income of the richest 10% was estimated to be 18 times higher than that of the poorest 50%. By 1910, the gap had widened to 41 to 1, with relative stability during the first half of the twentieth century (Oxfam, 2025). This was followed by a period of exceptionally high global inequality from the post-war years to the end of the twentieth century, partly due to the policies associated with the Washington Consensus (Stiglitz, 2002). By 1980, for instance, the top decile's income was 53 times higher than that of the bottom half. More recently, in the current phase, inequality has declined largely due to China's rapid growth and the expansion of its middle class. By 2020, the ratio had fallen to 38 to 1. In Milanović's view, future trends in global inequality will depend less on developments in China and increasingly on economic trajectories and internal inequalities in India and major African economies, as well as on the uneven impacts of climate change. At the same time, recent evidence suggests that the COVID-19 pandemic partially reversed the previously positive trend: while the economic conditions of 99% of the world's population deteriorated, the wealth of the ten richest individuals doubled (Oxfam, 2025).

The consequences of structural economic inequality are well documented and manifest themselves on multiple scales. On the one hand, inequality perpetuates and deepens the asymmetry between the Global North and South, reproducing imbalances in access to strategic resources, resilience to global crises—such as climate change or pandemics—and the fiscal capacity of states. On the other hand, inequality has a direct impact on key indicators of human well-being, including life expectancy, health, education, and intergenerational social mobility. In short, global economic inequality is neither a circumstantial phenomenon nor the inevitable outcome of market mechanisms, but rather the product of political decisions, institutional architectures, and ideological regimes that have historically favoured and protected the concentration of wealth in the hands of a few (Piketty, 2020).

2 UN Proposals

In response to global inequality, several international organisations—most notably the United Nations—have put forward proposals for action. In his speech outlining the UN's priorities for 2025, Secretary-General António Guterres identified inequality as one of the four problems of today's Pandora's box, alongside armed conflict, the climate crisis, and out-of-control technology (Guterres, 2025). The UN's vision reflects a multidimensional and integrated approach. It considers geographical conditions (such as inner countries, island states, and disadvantaged rural regions), focuses on historically vulnerable groups (including women, children, indigenous peoples, migrants, refugees, and ethnic minorities), and goes beyond the strictly economic dimension to include human development indicators such as life expectancy, access to healthcare, education, safe water, sanitation, and other fundamental rights.

Inequality is explicitly addressed in Sustainable Development Goal 10 (SDG 10), which seeks to "reduce inequality within and among countries". The goal sets out several specific targets: ensuring income growth for the bottom 40% of the population at a rate higher than the national average, guaranteeing equal opportunities and reducing outcome inequalities, facilitating safe, orderly, and regular migration, and lowering the transaction costs of remittances to below 3%, while eliminating corridors with costs above 5%. The aim is to facilitate these transfers, which constitute a vital source of income for millions of households in vulnerable situation.

The UN has also developed metrics to assess inequality more accurately, such as the Inequality-adjusted Human Development Index (IHDI), compiled by the United Nations Development Programme (UNDP). Unlike the traditional HDI, which relies on national averages, the IHDI introduces a corrective factor that reduces the value according to the level of inequality present in each of its dimensions: health, education, and income. The result is a more realistic indicator, one that reflects not only the average level of development but also how these achievements are distributed across the population. When inequalities are minimal, the IHDI and the HDI coincide. However, as internal disparities increase, the IHDI decreases, revealing the losses suffered by a society when progress is not shared. This methodology therefore offers a more critical and nuanced analysis of development, explicitly incorporating the issue of internal inequality.

Explicit proposals for reducing inequality are set out above all in the reports produced by the Department of Economic and Social Affairs (UN DESA), one of the UN's principal technical bodies responsible for economic, social, and environmental analysis. The *World Social Report 2020* (UN DESA, 2020), devoted specifically to inequality, emphasised the importance of ensuring quality education as a tool to break the intergenerational cycle of disadvantage, while also recognising that in many contexts educational systems tend to reproduce inequality rather than correct it. The report further advocated strengthening labour institutions and worker representation in order to reduce disparities in the labour market. Another key priority was the need for greater fiscal redistribution, in contrast with austerity policies that have eroded social spending in numerous countries. However, according to the report, reducing inequality is not merely a technical challenge but also a deeply political one that requires institutional resistance to be overcome and coordinated action to be mobilised at the international level. From this perspective, multilateralism is presented not only as desirable but also as a necessary condition for addressing the cross-border effects of inequality in an increasingly interdependent world.

The *World Social Report 2024* (UN DESA, 2024) focused more explicitly on social protection as a means of tackling inequality. It underlined that, although social security is recognised as a universal human right, its implementation remains highly uneven, often perpetuating and in some cases exacerbating socio-economic divides. The report therefore called for an urgent reformulation of social development strategies and policies aimed at expanding and consolidating inclusive and universal social protection systems that account for differentiated vulnerabilities, especially those linked to climate risks that disproportionately affect the groups most exposed to inequality. It also warned against the growing concentration of social security schemes in the hands of a small number of private corporations, a phenomenon that restricts equitable access and intensifies exclusion. For this reason, the UN stressed the importance of regulated public and community-based mechanisms to guarantee fair and sustainable distribution of social protection.

In its most recent edition, the *World Social Report 2025* (UN DESA, 2025) provided a rigorous diagnosis of the worsening of global inequality, fuelled by disruptive technologies and the impacts of climate change. In response, the report called for the construction of a new people-centred narrative, grounded in equality of opportunity, solidarity, and social protection. This vision demands a global consensus on public policies with a clear social orientation, referred to as "social lenses". These lenses are envisaged as the instrument to ensure universal access to essential services such as education, healthcare, housing, and clean energy, alongside the promotion of decent work and social protection across the life course. To make this agenda viable, progressive taxation is required to provide the necessary fiscal space, as well as more inclusive institutions. In this regard, the UN highlighted the importance of constitutional and legal frameworks that safeguard fundamental rights and ensure equitable access to justice, particularly for vulnerable groups. It also stressed the value of legal and administrative recognition of all people—including those who remain "invisible"—as a precondition for fair distribution of resources. Finally, the report underlined that building more legitimate institutions depends on effective citizen participation, transparency, and social cooperation, all within a framework of determined multilateral action.

Beyond the multidimensional proposals contained in the *World Social Reports*, the United Nations has advanced more specific initiatives to address inequality, most notably the taxation of wealth. UN DESA itself has highlighted the need to strengthen wealth taxes as a means of financing sustainable development and reducing the extreme concentration of wealth, taking advantage of the opportunities offered by digitalisation to improve administrative efficiency and tax oversight (Ritter et al., 2024). In the same direction, the UN Committee of Experts on International Cooperation in Tax Matters has recommended integrating wealth taxes into existing fiscal systems, whether through recurring levies or one-off solidarity charges, while prioritising administrative feasibility and political viability (Economic and Social Council, 2024). The committee argues that those who benefit most from a country's institutions and resources should bear a proportionately greater fiscal burden, and it further warns that extreme wealth accumulation is linked to higher environmental impacts, as the richest individuals produce levels of greenhouse gas emissions far above the average. International cooperation, along with information exchange and the fight against tax evasion, is therefore presented as essential to the effectiveness of such measures.

Finally, the International Labour Organization (ILO), in collaboration with the OECD, has advanced a set of concrete proposals to reduce global inequality, centred on wage and employment conditions. Among its priorities are strengthening collective bargaining and trade unions, as well as revaluing minimum wages, recognising that wage-setting should take into account not only economic factors but also the basic needs of workers and their families. The ILO further advocates for the formalisation of informal employment, the reinforcement of progressive fiscal policies, and greater investment in social protection and public services. All of this, it argues, should be articulated through country-specific policies tailored to address the structural causes of low wages (ILO & OECD, 2025).

3 Assessment

For decades, the fight against global inequality has stood at the heart of the normative agenda of the United Nations and its agencies. Yet, despite the clarity of the diagnosis and the growing technical consensus around measures such as progressive taxation, greater investment in public services, and the strengthening of labour rights, the translation of these proposals into practice has often been limited, fragmented, and in many respects insufficient. Structural resistance, entrenched power imbalances, and the widening gap between global normative frameworks and the realities of economic governance continue to obstruct meaningful progress. Against this backdrop, there are several areas that deserve greater prominence in the UN's response to the challenge of global inequality.

To begin with, reducing inequality is not simply a technical undertaking; it is also a deeply historical and political one. Inequality is rooted in a legacy of colonialism, armed conflict, and illicit financial flows. Addressing it therefore requires not only redistributive policies with medium- and long-term horizons but also a reparative dimension, one that recognises inherited imbalances and responds realistically to the most immediate and pressing effects of inequality. For instance, this calls for accelerated efforts in contexts that are becoming ever more complex, such as climate change, which disproportionately exposes countries and communities already burdened by vulnerability and inequality. Mitigation and adaptation policies must be explicitly framed around distributive and climate justice—including reparative measures—, acknowledging that those who contributed least to the problem are, paradoxically, those who suffer the most.

Equally, rethinking the response to inequality requires a thorough re-examination of fiscal and redistributive systems in the face of new forms of capital, such as digital or "cloud" capital—in the sense articulated by Varoufakis (2023)—whose concentration is even greater than that of traditional forms of capital. These forms of assets are reshaping economic power and widening the divide not only between North and South globally, but also within the Global North itself. At the same time, the technological exclusion of large sections of society not only limits their access to capital and employment but also reduces their ability to engage with basic services that are increasingly digitalised, thereby deepening the vicious cycle of inequality.

All of this, in turn, raises fundamental questions about the feasibility of forging effective international alliances in an international order that is becoming increasingly fragmented. The steady retreat of the United States from multilateral cooperation and its recent aggression to Venezuela and Iran, the persistence of conflicts in the east of Europe and West Asia, and the European Union's failure to articulate a coherent political project rooted in a rational identity with a Mediterranean scope—as argued by Naïr (2025)—all make the construction of common frameworks of action more difficult. What is needed now are new, action-oriented narratives adapted to the realities of the twenty-first century, built on social justice, international solidarity, and sustainability. Only if these principles are embraced by public actors, social movements, and intergovernmental coalitions will it be possible to open a path towards more effective global governance in tackling inequality. Despite all its limitations, the United Nations remains the institution best placed to lead this endeavour and to preserve hope in a world that is, little by little, losing its sense of possibility.

References

Chancel, L., Gómez-Carrera, R., Moshrif, R., Piketty, T. (2026). *World Inequality Report 2026*. World Inequality Lab. wir2026.wid.world.

Economic and Social Council. (2024). *UN handbook on wealth and solidarity taxes*. United Nations Committee of Experts on International Cooperation in Tax Matters.

Guterres, A. (2025, January 15). *Secretary-General's address to the General Assembly on his Priorities for 2025*. United Nations. https://www.un.org/sg/en/content/sg/statements/2025-01-15/secretary-generals-address-the-general-assembly-his-priorities-for-2025-bilingual-delivered-scroll-down-for-all-english-and-all-french

ILO & OECD. (2025). *Policy measures to address inequalities and increase the labour income share*. Paper prepared under South Africa's G20 Presidency. https://www.ilo.org/sites/default/files/2025-04/G20_Technical Paper%232_Policy%20measures%20to%20address%20inequalities%20and%20increase%20the%20labour%20income%20share.pdf

Milanovic, B. (2024). The three eras of global inequality, 1820-2020 with the focus on the past thirty years. *World Development, 177*, 106516. https://doi.org/10.1016/j.worlddev.2023.106516

Naïr, S. (2025). *Europa encadenada: El neoliberalismo contra la Unión*. Galaxia Gutenberg.

Oxfam. (2025). *Takers not makers. The unjust poverty and unearned wealth of colonialism*. Oxfam International. https://oi-files-d8-prod.s3.eu-west-2.amazonaws.com/s3fs-public/2025-01/English%20-%20Davos%20Full%20Report%202025.pdf.

Piketty, T. (2020). *Capital and ideology*. Harvard University Press (original version published in 2019).

Ritter, I., Burt, L., & Ferreira, B. (2024). *Net wealth taxes: How they can help fight inequality and fund sustainable development* (Policy Brief No. 168). United Nations Department of Economic and Social Affairs. https://desapublications.un.org/policy-briefs/un-desa-policy-brief-no-168-net-wealth-taxes-how-they-can-help-fight-inequality-and

Stiglitz, J. E. (2002). *Globalization and its discontents*. W. W. Norton & Company.

UBS. (2024). *Global wealth report 2024: Crafted wealth intelligence*. UBS. https://www.ubs.com/global/es/wealthmanagement/latamaccess/wealth-planning/global-wealth-report-2024.html

UN DESA (2020). *World social report 2020: Inequality in a rapidly changing world*. United Nations Department of Economic and Social Affairs. https://www.un.org/en/desa/world-social-report-2020

UN DESA (2024). *World social report 2024: Social development in times of converging crises: A call for global action*. United Nations Department of Economic and Social Affairs. https://desapublications.un.org/publications/world-social-report-2024-0

UN DESA (2025). *World social report 2025: A new policy consensus to accelerate social progress*. United Nations Department of Economic and Social Affairs. https://desapublications.un.org/sites/default/files/publications/2025-04/250422%20BLS25022%20UDS%20UN%20World%20Social%20Report%20WEB.pdf

Varoufakis, Y. (2023). *Technofeudalism: What killed capitalism*. Bodley Head.

CHAPTER 19

Decent Work

Joan Sanchis

1 The Challenge

In 1919, the leaders of Germany and the Allied Powers gathered in the French city of Versailles to sign the treaty that would officially end of World War I. Throughout the negotiations, there was a widespread belief that steps needed to be taken to prevent such a devastating conflict from happening again. International cooperation had to be strengthened and social unrest alleviated, through bold policy reforms. The heightened attention given to the needs of the working class following the 1917 Russian Revolution, coupled with the strength of the trade union movements in Europe and North America, presented an opportunity to address these demands politically. It was precisely with this spirit in mind that the International Labour Organization (ILO) was founded in 1919 as part of the Treaty of Versailles. The ILO's main goals were to promote social justice and improve working conditions worldwide as a prerequisite for peace and social inclusiveness (ILO, 1919).

J. Sanchis (✉)
University of Valencia, Valencia, Spain
e-mail: joan.sanchis@uv.es

R. de Arriba (ed.), *United Nations Facing Global Economic Disorder: Assessing 20 Policy Proposals*,
https://doi.org/10.1007/978-3-032-21952-7_19

In 1946, in the aftermath of World War II, the ILO became the first specialised agency of the newly established United Nations. The organisation played a pivotal role in the 1946–1980 period promoting the adoption of international labour standards through conventions and recommendations. Relevant issues addressed include supporting reduced working time schedules (ILO, 1962) and implementing measures against all forms of discrimination in the workplace (ILO, 1958).

The advent of globalisation in 1980s posed significant challenges to the ILO's mission. Harsh neoliberal reforms were promoted by conservative governments, particularly in the United States and the United Kingdom. These reforms severely eroded collective bargaining provisions and labour protections. On the other hand, the relocation of economic activity to lower-wage countries created new problems for global labour markets, such as dealing with unethical working conditions (forced labour and child labour) and coping with increased competitive pressures to make contractual labour relationships more flexible (Hermann, 2014).

Despite the economic opportunities generated by globalisation in developing countries, higher employment levels proved clearly insufficient to lift people out of poverty and exploitation. At the start of the millennium in 2000, the ILO estimated that 206 million children were still involved in production processes worldwide and its Director-General stated that globalisation had significantly worsened labour conditions for workers in the informal economy and rural communities of developing countries (ILO, 2002). Furthermore, the ILO argued that a new type of worker was emerging: the working poor. This category was comprised of 550 million people who, despite having a job earned less than one US dollar per day (ILO, 2003).

The situation in the labour market was becoming no less complicated in Western countries. In Europe, the notion of the Standard Employment Relationship (SER) as a reference for quality and predictable jobs was under severe threat (Bosch, 2004). The transition to a post-industrial, decentralised, global economy imposed high levels of competition that resulted in an increase in precarious, atypical forms of employment, and fuelled a destandardisation process of working time (Boulin et al., 2006; Burchell et al., 2024). Consequently, working conditions became harder, more uncertain, and insecure for a significant proportion of the population in both the Global South and industrialised countries during the 1990s and early 2000s.

In addition to these disruptive structural changes in global labour markets, there has been a notable growth in academic and social interest in the qualitative aspects of employment since at least the 1960s and 1970s. Issues such as health, wellbeing, and work-life balance became increasingly prevalent in the public debate, particularly during the 1990s (Burchell et al., 2013). Evidence in this regard accumulated over the years and was unequivocal. Having a job, regardless of its characteristics, was no longer enough for an increasing number of people, particularly for women and other disadvantaged workers in the informal economy. As evidence of this, in 2001 the ILO highlighted that 20% of the global workforce had no access to adequate social protection, a dire situation with profound economic and social consequences for both workers and companies (ILO, 2001).

In this context, meeting the ILO's foundational goal of promoting better and fairer working conditions worldwide had become a significant challenge for the organisation. There was a need to transition from focusing on quantitative indicators, such as the unemployment rate, to analysing more intricate qualitative indicators that could serve to assess real working conditions and the extent to which work improves people's lives. However, this is easier said than done. Setting new global benchmarks for employment standards required the development of a new analytical approach and a new comprehensive policy framework to support this mission. This was technically challenging due to the lack of internationally comparable data and politically complex given the ILO's tripartite structure, which gives equal voice to workers, employers, and governments.

2 UN Proposals

In response to the challenges posed by globalisation, the ILO adopted the Declaration on Fundamental Principles and Rights at Work in 1998 (ILO, 1998). This document reaffirms the previously adopted conventions and extends their applicability to all ILO Member States, even those that have not ratified each convention individually. The principles included in these conventions are:

a) Freedom of association and the effective recognition of the right to collective bargaining.

b) The elimination of all forms of forced or compulsory labour.
c) The effective abolition of child labour.
d) The elimination of discrimination with respect to employment and occupation.

In 1999, these set of principles were formalised in the concept of Decent Work, introduced by the Director-General of the ILO in his Report to the 87th International Labour Conference. Decent Work, as a proxy for job quality, was defined as "productive work for women and men in conditions of freedom, equity, security and human dignity" (ILO, 1999). The Decent Work framework is composed of four "inseparable, interrelated, and mutually supportive strategic objectives":

1. Increase employment opportunities with equal access for men and women.
2. Uphold the fundamental principles and rights at work established in ILO conventions.
3. Extend the social protection coverage, including social security and occupational safety and health.
4. Strengthen social dialogue between employers, workers, and governments.

Additionally, gender equality and non-discrimination are established as "cross-cutting principles of Decent Work"(ILO, 1999).

The Decent Work concept recognises the importance of employment in improving people's lives, while also acknowledging the need to consider the regulatory and social conditions under which work is carried out. In this sense, the Decent Work framework can be portrayed as the result of the ILO's efforts to provide a "social dimension" to globalisation, which has contributed to establish new principles for a "human-oriented" approach to international labour standards (Rantanen et al., 2020).

To deploy the Decent Work Agenda globally, the ILO has promoted the adoption of Decent Work Country Programmes (DWCPs). These programmes are designed at a national level by local stakeholders, with the support of the ILO's office. These plans establish priorities according to each country's specific situation and must engage employers' and workers' organisations in the design process. By May 2025, 51 countries had

had their DWCPs approved by their Regional ILO Director, and a further 15 were in the process of drafting them in consultation with social partners. Notably, the African continent has adopted the highest number of DWCPs (22), followed by Asia and the Pacific (16). Notably, only six European countries had adopted DWCPs by the aforementioned date (ILO, 2025).

The Decent Work Agenda has been tightly integrated into the United Nations' 2030 Sustainable Development Goals (SDG), which were adopted in 2015. The concept of decent work is directly integrated through SDG 8, which aims to: "Promote sustained, inclusive and sustainable economic growth, full and productive employment and decent work for all" (United Nations, 2015). As with all SDGs, a set of specific targets and indicators have been established to assess progress, most of which are directly related to the ILO's four core defining principles of decent work. Moreover, the ILO has been designated as a "custodian agency" responsible for reporting labour statistics on 14 decent work indicators spanning five of the 17 SDGs.

3 Assessment

The ILO's implementation of the Decent Work Agenda has been met with considerable scepticism resulting in limited engagement from both the academic community and local policymakers, particularly in Global North countries. This limited engagement with such an ambitious proposal can be partially attributed to the contrasting political interests embedded in the ILO but is also related to the significant limitations of the proposed approach. At least four critiques can be developed can be developed that severely constrain the capacity of the Decent Work Agenda to transform work globally for the better.

Firstly, an operationalisation effort is missing in the ILO initial inception of the framework. This implies that the concept of Decent Work is defined very broadly and relies mostly on subjective definitions that are, in practice, hard to measure. For instance, the concepts of "freedom" or "dignity" seem merely aspirational and can have very different meanings depending on the context. Moreover, as Burchell et al. (2013) point out, certain aspects that mainly concern individual workers—such as child and forced labour—are mixed with issues that have to be addressed at the aggregate level—for instance social protection legislation—with no coherent solutions proposed to conduct this integrated assessment. In these sense, the authors define Decent Work as "prematurely mandated", "extremely vague", and "all-encompassing".

In recent decades, efforts to operationalise the ILO's Decent Work framework have been identified in the academic literature. For example, Anker et al. (2003) have proposed a series of measurement categories and specific statistical indicators that aim to reflect the core principles of Decent Work. Similarly, Fields (2003) has discussed the practical implications of the concept from the point of view of consumer choice theory and conventional economic theory. More recently, the integration of the Decent Work Agenda into the 2030 SDGs has meant that specific indicators have been set for each target, helping to define some of the Decent Work dimensions more precisely (United Nations, 2015).

Secondly, even if the concept of Decent Work could be effectively operationalised in some manner, the lack of internationally comparable data is a severe limitation. The available labour statistics and measurement methods vary substantially across jurisdictions, hampering the universal approach that the Decent Work Agenda aspires to embody. Therefore, as Fields (2003) also discusses, any set of Decent Work indicators should be minimal and the ILO maybe often forced to use additional indicators in cases where comparable data does not exist. In contrast with these problems, Burchell et al. (2013) highlight the notable success of the European Union in producing a comparable set of labour statistics gathered through a harmonised survey methodology.

Thirdly, the aforementioned deficits in operationalisation and data gathering have often been linked to the political nature of the ILO. As a tripartite organisation in which workers, employers and governments are equally represented, reaching a consensus on action is often difficult due to contrasting interests. Employers' associations, for instance, seem to have usually opposed the collection of international data on sensitive labour issues. In this sense, Burchell et al. (2013) refer to their experience of conducting interviews with senior ILO officials to confirm the extent of these constraints and draw attention to the ILO's lack of political will to conduct more extensive data-gathering efforts on an international scale.

Finally, degrowth and post-work scholars have argued that the Decent Work Agenda contributes to reinforce a work-centred approach to social policy that ignores planetary boundaries and the unsustainability of the infinite economic growth paradigm. Despite the Decent Work definition encompassing multiple qualitative aspects of a job, increasing absolute employment and social inclusion through work still remains a core priority. As a response, Kreinin and Aigner (2022) have proposed an alternative vision for SDG 8 based on "sustainable work" and economic degrowth. The rationale for this critique seems well founded, as there is a proven correlation between working longer hours and higher carbon dioxide emissions (Schor, 2005). From this perspective, Strunk (2025) has discussed the potential of work-time reduction as an alternative paradigm to Decent Work, which could contribute to revalue non-work activities and reduce emissions in order to uphold the planet's biophysical boundaries.

In conclusion, it can be asserted that the ILO's Decent Work framework has been a significant milestone in the organisation's efforts to address labour market challenges on a global scale within the UN institutional framework. The formulation of Decent Work as a multifaceted concept that transcends mere quantitative approaches to employment rates has opened up new policy frontiers and set a global benchmark for labour quality standards. However, the concept's vague definition, the absence of concrete measurement methodologies and internationally comparable data, and the ILO's internal political differences have hindered the real impact of this novel approach. At least two crucial tasks remain if a modern, global approach to labour policy is to be achieved. The first involves greater data-gathering efforts, and the second involves transitioning to a more ambitious Decent Work formulation that encompasses environmental sustainability and a more holistic vision of work, not exclusively limited to remunerated activities.

References

Anker, R., Chernyshev, I., Egger, P., Mehran, F., & Ritter, J. A. (2003). Measuring decent work with statistical indicators. *International Labour Review, 142*(2), 147–178. https://doi.org/10.1111/j.1564-913x.2003.tb00257.x

Bosch, G. (2004). Towards a new standard employment relationship in Western Europe. *British Journal of Industrial Relations, 42*(4), 617–636. https://doi.org/10.1111/j.1467-8543.2004.00333.x

Boulin, J.-Y., Lallement, M., Messenger, J. C., & Michon, F. (2006). *Decent working time: New trends, new issues*. International Labour Office.

Burchell, B., Deakin, S., Rubery, J., & Spencer, D. A. (2024). The future of work and working time: Introduction to special issue. *Cambridge Journal of Economics, 48*(1), 1–24. https://doi.org/10.1093/cje/bead057

Burchell, B., Sehnbruch, K., Piasna, A., & Agloni, N. (2013). The quality of employment and decent work: Definitions, methodologies, and ongoing debates. *Cambridge Journal of Economics, 38*(2), 459–477. https://doi.org/10.1093/cje/bet067

Fields, G. S. (2003). Decent work and development policies. *International Labour Review, 142*(2), 239–262. https://doi.org/10.1111/j.1564-913x.2003.tb00260.x

Hermann, C. (2014). *Capitalism and the political economy of work time.* Routledge.

ILO. (1919). *Constitution of the International Labour Organisation.* International Labour Organisation. https://www.refworld.org/legal/agreements/ilo/1919/en/47521

ILO. (1958). *Discrimination (employment and occupation) recommendation.* International Labour Organization.

ILO. (1962). *R116-reduction of hours of work recommendation (no. 116).* International Labour Organisation. https://normlex.ilo.org/dyn/normlex/en/f?p=NORMLEXPUB:12100:0::NO::P12100_ILO_CODE:R116

ILO. (1998). *Declaration on fundamental principles and rights at work.* International Labour Organisation. https://www.ilo.org/declaration/thedeclaration/textdeclaration/lang–en/index.htm

ILO. (1999). *Report of the director-general: Decent work.* International Labour Organisation. https://webapps.ilo.org/public/english/standards/relm/ilc/ilc87/rep-i.htm

ILO. (2001). *Reducing the decent work deficit: A global challenge.* International Labour Organization.

ILO. (2002). A future without child labour: Global report under the follow-up to the ILO declaration on fundamental principles and rights at work. International Labour Organization. https://www.ilo.org/publications/future-without-child-labour-global-report-under-follow-ilo-declaration

ILO. (2003). *Global employment trends 2003.* International Labour Organization. https://www.ilo.org/publications/global-employment-trends-2003

ILO. (2025). *Status of Decent Work Country Programme Development by Region (as at 15 May 2025).* https://www.ilo.org/resource/other/status-decent-work-country-programme-development-region-15-may-2025

Kreinin, H., & Aigner, E. (2022). From "decent work and economic growth" to "sustainable work and economic degrowth": A new framework for SDG 8. *Empirica, 49*(2), 281–311. https://doi.org/10.1007/s10663-021-09526-5

Rantanen, J., Muchiri, F., & Lehtinen, S. (2020). Decent work, ILO'S response to the globalization of working life: Basic concepts and global implementation with special reference to occupational health. *International Journal of Environmental Research and Public Health, 17*(10), 3351. https://doi.org/10.3390/ijerph17103351

Schor, J. (2005). Sustainable consumption and Worktime reduction. *Journal of Industrial Ecology, 9*(1–2), 37–50. https://doi.org/10.1162/1088198054084581

Strunk, B. (2025). Degrowth and decent work. *Chapters*, 526–537. https://ideas.repec.org//h/elg/eechap/21934_42.html

United Nations. (2015). *Transforming our world: The 2030 agenda for sustainable development*. United Nations. https://sdgs.un.org/2030agenda

CHAPTER 20

Migration

Carlos Ochando Claramunt

1 The Challenge

While most migration occurs within national borders as internal movement, international migration flows remain significant and have continued to increase over time. According to the United Nations estimates, there are approximately 281 million international migrants worldwide, accounting for 3.6% of the global population in 2020. Of this total, 135 million are women (3.5% of the global female population) and 146 million are men (3.7% of the global male population), meaning that 51.9% of international migrants are male and 48.1% are female. Additionally, around 28 million migrants are children, representing 1.4% of the world's child population (McAuliffe & Oucho, 2024).

Historical data show that the number of people forced to move—both within their own countries and to neighboring ones—is steadily increasing. In other words, international migration is on a clear upward trend. Estimates indicate there were 84.5 million international migrants in 1970, around 153 million in 1990, and nearly 281 million in 2020

C. O. Claramunt (✉)
University of Valencia, Valencia, Spain
e-mail: carlos.ochando@uv.es

R. de Arriba (ed.), *United Nations Facing Global Economic Disorder: Assessing 20 Policy Proposals*,
https://doi.org/10.1007/978-3-032-21952-7_20

(McAuliffe & Oucho, 2024). These figures do not include internal migrants, who account the majority of migration within continents, with an estimated 800 million people moving within their own countries. The main drivers of migration are well established: violent conflicts (wars), disparities in development, climate-related disasters, lack of opportunities for highly skilled populations, and gender discrimination.

Migration is a phenomenon that profoundly affects economic growth, employment, demographics, the welfare state, and the social and political cohesion of societies. Although immigration offers significant benefits to host countries—such as boosting economic growth, filling labor gaps, and supporting the funding and sustainability of welfare systems—it also poses considerable social and political challenges.

Undoubtedly, a major challenge is preventing migrant deaths and improving the safety of journeys to other countries. According to the latest UN data for 2023, there were 8500 recorded deaths—the highest figure in the series (McAuliffe & Oucho, 2024).

While this is the most urgent issue, it is far from being the only one. Increasing international migration flows pose significant challenges for both the United Nations and individual countries, whether they are sending or receiving migrants. Some of these challenges include:

- Safeguarding the human rights of migrants.
- Countering rising xenophobia, particularly with the growth of far-right movements.
- Developing solutions to regularize migrants in host countries and address irregular migration.
- Managing and regulating the entry of migrants at borders.
- Supporting economic development and expanding opportunities in countries of origin, to mitigate the loss of talent and human capital.
- Combating criminal networks that traffic and profit from exploiting migrants.

One key challenge affecting not only the United Nations but also governments, institutions, political parties, and citizens committed to human rights is the fight against misinformation, myths, and falsehoods spread by far-right parties and ideologues who exploit migration to polarize and divide the population ideologically (De Haas, 2024). Far-right populists falsely claim that international migration is to blame for the problems facing developed economies and democracies, even though it in fact makes a significantly positive contribution to the welfare-state economics of developed host countries. Actually, the fiscal impact of migration is typically positive, supporting the economic sustainability of social welfare systems. While there is extensive empirical evidence to back this, clear and transparent communication to the public remains insufficient (Damas de Matos, 2021; Dustmann & Frattini, 2014; Fernández & Vargas-Silva, 2022; Giulietti & Wahba, 2013; Giulietti, 2014; Rowthorn, 2008; Sriskandarajah et al., 2005; Vargas-Silva, 2014).

2 UN Proposals

The United Nations does not pass mandatory or legally binding laws. Instead, its role is to promote principles and policy recommendations on migration, serving as guidance for countries. Its primary aim is to encourage the development of more coordinated, comprehensive, and humane migration policies. These principles and recommendations can be traced through:

1. The documents, pacts, and agreements that have been approved.
2. The declarations and resolutions of the General Assembly
3. The institutions that have been established, primarily UN Migration, the International Organization for Migration (IOM), the United Nations Human Rights Council, and the United Nations High Commissioner for Refugees (UNHCR).

Among the key documents and agreements adopted by the UN since 1948, the following are particularly noteworthy:

- *Universal Declaration of Human Rights*. Adopted by the General Assembly on 10 December 1948, UN Doc A/RES/217(III).
- *Convention Relating to the Status of Refugees* (adopted 28 July 1951, entered into force 22 April 1954) and ***Protocol Relating to the Status of Refugees*** (adopted 31 January 1967, entered into force 4 October 1967).
- ***International Convention on the Protection of the Rights of All Migrant Workers and Members of Their Families* (1990).** Adopted 18 December 1990, UN Doc A/RES/45/158.

- *Guidelines on Migration and Development*. High-level Dialogue on International Migration and Development (United Nations General Assembly, 2006).
- *Declaration of the High-level Dialogue on International Migration and Development*. Resolution A/RES/68/4.
- *New York Declaration for Refugees and Migrants*. Resolution A/RES/71/1.
- *Global Compact for Safe, Orderly and Regular Migration* (A/RES/73/195). Adopted 19 December 2018 (United Nations General Assembly, 2018).
- *Towards a Human Rights-Based Approach to Migration: Training Guide* (Professional Training Series No. 26). United Nations Office of the High Commissioner for Human Rights (OHCHR, 2023).

In summary, the United Nations' efforts on migration can be grouped into two focus areas:

1. To strengthen global migration governance and
2. To promote a comprehensive approach to migration policies.

The priority has undoubtedly been on advancing global migration governance, encouraging member states to work toward shared objectives and a common vision on migration. This effort has been developed through a networking approach, including numerous meetings, commissions, and forums. It began with the creation of the 2003 Global Commission on International Migration (GCIM). Later, two key networks were established: the Global Refugee Network and the United Nations Network on Migration. Following the 2013 Global Forum on Migration and Development (GFMD), the most important milestone was the 2018 Global Compact for Safe, Orderly, and Regular Migration. In 2022, the Compact was evaluated through the First International Migration Review Forum, resulting in the Progress Declaration.

The United Nations describes migration governance as a multi-stakeholder system—led by the UN—that emphasizes greater transparency, a rights-and obligations-based approach, and the implementation of innovative policies in collaboration with states and international organizations. According to the IOM, migration governance consists of a combination of legal frameworks, laws, regulations, policies, and traditions, as well as organizational structures at subnational, national, regional, and international levels, along with processes that guide and regulate state actions. A key objective of this governance model is to promote international cooperation.

The 2018 Global Compact for Safe, Orderly, and Regular Migration represents the most important milestone for the United Nations in the field of migration. Endorsed by 150 countries, the Compact advances Target 10.7 of the Sustainable Development Goals (SDG 10) from the 2030 Agenda, which aims to "facilitate orderly, safe, regular, and responsible migration, including through well-managed and planned migration policies." It also supports SDG 8, which focuses on decent work and economic growth. Serving as the UN's main framework for migration action, the 2018 Global Compact sets out 23 non-binding objectives:

1. Collect and use accurate, disaggregated data to inform evidence-based policies.
2. Minimize adverse and structural factors that force people to leave their countries of origin.
3. Provide timely and accurate information at all stages of migration.
4. Ensure that all migrants have proper legal and documented proof of identity.
5. Increase the availability and flexibility of regular migration pathways.
6. Facilitate fair and ethical recruitment and safeguard conditions that guarantee decent work.
7. Address and reduce vulnerabilities in migration.
8. Save lives and undertake coordinated international initiatives for missing migrants.
9. Strengthen transnational responses to the illicit trafficking of migrants.
10. Prevent, combat, and eradicate human trafficking in the context of migration.
11. Manage borders in an integrated, safe, and coordinated manner.
12. Enhance the certainty and predictability of migration procedures for proper background checks, assessment, and referral.
13. Use migrant detention only as a last resort and seek alternative measures.
14. Improve protection, assistance, and consular cooperation throughout the migration cycle.

15. Provide migrants with access to basic services.
16. Empower migrants and societies to achieve full inclusion and social cohesion.
17. Eliminate all forms of discrimination and promote evidence-based public discourse to change perceptions of migration.
18. Invest in skills development and facilitate the mutual recognition of skills, qualifications, and competencies.
19. Create the conditions for migrants and diasporas to fully contribute to sustainable development in all countries.
20. Promote faster, safer, and more affordable remittance transfers and encourage the financial inclusion of migrants.
21. Collaborate to facilitate safe return and readmission, as well as sustainable reintegration.
22. Establish mechanisms for the portability of social security and acquired benefits.
23. Strengthen international cooperation and global partnerships for safe, orderly, and regular migration.

The second key focus of the United Nations has been on promoting a comprehensive approach to migration policies. What does this UN-endorsed approach entail? (IOM, 2023; UN DESA, 2023; United Nations Secretary-General, 2024). Its core principles are naturally based on the objectives outlined in the 2018 Global Compact. Some of the main recommendations are summarized below:

1. Advocate for safe, orderly, and regular migration (promote multilateral agreements to facilitate legal pathways and support the elimination of dangerous irregular routes).
2. Protect and promote the rights of all migrants (protection from abuse, right to life, security, and freedom; prevention of arbitrary detention and discrimination; right to seek asylum and international protection).
3. Provide guidance, recommendations, and principles to improve effective and inclusive migration policies (responsible management of international migration flows).
4. Strengthen and promote international cooperation (address root causes such as poverty, violence, and climate change; improve

economic opportunities in countries of origin; exchange of data and information, etc.).

5. Support countries of origin, transit, and destination (ensure a fairer distribution of responsibilities among countries).
6. Conduct campaigns to combat xenophobia and discrimination (raise public awareness and provide education on the benefits of migration).
7. Promote the socio-economic inclusion of migrants (access to basic services such as health and education).
8. Combat human trafficking, migrant smuggling, and irregular migration.
9. Encourage policies for migrant integration and inclusion (social cohesion, intercultural understanding, life opportunities, recognition of qualifications and skills, etc.).
10. Reduce vulnerabilities in migration and facilitate safe and dignified return and reintegration.

3 Assessment

It is difficult to take issue with the United Nations' well-intentioned migration proposals, which are based on respect for human rights, international cooperation, integration and inclusion, safe, orderly, and regular migration, and sustainable development. However, there are valid reasons for adopting a critical perspective—not because the goals themselves lack merit, but because their effectiveness and real-world impact are limited. The main weakness of these proposals, which hinders their implementation, is their non-binding nature, such as the 2018 Global Compact for Safe, Orderly, and Regular Migration. Their broad and vague language further reduces their practicality for enacting concrete measures. Additionally, despite the emphasis on international cooperation, migration policy remains the sovereign responsibility of each state. Another limitation is the insufficient funding of key agencies like the IOM and UNHCR, which often rely on voluntary contributions.

These four factors—the voluntary nature of objectives, the generality of proposals, lack of authority over state policies, and limited financial resources—significantly weaken the UN's ability to coordinate and regulate international migration flows. This weakness is further amplified by the rise of authoritarian and xenophobic governments, including autocratic, nationalist, populist, and far-right regimes, that scapegoat migration for economic challenges in developed societies. These governments actively foster distrust toward multilateral institutions like the UN, often through misinformation and falsehoods about migration, while criticizing their effectiveness and reinforcing restrictive, authoritarian national control over borders.

Despite these criticisms, it is worth considering a counterfactual scenario: what would the state of international migration be like without a transnational institution such as the United Nations that has helped establish fundamental global principles? Undoubtedly, the situation would be far worse. Therefore, the solution lies in genuinely strengthening the UN's role, rather than weakening it as far-right governments and parties attempt to do. Unfortunately, current geopolitical trends seem to be moving in the opposite direction.

References

Damas de Matos, A. (2021). The fiscal impact of immigration in OECD countries since the mid-2000s. In *OECD international migration outlook 2021* (pp. 111–162). OECD Publishing.

De Haas, H. (2024). *How migration really works 22 things you need to know about the Most divisive issue in politics*. Penguin Books.

Dustmann, C., & Frattini, T. (2014). The fiscal effects of immigration to the UK. *The Economic Journal, 124*(580), 593–643. https://doi.org/10.1111/ecoj.12181

Fernández, M., & Vargas-Silva, C. (2022). *Migrants and housing in the UK*. Migration Observatory, University of Oxford.

Giulietti, C. (2014). The welfare magnet hypothesis and the welfare take-up of immigrants. IZA world of labor, 37. IZA Institute of Labor Economics.

Giulietti, C., & Wahba, J. (2013). Welfare migration. In A. F. Constant & K. F. Zimmermann (Eds.), *International handbook on the economics of migration* (pp. 489–504). Edward Elgar Publishing.

IOM. (2023). *International migration policies and governance*. United Nations International Organization for Migration.

McAuliffe, M., & Oucho, L. A. (Eds.). (2024). *World migration report 2024*. International Organization for Migration.

OHCHR (2023). Towards a human rights-based approach to migration: Training guide (Professional Training Series No. 26). United Nations Office of the High Commissioner for Human Rights.

Rowthorn, R. (2008). The fiscal impact of immigration on the advanced economies. *Oxford Review of Economic Policy, 24*(3), 560–580. https://doi.org/10.1093/oxrep/grn023

Sriskandarajah, D., Cooley, L., Reed, H., & Latorre, M. (2005). *Paying their way: The fiscal contribution of immigrants in the UK*. Institute for Public Policy Research.

UN DESA. (2023). *International migration and sustainable development* (UN DESA/POP/2023/TR/no. 7). United Nations Department of Economic and Social Affairs, Population Division.

United Nations General Assembly (2018). Global compact for safe, orderly and regular migration. Resolution A/RES/73/195. United Nations.

United Nations Secretary-General. (2024). *Report on the implementation of the global compact for safe, orderly and regular migration (a/79/590)*. United Nations.

Vargas-Silva, C. (2014). *The fiscal impact of immigration in the UK*. Migration Observatory, University of Oxford.

CHAPTER 21

Tourism

Paula Simó-Tomás

1 The Challenge

Tourism is one of the most visible faces of globalization. It symbolizes mobility, cultural contact, and economic integration, but also reflects the contradictions and vulnerabilities of the current international order. As the United Nations has recognized, tourism has the potential to contribute directly to sustainable development, poverty reduction, and intercultural dialogue (United Nations, 2015). Yet, its rapid and largely uneven expansion over the last decades has generated environmental pressures, social tensions, and economic dependencies that pose major challenges for governance at both the national and international level.

Environmental pressure and climate change remain among the most pressing issues. Transport associated with tourism, particularly aviation, contributes substantially to greenhouse gas emissions. Recent estimates indicate that global tourism accounted for 8.8% of greenhouse gas emissions in 2019, or 5.2 Gt of CO_2 equivalent, a significant increase from

P. Simó-Tomás (✉)
University of Valencia, Valencia, Spain
e-mail: paula.simo@uv.es

R. de Arriba (ed.), *United Nations Facing Global Economic Disorder: Assessing 20 Policy Proposals*,
https://doi.org/10.1007/978-3-032-21952-7_21

earlier figures (Sun et al., 2024). Beyond emissions, tourism places enormous pressure on fragile ecosystems, including coastal and mountain areas, accelerating biodiversity loss and resource scarcity (Gössling & Higham, 2021). The paradox is that the very landscapes and ecosystems that attract tourists are those most at risk from their uncontrolled expansion.

The phenomenon of overtourism further illustrates tourism's contradictions. Defined by UNWTO (2018) as the excessive impact of tourism on residents' quality of life and visitor satisfaction, overtourism has become acute in emblematic urban and heritage destinations such as Venice, Barcelona, and Machu Picchu. These dynamics produce housing shortages, rising costs of living, and social conflict, while degrading the visitor experience (Milano et al., 2019). The growth of digital platforms such as Airbnb and Booking.com has exacerbated these pressures, encouraging speculative investment in housing markets and accelerating gentrification. What once was a local issue has become globalized, with similar complaints emerging from Amsterdam to Lisbon, from Prague to Kyoto.

Tourism also generates sociocultural disruptions. While it can foster appreciation of cultural heritage, it often commodifies traditions, displaces communities, and erodes intangible practices. Urban congestion, noise, and waste aggravate local resistance, while speculative investment linked to tourism accelerates gentrification processes (Smith & Richards, 2013). Moreover, cultural homogenization is a growing concern: standardized tourism products and the dominance of global hotel chains and restaurant franchises reduce cultural distinctiveness, replacing local diversity with uniform global brands.

Economic vulnerability is another central challenge. Tourism represents—approximately—the 10% of global GDP and one in ten jobs before the COVID-19 crisis (UNWTO, 2021). Yet this dependence exposes entire economies to external shocks. The pandemic precipitated a collapse of 72% in international arrivals in 2020, threatening the fiscal stability of many states, particularly Small Island Developing States (SIDS), where tourism accounts for over 40% of GDP (UNWTO, 2023a). Similar patterns of vulnerability linked to high tourism dependency have also been identified in comparative policy analyses conducted by the Organisation for Economic Co-operation and Development (OECD, 2024). Beyond pandemics, natural disasters, financial crises, and geopolitical instability all demonstrate how fragile an overdependence on tourism can be. The war in Ukraine, for example, has severely reduced flows to Eastern Europe and disrupted global air connectivity, illustrating how quickly external shocks reverberate across the sector.

Labor conditions are an additional area of concern. Tourism employment is often seasonal, low paid, and precarious, with limited access to social protection. Women and youth are overrepresented in these positions, reflecting wider patterns of inequality in the global labor market (Gössling & Hall, 2019). This raises questions about the quality of tourism-driven development: while it generates jobs, it often reproduces structural inequities rather than alleviating them. Migrant workers in the Gulf, seasonal workers in the Mediterranean, and informal service providers in Southeast Asia all exemplify the precarious realities behind the statistics.

Finally, governance and measurement gaps persist. Despite the explicit inclusion of tourism in the SDGs, many states lack institutional frameworks or data systems to monitor the sector's impacts. SDG target 12.b calls for the development of sustainable tourism monitoring tools, but progress remains uneven. The UNWTO's Measuring the Sustainability of Tourism (MST) framework offers a step forward, but adoption has been slow. Without robust and comparable data, policymaking is reactive and fragmented, undermining accountability and long-term planning (United Nations, 2015). Moreover, fragmented governance across different UN agencies (UNWTO, UNEP, UNDP, ICAO) complicates coordination and dilutes effectiveness.

In sum, the challenges of tourism in the context of globalization are multidimensional. They encompass climate change, environmental degradation, overtourism, cultural homogenization, labor precarity, economic vulnerability, and institutional weakness. These tensions underscore the urgency of coherent and effective governance at the global level, as well as the central role of the United Nations in shaping the future of tourism.

2 UN Proposals

The United Nations, through UNWTO and in cooperation with other agencies, has advanced a broad set of proposals to align tourism with sustainable development and global governance. One key achievement has been the integration of tourism into the 2030 Agenda. SDG target 8.9 emphasizes policies for sustainable tourism that generate jobs and promote local culture. Target 12.b calls for monitoring systems to assess tourism's impacts. And target 14.7 highlights the role of tourism in supporting economic benefits for SIDS and least developed countries (United Nations, 2015). These provisions provide a normative framework that positions tourism within global development priorities.

In terms of measurement, UNWTO has promoted the Measuring the Sustainability of Tourism (MST) initiative. Together with the UN Statistics Division and partner organizations, it developed a Statistical Framework for Measuring the Sustainability of Tourism (SF-MST), which establishes standardized concepts, definitions, and indicators. This complements the Tourism Satellite Account (TSA), which measures tourism's economic contribution within national accounts (UNWTO, 2015, 2023b).

Another major proposal concerns sustainable investment. In 2025, UNWTO and UNCTAD launched the Guiding Principles for Sustainable Investment in Tourism, establishing criteria for aligning financial flows with the SDGs. These principles address governance, economic, sociocultural, and environmental dimensions, encouraging investors and governments to prioritize projects that respect cultural heritage, generate quality employment, and mitigate environmental impacts (UNCTAD & UNWTO, 2025). Comparable , concerns regarding the need to reorient tourism investment toward resilience and sustainability have also been highlighted in recent OECD policy assessments (OECD, 2024).

The UN has also advanced proposals for climate action and biodiversity protection in the tourism sector. Climate action has been primarily articulated through the Glasgow Declaration on Climate Action in Tourism, launched at the twenty-sixth Conference of the Parties (COP26) as a voluntary global framework encouraging governments and tourism stakeholders to align the sector with the objectives of the Paris Agreement and to integrate tourism considerations into national climate strategies (UNWTO & UNEP, 2021). At COP29 in Baku in 2024, more than 50 countries signed the Declaration for Enhanced Climate Action in Tourism, committing to incorporate tourism into their Nationally Determined Contributions (NDCs) (Reuters, 2024). In parallel, biodiversity-related initiatives promoted within the UN system increasingly frame tourism within a "nature-positive" approach aligned with the Kunming–Montreal Global Biodiversity Framework. This perspective emphasizes the need to halt and reverse biodiversity loss across economic sectors, including tourism, through evidence-based and cross-sectoral strategies (Convention on Biological Diversity, 2022; UNDP, 2023).

Finally, symbolic initiatives have helped raise awareness. The General Assembly declared 2017 as the International Year of Sustainable Tourism for Development and 2027 as the International Year of Sustainable and Resilient Tourism. Both designations highlight tourism's potential for poverty reduction, gender equality, cultural preservation, and environmental sustainability (2024; United Nations General Assembly, 2017).

3 Assessment

The United Nations' proposals for tourism sector present significant strengths but also notable limitations. Among the most important strengths is the formal recognition of tourism within the Sustainable Development Goals. The inclusion of specific targets under SDG 8, SDG 12, and SDG 14 provides a shared global framework for action and has helped elevate the status of tourism from a marginal economic activity to a legitimate development priority. This institutional recognition has encouraged governments and international organizations to adopt policies that link tourism to employment generation, cultural preservation, and sustainable consumption. Countries such as Costa Rica have used SDG frameworks to justify investments in ecotourism, while Bhutan has linked its "high value, low volume" tourism strategy to broader sustainable development objectives.

Measurement initiatives also represent a notable advance. The Measuring the Sustainability of Tourism (MST) framework is a pioneering attempt to harmonize statistical approaches, enabling governments to assess tourism's economic, environmental, and social impacts in a comparable manner. Pilot projects in Mexico and the Philippines show that when adopted, MST indicators can significantly improve policy coherence, allowing tourism planning to be integrated into national accounts and environmental reporting systems. This not only enhances accountability but also reduces the risk of greenwashing, a common criticism of tourism strategies. However, the effectiveness of such tools ultimately depends on national administrative capacity and political commitment (OECD, 2024).

Another major strength is the attempt to redirect financial flows through the Guiding Principles for Sustainable Investment in Tourism. The explicit integration of governance, sociocultural, and environmental criteria into investment decisions helps counter the longstanding problem of capital leakage from host countries, where large portions of tourism revenue return to international airlines, hotel chains, or digital platforms. By encouraging community participation and local benefit-sharing, these principles create opportunities for more equitable forms of tourism development, particularly in Africa and Asia, where dependence on foreign investment is high. Early experiences in Kenya and Rwanda illustrate the potential of these guidelines, as governments have begun to integrate them into investment codes for ecotourism and cultural tourism projects (Hall et al., 2023).

Climate-oriented initiatives within the UN tourism agenda illustrate both progress and persistent limitations. The most prominent example is the Glasgow Declaration on Climate Action in Tourism. While the Declaration has contributed to raising awareness and mobilizing commitments, its voluntary nature and the absence of binding enforcement mechanisms have limited its capacity to deliver measurable emissions reductions to date (UNWTO & UNEP, 2021). In parallel, biodiversity-oriented approaches promoted within the UN system reveal both opportunities and constraints. While the adoption of a "nature-positive" framing aligned with the Kunming-Montreal Global Biodiversity Framework signals a growing awareness of tourism's dependence on healthy ecosystems, it largely remains at the level of strategic orientation rather than operational transformation. In practice, the translation of biodiversity commitments into tourism planning continues to rely on project-based interventions and voluntary uptake, with uneven impacts across regions. This limits the capacity of nature-positive narratives to systematically reconfigure tourism development pathways, particularly in highly resource-dependent contexts such as the Pacific Islands, where UNDP-supported community-based marine and coastal tourism initiatives illustrate how tourism can generate local income while directly contributing to conservation objectives and sustainable resource management (UNDP, 2021).

Finally, symbolic initiatives such as the International Years of Sustainable Tourism (2017 and 2027) have had tangible awareness-raising effects. In 2017, more than 1500 initiatives were launched worldwide, ranging from local educational campaigns to international conferences. While their impact on structural change is debatable, they have undeniably raised the visibility of tourism as a policy domain within the UN system and beyond. The upcoming International Year of Sustainable and Resilient Tourism in 2027 is expected to reinforce this momentum, particularly with a stronger focus on resilience in the aftermath of the COVID-19 crisis.

Despite these advances, important weaknesses persist. UN instruments remain non-binding, relying on voluntary compliance by states and private actors. This voluntarism undermines enforcement and creates highly uneven implementation across regions, a challenge also identified in recent European policy discussions on tourism transition (European Commission, 2022). In practice, European Union member states, which already have relatively strong regulatory frameworks, have been able to integrate MST indicators and sustainability criteria more effectively, while many African and Pacific states lack the financial and institutional resources to do so. The result is a widening gap between regions, with the risk of reproducing global asymmetries in sustainability governance (UNWTO, 2023b; United Nations, n.d.).

Climate initiatives face particular obstacles. Although tourism is increasingly mentioned in climate discussions, concrete measures to reduce emissions remain marginal. Aviation, the single largest contributor to tourism-related emissions, remains under the jurisdiction of the International Civil Aviation Organization, where progress toward binding emission reductions has been slow and contested. Similarly, cruise tourism, another high-emission subsector, has received little attention in UN proposals. This creates a credibility gap: while the UN promotes ambitious climate goals for tourism, the absence of binding measures in aviation and shipping undermines their effectiveness. Even the voluntary initiatives advanced under the Glasgow Declaration on Climate Action in Tourism have yet to generate measurable reductions in emissions, and most signatory organizations lack concrete roadmaps for achieving net zero (UNWTO & UNEP, 2021). As Peeters et al. (2019) argue, achieving sustainable futures for tourism transport requires systemic transformations that go far beyond voluntary commitments.

Social justice concerns also remain under-addressed. Tourism continues to rely on precarious labor, often informal, seasonal, and poorly paid. Women and young workers are disproportionately concentrated in these positions, and migrant laborers often face exploitative conditions. UN proposals emphasize aggregate sustainability outcomes but rarely confront these inequalities directly. Without explicit commitments to labor rights, social protection, and gender equity, there is a risk that the sector's contribution to inclusive development remains superficial. For example, while the UN has promoted women's participation in tourism entrepreneurship, less attention has been given to structural barriers such as access to credit, land ownership, and training.

Another weakness is governance fragmentation. Tourism touches on multiple domains including environment, trade, transport, and culture, but institutional responsibilities within the UN remain dispersed. UNWTO leads on tourism, UNEP addresses environmental dimensions, UNDP links tourism to development, UNESCO covers heritage, and ICAO oversees aviation. While inter-agency cooperation has increased, coordination remains ad hoc and limited. This fragmentation weakens the coherence of global tourism governance and complicates implementation for member states, especially those with limited administrative capacity. For instance, a state may adopt MST indicators but lack mechanisms to connect them with climate reporting to the United Nations Framework Convention on Climate Change (UNFCCC), or with cultural heritage reporting to UNESCO. The absence of a clear coordinating mechanism means that duplication and overlap persist, reducing efficiency and effectiveness.

Symbolic initiatives, although useful, also reveal the gap between discourse and practice. International Years generate momentum, but without binding follow-up mechanisms, their influence tends to fade once the commemorative year ends. This cyclical pattern risks producing what Gössling and Hall (2019) describe as soft governance without hard results. Awareness campaigns, conferences, and declarations alone cannot deliver the structural changes needed in global tourism, particularly when confronted with powerful interests in aviation, real estate, and digital platforms.

In conclusion, the United Nations has made notable progress in positioning tourism within global governance. Its proposals advance sustainability, measurement, investment, and environmental protection and represent a significant evolution in the way the sector is conceived internationally. Yet their effectiveness remains constrained by voluntarism, unequal capacities, fragmented governance, and insufficient mechanisms to address structural inequalities and climate emissions. Unless these gaps are resolved, there is a danger that UN proposals will remain aspirational rather than transformative. To avoid this outcome, the UN system must move toward stronger accountability frameworks, increased financial and technical support for vulnerable states, and a more explicit integration of equity and justice into its tourism agenda. Only by doing so can tourism genuinely contribute to sustainable globalization rather than reproducing its contradictions.

References

Convention on Biological Diversity. (2022). *Kunming-Montreal global biodiversity framework: Decision adopted by the conference of the parties to the convention on biological diversity (decision 15/4)*. United Nations Digital Library. https://www.cbd.int/doc/decisions/cop-15/cop-15-dec-04-en.pdf

European Commission. (2022). *Transition pathway for tourism: Building a more resilient, innovative and sustainable ecosystem*. Publications Office of the European Union. https://op.europa.eu/en/publication-detail/-/publication/678c08ab-bc06-11ee-b164-01aa75ed71a1

Gössling, S., & Hall, C. M. (2019). Tourism and the Anthropocene. *Channel View Publications*.

Gössling, S., & Higham, J. (2021). The low-carbon imperative: Destination management under urgent climate change. *Journal of Travel Research, 60*(6), 1167–1179. https://doi.org/10.1177/0047287520933679

Hall, C. M., Seyfi, S., & Naderi Koupaei, S. (2023). Politics and the sustainable development goals: Tourism agenda 2030 perspective. *Tourism Review, 78*(2), 314–320. https://doi.org/10.1108/TR-10-2022-0498

Milano, C., Cheer, J. M., & Novelli, M. (2019). *Overtourism: Excesses, discontents and measures in travel and tourism*. CABI.

OECD. (2024). *OECD tourism trends and policies 2024*. Organisation for Economic Co-operation and Development. https://www.oecd.org/en/publications/2024/07/oecd-tourism-trends-and-policies-2024_17ff33a3.html

Peeters, P., Higham, J., Kutzner, D., Cohen, S., & Gössling, S. (2019). Are technology myths stalling aviation climate policy? *Transportation Research Part D: Transport and Environment, 44*, 30–42. https://doi.org/10.1016/j.trd.2016.02.004

Reuters. (2024, November 20). *More than 50 countries sign UN sustainable tourism declaration*. Reuters. https://www.reuters.com/sustainability/more-than-50-countries-sign-un-sustainable-tourism-declaration-2024-11-20/

Smith, M. K., & Richards, G. (2013). *The Routledge handbook of cultural tourism*. Routledge.

Sun, Y. Y., Faturay, F., Lenzen, M., Gössling, S., & Higham, J. E. S. (2024). Drivers of global tourism carbon emissions. *Nature Communications, 15*, 10384. https://doi.org/10.1038/s41467-024-54582-7

UNCTAD & UNWTO. (2025). *Guiding principles for sustainable investment in tourism*. United Nations World Tourism Organization. https://doi.org/10.18111/9789284425389

UNDP. (2021). *Pacific multi-country programme document (2023–2027)*. United Nations Development Programme. https://www.undp.org/pacific/publications/multi-country-programme-document-2023-2027

UNDP. (2023). *Navigating towards a nature-positive future: Strategic uptake of evidence towards tangible biodiversity solutions*. United Nations Development Programme. https://www.undp.org/publications/navigating-towards-nature-positive-future-strategic-uptake-evidence-towards-tangible-biodiversity-solutions

United Nations. (2015). *Transforming our world: The 2030 Agenda for Sustainable Development* (A/RES/70/1). https://sdgs.un.org/2030agenda

United Nations. (n.d.). SIDS accelerated modalities of action (Samoa) pathway. United Nations Office of the High Representative for the Least Developed Countries, Landlocked Developing Countries and Small Island Developing States. https://www.un.org/ohrlls/content/samoa-pathway

United Nations General Assembly (2017). International year of sustainable tourism for development. Resolution A/RES/70/193. United Nations.

United Nations General Assembly (2024). International year of sustainable and resilient tourism. Resolution A/RES/78/260. United Nations.

UNWTO. (2015). *Tourism Satellite Account: Recommended methodological framework 2008*. United Nations World Tourism Organization, United Nations Statistics Division, Organisation for Economic Co-operation and Development & Eurostat. https://unstats.un.org/unsd/publication/seriesf/seriesf_80rev1e.pdf

UNWTO. (2018). *'Overtourism'? Understanding and managing urban tourism growth beyond perceptions*. United Nations World Tourism Organization. https://doi.org/10.18111/9789284420070

UNWTO. (2021). *2020: Worst year in tourism history with 1 billion fewer international arrivals*. United Nations World Tourism Organization. https://www.untourism.int/news/2020-worst-year-in-tourism-history-with-1-billion-fewer-international-arrivals

UNWTO. (2023a). *Tourism and rural development: A policy perspective*. United Nations World Tourism Organization. https://www.e-unwto.org/doi/10.18111/9789284424306

UNWTO. (2023b). *Measuring the sustainability of tourism (MST): Proposals for a set of indicators*. United Nations World Tourism Organization. https://webunwto.s3.eu-west-1.amazonaws.com/s3fs-public/2023-09/MST_Indicators_EG_version_Sep2023_13092023_REV1.pdf

UNWTO & UNEP. (2021). *Glasgow declaration on climate action in tourism*. United Nations World Tourism Organization & United Nations Environment Programme. https://www.unwto.org/the-glasgow-declaration-on-climate-action-in-tourism

Index

R. de Arriba (ed.), *United Nations Facing Global Economic Disorder: Assessing 20 Policy Proposals*,
https://doi.org/10.1007/978-3-032-21952-7

The manufacturer's authorised representative in the EU is Springer Nature Customer Service Centre GmbH, Europaplatz 3, 69115 Heidelberg, Germany. If you have any concerns regarding our products, please contact ProductSafety@springernature.com

Printed and bound by CPI Group (UK) Ltd, Croydon, CR0 4YY

22/09/2026

02220991-0005